THE QUEST FOR
MARY MAGDALENE

THE QUEST FOR MARY MAGDALENE

~

MICHAEL HAAG

P

PROFILE BOOKS

First published in Great Britain in 2016 by
Profile Books:
3 Holford Yard, Bevin Way
London WC1X 9HD
www.profilebooks.com

1 3 5 7 9 10 8 6 4 2

The moral right of the author has been asserted.

A CIP catalogue record for this book is available from the British Library.
320pp

ISBN 978-1846684524
e-ISBN 978-1847659385

Printed and bound in Great Britain by Clays, Bungay, Suffolk
on Forest Stewardship Council (mixed sources) certified paper

MIX
Paper from
responsible sources
FSC® C018072
FSC
www.fsc.org

Pour Dasha derrière ces mots

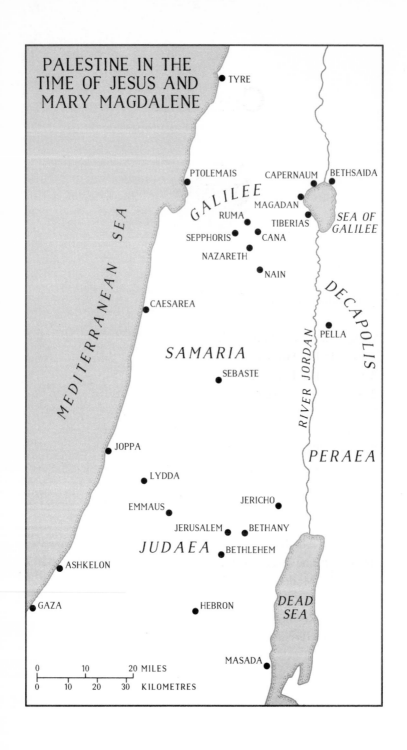

PALESTINE IN THE
TIME OF JESUS AND
MARY MAGDALENE

TYRE

MEDITERRANEAN SEA

PTOLEMAIS

GALILEE

CAPERNAUM   BETHSAIDA

MAGADAN

RUMA   TIBERIAS   SEA OF
                            GALILEE

SEPPHORIS   CANA

NAZARETH

NAIN

CAESAREA

DECAPOLIS

PELLA

SAMARIA

SEBASTE

RIVER JORDAN

PERAEA

JOPPA

LYDDA

EMMAUS   JERICHO

JERUSALEM   BETHANY

JUDAEA   BETHLEHEM

ASHKELON

GAZA   HEBRON   DEAD
                                   SEA

0   10   20 MILES
0   10   20   30   KILOMETRES

MASADA

Contents

Spikenard and myrrh – the anointing oils

Introduction

IN 1969 DURING THE PAPACY of Paul VI the Vatican made
some discreet alterations to the Latin mass. Until then the reading
for the feast day of Mary Magdalene on 22 July was from chapter 7
of the gospel of Luke in which an unnamed woman enters a house
where Jesus is a dinner guest and abases herself to him.

> And, behold, a woman in the city, which was a sinner,
> when she knew that Jesus sat at meat in the Pharisee's
> house, brought an alabaster box of ointment, And stood
> at his feet behind him weeping, and began to wash his feet
> with tears, and did wipe them with the hairs of her head,
> and kissed his feet, and anointed them with the ointment.
> ... And he said unto her, Thy sins are forgiven.

This story was replaced in 1969 by a very different reading, this
time from chapter 20 of the gospel of John in which a woman
identified as Mary Magdalene commands attention not because of

her supposed sins but because Jesus first reveals himself to her at the resurrection.

> Jesus saith unto her, Woman, why weepest thou? whom seekest thou? She, supposing him to be the gardener, saith unto him, Sir, if thou have borne him hence, tell me where thou hast laid him, and I will take him away. Jesus saith unto her, Mary. She turned herself, and saith unto him, Rabboni; which is to say, Master.

Without making an unmistakeable public apology the Vatican was in effect saying that it had got it wrong about Mary Magdalene for one thousand four hundred years, ever since 591 when Pope Gregory the Great delivered his homily which declared that Mary Magdalene was a whore.

Not that anyone was listening to the Vatican's retraction in 1969, or perhaps they simply preferred the whore to the woman who witnessed the resurrection, the event that stands at the centre of the religion that has shaped the history and culture of the greater part of the world for the last two thousand years. Whatever the reason, in 1970, just a year after the Catholic Church changed its mind about Mary Magdalene, she scored a worldwide hit in the *Jesus Christ Superstar* album (followed by the stage musical in 1971 and the film in 1973) when in the person of Yvonne Elliman she sang a torch song, 'I Don't Know How to Love Him', about her passion for Jesus:

> I don't see why he moves me.
> He's a man. He's just a man.
> And I've had so many men before,
> In very many ways,
> He's just one more.

Since then Mary Magdalene's reputation as a prostitute has grown as film after film presents her as a whore. In Martin Scorsese's 1988 film *The Last Temptation of Christ* Mary Magdalene is the woman taken in adultery in John 8 but is defended from stoning by Jesus; her repentance is made a driving theme in the film. Even Mel Gibson's 2004 *Passion of the Christ*, though it is set entirely within the week leading up to the crucifixion, feels compelled to include a flashback falsely alluding to Mary Magdalene as the woman taken in adultery.

The public appetite for Mary Magdalene the whore is matched only by that for Mary Magdalene the wife of Jesus and even as the mother of his child. Witness to this is the huge media attention given to Harvard University's professor Karen King's announcement in 2012 of the discovery of an ancient papyrus fragment bearing the words 'Jesus said unto them, "my wife"' – not to mention the vast popularity of Dan Brown's *The Da Vinci Code* in which Mary Magdalene flees the Holy Land with her child by Jesus and founds the Merovingian dynasty of French kings.

Certainly in the Middle Ages the Cathars in France saw Mary Magdalene as the wife of Jesus in the divine world and as his concubine in the world of illusion, the world that they believed we inhabit in our everyday lives; while in the early centuries of the Christian era the gnostic gospels portray Mary Magdalene as the 'companion', 'consort' and even 'wife' of Jesus, as the woman he loved more than all the other disciples, their relationship often described in erotic terms. For that matter there are incidents even in the canonical gospels of the New Testament that have suggested to scholars that Mary Magdalene was indeed the wife of Jesus. For some the argument is not whether it was true but why the truth was edited out.

This touches on the larger question of Mary Magdalene's vision, the vision she shared with Jesus – and how much of that was suppressed or lost in the controversies that shaped the new religion which some have described not as Christianity but as Churchianity, an institution utterly alien to the vision of Jesus and Mary Magdalene.

Mary Magdalene is a larger figure than any text, larger than the Bible or the Church; she has taken on a life of her own. In medieval times she was called 'the light-bearer', recalling her gnostic epithet 'inheritor of light' in her search for the truth. She is the mediator of the divine mystery and she has remained a potent and mysterious figure ever since. In the manner of a quest this book follows Mary Magdalene through the centuries, explores how she has been reinterpreted for every age and examines what she herself reveals about woman and man and the divine.

Jesus and Mary Magdalene

MARY MAGDALENE WAS WITH Jesus in Galilee where he preached the kingdom of God to people in their thousands and healed the sick and lame. And she accompanied Jesus as he journeyed to Jerusalem and entered the holy city in accordance with the prophecy, 'humble and mounted on a donkey' (Zechariah 9:9), but a challenge all the same, and where multitudes greeted him, waving palm branches and casting their garments before him and calling out hosanna. 'Hosanna to the son of David: Blessed is he that cometh in the name of the Lord: Hosanna in the highest.' When he came into Jerusalem, and 'all the city was moved', Mary Magdalene was there (Matthew 21:10).

When the Romans nailed Jesus to the cross, abandoned by his disciples, and he cried out, 'My God, my God, why hast thou forsaken me?', Mary Magdalene was there. And when it was finished, Mary Magdalene followed as they carried his body to the tomb and she watched as the stone was rolled into place.

On the third day Mary Magdalene went to the tomb and found that it was empty. 'Mary', said a voice, and she turned and saw that it was Jesus. 'Rabboni', she said, using the familiar Aramaic word for master, and reached out to touch him. 'Touch me not', Jesus said to Mary Magdalene, she who had touched him many times

'Touch me not,' Jesus says to Mary Magdalene in the garden of the resurrection, she who had touched him so many times before. *Noli Me Tangere* by Fra Angelico, Convent of San Marco, Florence, 1442.

before. 'Touch me not; for I am not yet ascended to my Father: but go to my brethren, and say unto them, I ascend unto my Father, and your Father; and to my God, and your God' (John 12:17).

Passionately and spiritually, Mary Magdalene understood, and following Jesus' command she faithfully carried his message to the disciples, his apostle to the apostles; Mary Magdalene, witness to the resurrection.

Yet Mary Magdalene is mentioned by name only fourteen times in the Bible – and only in the four gospels, never in Acts or anywhere else in the New Testament. But as little as that seems, it compares favourably to mentions of Mary the mother of Jesus. Apart from the accounts of the nativity and a few stories of Jesus' childhood, Mary the mother of Jesus hardly figures at all – only seven times, and that includes occasions when she is unnamed. 'The reader of the gospels', says *The Catholic Encylopaedia*, referring to the mother of Jesus, 'is at first surprised to find so little about Mary'.

As Jesus grows up, the role of his mother sharply decreases. She is mentioned in passing as he travels round Galilee where he is dismissive towards her (Matthew 12:47-49 and John 2:1-4), and again at the crucifixion though only in the gospel of John, and once more in Acts in the story of the Pentecost. And that is it for Mary the mother of Jesus. Her fame and the cult that surrounds her, her perpetual virginity, the reports of her Assumption, her title Mother of God, these and much more arose centuries later and are not found in the Bible at all.

Mary Magdalene, on the other hand, though she is mentioned only fourteen times, and though the gospels repeat themselves, telling and retelling their stories so that really she appears only on four distinct occasions – nevertheless, each of those occasions in which Mary Magdalene appears is crucial.

Mary Magdalene is at the crucifixion, she is at the burial, and she is at the resurrection, and before that she is with Jesus throughout his ministry in Galilee. As a woman and companion of Jesus she is the only person close to him at the critical moments that define his purpose, that describe his fate, and that will give rise to a new

3

religion; she helps support Jesus in his works, she is utterly fearless, and she is a woman of vision. Her character holds the secret of her name. At the beginning there is Jesus and Mary called Magdalene.

Mary Magdalene and Mary the Mother of Jesus

Mary the mother of Jesus appears primarily in chapters 1 and 2 of the gospels of Matthew and Luke which tell the story of the nativity and the infancy of Jesus – the virgin birth in a Bethlehem manger, the shepherds in the field, the star in the east, the worshipping magi – a story entirely ignored by the gospels of Mark and John which begin with the baptism of Jesus the man by John the Baptist.

Various scholars, among them Geza Vermes, a leading authority on Jesus, consider the birth narratives as legendary and say they were added to Luke and Matthew at a later date. These nativity stories, which in any case contradict one another (for example Matthew has the Holy Family, fearful for Jesus' life, fleeing Bethlehem to Egypt, while Luke has them returning to Nazareth after spending forty days peacefully in Bethlehem and Jerusalem), are unsupported by the other two gospels. Mark and John say Jesus came 'out of Galilee'; Mark makes no mention of Bethlehem while John does not contradict the assertion of the Pharisees that Jesus was born in Galilee, not Bethlehem (John 7:41-42). Apart from these birth and infancy chapters of Matthew and Luke, Mary appears in the gospels only seven times, five of those times described as the mother of Jesus but otherwise unnamed, and once in Acts.

Three of the references to Jesus' unnamed mother relate to one event which is described in Mark 3:31-35, Matthew 12:46-50 and Luke 8:19-21. Jesus has been healing and preaching and driving out devils and has attracted crowds of people up and down Galilee, but his friends and family fear that he is deranged and possessed by Beelzebub and they come for him. Instead he dismissively waves his mother and brothers away, saying his true mother and brothers are those who do the will of God.

The fourth time when the mother of Jesus is mentioned but not named is at the marriage of Cana where again she makes a

Mary Magdalene addressing the disciples – the apostle to the apostles.
From the Albani Psalter, c.1100.

nuisance of herself and Jesus turns on her and says, 'Woman, what
have I to do with thee?' (John 2:4). For other reasons the marriage
at Cana (whose marriage is it?) is an important event and will be
mentioned later.

When she appears at the crucifixion in John 19:25 she is likewise
not named, only identified as the mother of Jesus. John is the only

gospel which has Mary at the crucifixion of Jesus; she is not at the burial or the resurrection at all.

Mary the mother of Jesus is, however, named in the gospels of Mark and Matthew when villagers in Galilee are irate that Jesus should be preaching at their synagogue. They believe him to be a carpenter, or the son of a carpenter, from Nazareth and do not realise that he is a rabbi: 'Is not this the carpenter, the son of Mary, the brother of James, and Joses, and of Juda, and Simon? and are not his sisters here with us?' (Mark 6:3). Matthew 13:55 also mentions Mary and her sons by name but makes no mention of her daughters.

And finally Mary the mother of Jesus is mentioned by name in Acts 1:14 at Pentecost where after the resurrection the Holy Spirit descends upon those in the Upper Room.

Mary has the distinction of being the mother of Jesus, but there is nothing in their relationship to suggest that she had any understanding of what he was about. In the end there was a reconciliation of sorts when according to the gospel of John, though no one else, Mary came to see Jesus hanging on the cross and he acknowledged her with his dying breath, saying 'Woman, behold thy son!' (John 19:26).

In contrast, Mary Magdalene was Jesus' constant companion throughout his ministry in Galilee and helped organise and finance the scores of people involved in his mission to heal and bring salvation to the sick and the poor (Luke 8:1-3). She came with Jesus to Jerusalem, witnessed his crucifixion (Matthew 27:56; Mark 15:40; John 20:1), watched to see where his body was laid (Matthew 27:61; Mark 15:47), returned to anoint him on the third day and witnessed his resurrection from the dead (Matthew 28:1; Mark 16:1, 16:9; Luke 24:1; John 20:1, 20:11, 20:16, 20:18) – fourteen mentions of Mary Magdalene by name, as well as other mentions, as when she is included among 'the women from Galilee'.

Readers will be familiar with the notions of Mary the mother of Jesus as a perpetual virgin, the perfect mother and the Theotokos, 'the mother of God', of having been conceived immaculately, of ascending into heaven, of being an intercessor between God and man, the one who knows the deepest human suffering, the woman always gentle and obedient to God's will. But nothing of this model of the 'perfect' woman is found in the Bible where she is a somewhat irritating woman who has no comprehension of what her son is about; instead she is an invention who belongs entirely to later centuries, a relatively minor biblical figure who was transformed into a major cult – while Mary Magdalene, the woman who knew Jesus, was turned into a whore.

CHAPTER ONE

The Woman Called Magdalene

MARY MAGDALENE FIRST APPEARS in the chronology of Jesus' life in Galilee where she is travelling with Jesus as he proclaims the kingdom of God. 'And the twelve were with him', writes Luke in his gospel, 'and certain women, which had been healed of evil spirits and infirmities'. Among these women three are mentioned by name, and the first is Mary Magdalene, 'out of whom went seven devils'.

We are told more, for Jesus and the twelve disciples have to be fed and cared for as they travel round Galilee, and it is Mary Magdalene who provides the means, along with Joanna the wife of Chuza, steward of Herod Antipas who is ruler of Galilee and Perea, and a woman called Susanna, and many other women who go unnamed.

This is how the Gospel of Luke 8:1-3 describes Mary Magdalene as she travels with Jesus round Galilee.

> And it came to pass afterward, that he went throughout every city and village, preaching and shewing the glad

tidings of the kingdom of God: and the twelve were with him, and certain women, which had been healed of evil spirits and infirmities, Mary called Magdalene, out of whom went seven devils, and Joanna the wife of Chuza Herod's steward, and Susanna, and many others, which ministered unto him of their substance.

This account of Luke's is all we have of Mary Magdalene in any of the gospels until we encounter her again at the crucifixion in Jerusalem. But though Luke is very brief, what he tells us of Mary Magdalene with Jesus in Galilee is full of clues and revelations about her life – her character, her wealth, her social and political connections, her mental and emotional and spiritual state, her origins and the nature of her relationship with Jesus and his circle – and it is full of mysteries too.

A Place Called Magdala

In the quest for Mary Magdalene we should begin with her name. In the original Greek of the gospels she is never 'Mary Magdalene'.

View of the Sea of Galilee looking south from Safed, 19th century.

When she travels with Jesus round Galilee, Luke describes her as 'Mary called Magdalene'. Later, at the resurrection, the original Greek of Luke describes her as 'the Magdalene Mary'. In Matthew, Mark and John the Greek is 'Mary the Magdalene'. She wears the name Magdalene as though it has been conferred on her like a title.

Though the New Testament never describes Mary Magdalene as *from* or *of* anywhere, the usual assumption is that Mary Magdalene means Mary from Magdala.

Magdala, 'the birthplace of Mary Magdalene', was a 'miserable village' according to the 1912 edition of Baedeker's *Guide to Palestine and Syria*. Galilee had suffered centuries of neglect and desolation under the Ottoman Empire, and under the Mamelukes before them. Mejdal, as Magdala was called in Arabic, was frequently described by travellers as impoverished and barely inhabited; it might have been entirely abandoned had it not been resettled in the nineteenth century by Egyptian fellahin. And even then, as Mark Twain wrote in *Innocents Abroad*, his book about his travels in the Holy Land published in 1867, Magdala was 'thoroughly ugly, and cramped, squalid, uncomfortable, and filthy', and the shores of the Sea of Galilee, whose ancient name, Genneret, meant a garden of riches, had become 'a silent wilderness'. Nor did much change at Mejdal throughout the twentieth century; if anything the scene became more desolate and depressing; all there was to see at Magdala were chickens scratching up what was left of ancient mosaics.

Yet among those mosaics today archaeologists are uncovering a vast city that flourished at the time of Jesus on this northwestern shore of the Sea of Galilee, a large freshwater lake fed by the River Jordan. Excavations show that Magdala was a Hellenistic city founded in the second century BC by the Hasmoneans, an independent Jewish dynasty that owed its origins to the Maccabean Revolt of the 160s BC against Seleucid Greek rule, though a dynasty nevertheless deeply imbued with Greek culture. Comparable in plan and size to some of the more important cities in Greece and Asia Minor, Magdala served to bring the Mediterranean world

For many centuries Mejdal was an impoverished and barely inhabited settlement where the chickens scratched up the ancient mosaics.

into the heart of Galilee. Large portions of its main avenues, the decumanus maximus, running from north to south, and the cardo maximus, running from east to west, have been uncovered – and beneath them water channels which fed the city's wells, fountains and a large public baths complex. Still more impressive were the harbour installations, including a quay and mooring stones, an L-shaped inner basin protected by a breakwater, and the massive foundations of a tower.

Construction on this scale could only have been undertaken with the support of the Hasmonean rulers with the intention of making Magdala the largest port on the western shore of the Sea of Galilee and a major centre for the fishing industry, catching and preserving fish for wide distribution and export.

The city was further embellished and enlarged after the Hasmoneans were overturned in 37 BC by the Romans who established a client state under the rule of Herod the Great and his successors. Excavations have revealed a synagogue decorated with a floor mosaic and painted walls; a coin found within the synagogue dates

Magdala from the north showing the recent synagogue excavations. A coin found within the synagogue dates it to AD 29, about the year that Jesus was announcing the imminent kingdom of God throughout the towns and villages of Galilee.

it to AD 29, about the year that Jesus was announcing the imminent kingdom of God throughout the towns and villages of Galilee.

Near the remains of the ancient synagogue a modern pilgrimage centre has been built, reviving an old tradition, welcoming those who come hoping to find Mary Magdalene. Perhaps in this synagogue Mary Magdalene came to pray and Jesus came to speak. Certainly on 26 May 2014, during his visit to Jerusalem, Pope Francis gave his blessing to the tabernacle that will stand in the new church being built at Magdala.

Altering the Gospel to Put Mary Magdalene on the Map

But despite the modern excavations at Magdala and the claims that it is associated with Mary Magdalene – and despite the blessing of Pope Francis in 2014 – there is no place called Magdala in the Bible except in one corrupted phrase in the gospel of Matthew 15:39 where after feeding the multitude with the loaves and fishes Jesus 'took ship, and came into the coasts of Magdala', which is how the King James Version has it. The Greek source that was followed in this instance, however, dates only from the fifth century; but older and more reliable Greek sources such as the early fourth-century manuscripts known as the Codex Sinaiticus and the Codex Vaticanus make no mention of 'Magdala' at all. The Codex Vaticanus, for example, says that Jesus 'took ship, and came into the coasts of Magadan' – exactly what appears in modern scholarly editions such as *The Revised English Bible* as well as in Catholic and Orthodox Bibles. This is supported by the evidence of the Church Fathers Eusebius and Jerome, the first writing in the early fourth century, the second in the late fourth century, who make no mention of any place called Migdal or Magdala; they wrote only of Magadan.

In what was apparently an act of creative editing, a Byzantine copyist turned Magadan into Magdala. As similar as the names are, Magadan and Magdala mean two different things. Magadan derives from the Aramaic word *magad* meaning precious ware, while Magdala derives from the Aramaic *magdal* and the Hebrew *migdal* meaning tower.

But the identification of Magdala with Magadan began working its effect. Before the Byzantine alteration of the text in the gospel of Matthew, pilgrims who travelled in the Holy Land were silent about any place called Magdala. In the early sixth century, however, a pilgrim called Theodosius came upon Magadan on the western shore of the Sea of Galilee and, influenced by the invented text, declared that he had come to Magdala; 'Magdale, ubi domna Maria nata est', he wrote in Latin: Magdala, where the lady Mary was born.

Pilgrims travelling to the Holy Land thrived on associations with the gospels and those following in the wake of Theodosius were happy to agree that Magadan was the birthplace of Mary Magdalene. By the ninth century pilgrims were reporting a church at 'Magdala' which supposedly enclosed the very house of Mary Magdalene where the seven devils were driven out, and which they could go inside. The church, they were told, had been built by the redoubtable empress Helena, mother of Constantine the Great, who in 326-328 at about the age of eighty visited the Holy Land and had churches built on the site of Jesus' birth in Bethlehem and his ascension atop the Mount of Olives. Her son, the emperor Constantine, built the Church of the Holy Sepulchre at the spot in Jerusalem where Helena was said to have discovered the tomb of Jesus. But though Helena's visit to Bethlehem and Jerusalem were recorded at the time, there is no contemporary record of her having visited Galilee; and had she built a church which claimed to enclose the house of Mary Magdalene it certainly would have been a famous feature on the pilgrimage route already in the fourth century – instead not a single pilgrim is known to have mentioned the name Magdala at all. The church seen by the ninth-century pilgrims may have been old – Christianity had been winning con- verts in Palestine since the first century – but its association with the house of Mary Magdalene was a pious invention in keeping with the substitution of Magdala for Magadan.

The alteration of Matthew's gospel by a fifth-century Byzantine copyist was turning Mary Magdalene's name into a place on a map. She was now Mary from Magdala. Any thought that her name might have some other and profound meaning was lost.

The Watch-Tower

Magdala derives from *magdal* which means tower in Aramaic, the language spoken by Jesus and his disciples and others in Palestine and Syria at the time. The Hebrew word for tower in the Old Tes- tament is migdal. But Migdal never appears on its own as a place name anywhere in Palestine; it always occurs as Migdal-Something, so for example there is Migdal Eder (Genesis 35:21, Micah 4:8), Migdal Gad (Joshua 15:37), and Migdal El (Joshua 19:38).

Had Mary been named Magdalene for a place she would have had a double-barreled name. Instead Mary Magdalene's name says what it means; Mary the Tower, or Mary who is like a Tower.

But in what sense was she like a tower? Migdal Gad and Migdal

Migdal means tower, including towers built by farmers to safeguard their fields. This tower, photographed in 1890, watched over sheep near Bethlehem.

El were fortified places, but Migdal Eder was something altogether different. Eder (or edar) is the Hebrew for flock; in large pastures shepherds would erect a high wooden tower in order to oversee their flock.

According to Genesis 35:19-21, Migdal Eder or the Tower of the Flock was near Bethlehem, five miles southeast of Jerusalem.

The prophetic Old Testament book of Micah is part of a Jewish tradition which expected the messiah to come from Bethlehem, from the line of David, who was a shepherd before he was a king. Micah 5:2 reads, 'But from you, Bethlehem in Ephrathah, small as you are among Judah's clans, from you will come a king for me over Israel, one whose origins are far back in the past, in ancient time.'

A bit earlier Micah 4:6-8 talks of the Last Days which are marked by the appearance of the Lord who like a shepherd gathers in the lost, the dispersed and the afflicted of his flock.

> In that day, saith the Lord, will I assemble her that halteth,
> and I will gather her that is driven out, and her that I have

afflicted; And I will make her that halted a remnant, and her that was cast far off a strong nation: and the Lord shall reign over them in mount Zion from henceforth, even for ever.

Micah's comparison of Lord and shepherd concludes with this verse about the tower of the flock.

And thou, O tower of the flock, the strong hold of the daughter of Zion, unto thee shall it come, even the first dominion; the kingdom shall come to the daughter of Jerusalem.

As the shepherd watches over his flock, so David established Jerusalem as the capital of his kingdom and watched over his people from his citadel on Mount Ophel, a rocky outcrop opposite Jerusalem's Temple Mount – and likewise this tower, this migdal, this magdala, will become a watchtower for looking after the Lord's flock, those people the messiah has come to save. So Mary Magdalene's name alludes to this biblical prophecy of watching over the flock and carries a sense of salvation to come.

But this image of the watchtower and the flock applied also to the Sea of Galilee where fishing was the mainstay of towns and villages round its shores. For example, Magadan, the place subsequently known as Magdala thanks to the Byzantine scribe, was a big port for catching and processing and exporting fish, and excavations there today reveal the foundations of a massive tower that once rose above the harbour. The purpose of the tower was likely a lighthouse, a beacon for fishermen out on the lake – for as we are told by John 21:3, they fished by night. Other ports would have had lighthouses or beacons too. And so the tower was very much like the Tower of the Flock near Bethlehem, a means for looking after the flock who in this case were fishermen. Several of Jesus' own disciples were fishermen before they became, in his words, fishers of men.

Jesus was fond of giving his disciples nicknames, as we are told in Mark 3.16-17: 'And Simon he surnamed Peter; And James the son of Zebedee, and John the brother of James; and he surnamed them Boanerges, which is, The sons of thunder'. Peter comes from the Greek Petros which in turn comes from Jesus' use of the original Aramaic which was Cephas, both Cephas and Petros meaning rock. Mary Magdalene would have received her name in the same way, Mary the migdal, the watchtower, the lighthouse, the beacon; a powerful name, the woman who helped the Good Shepherd protect his flock; and also a beacon at night, an illuminator, a visionary – contrasted with the rock of Peter; rock versus light.

Debauchery, Salted Fish and Biblical Scholars

Rabbinical writings dating from the fourth to fifth centuries AD mention a place called Migdal Tsebaya, meaning Tower of the Dyers, and another called Migdal Nunya, meaning Tower of the Fishes.

An old field tower built by a farmer to watch over his crops and flocks and to warn of approaching danger. Such watchtowers were especially common during the first century AD.

How long they had been in existence is not known; certainly they appear nowhere in the Old or New Testaments. Likewise the location of both is uncertain; but the latter is thought to be about a mile north of Tiberias, not far enough north to be anywhere near the place now called Magdala. The place might correspond to Tel Rakat (or Tel Raqqat); a tel is an ancient mound of debris that grows up over abandoned villages or other structures, and though Tel Rakat is set back from the lake, that might not always have been so; perhaps there was a lighthouse here, or maybe this was a place for processing fish. Without excavating the site we will not know more.

As Migdal Tsebaya means Tower of the Dyers and dyeing is usually done near water, so possibly this was also on the shores of the Sea of Galilee but the rabbinical literature does not say. Instead it makes one comment, that Migdal Tsebaya was destroyed for its prostitution, but it does not explain when or how or by whom – no context is provided whatsoever.

That has not stopped Migdal Tsebaya being identified with Tarichaea (Taricheae is a variant spelling), its name, which is Greek, meaning place of salted fish. The identification was made in the 1920s by the American biblical archaeologist William F. Albright, pretty much because he thought so. Albright also identified Tarichaea with the place now called Magdala in spite of the evidence to the contrary.

The evidence points to Tarichaea being three and a half miles south of Tiberias on the west bank of the river Jordan where it emerges from the southern end of the Sea of Galilee, not three and a half miles north, the site of present-day Magdala. The first century AD Roman historian Pliny, for example, described the Sea of Galilee in his *Natural History* as 'surrounded by the pleasant towns of Julias and Hippos in the east, Tarichaea in the south ... and in the west Tiberias' – which places Tarichaea south of Tiberias while Magadan, known since Byzantine times as Magdala, is to the north of Tiberias.

Moreover Tarichaea was the site of a famous battle in AD 67 during the Jewish Revolt; the historian Flavius Josephus, who was a commander of Jewish forces during the early part of the uprising in Galilee, described the Roman siege and occupation of the city and the fierce naval battle that ensued that left 6700 Jewish fighters dead and turned the lake water red. Yet excavations at present-day Magdala reveal no signs whatsoever of fighting or damage from the time of the revolt, while Josephus' account of Roman movements makes it clear that Tarichaea was south of Tiberias. Quite simply, Magdala and Tarichaea were two different places.

Nevertheless Albright's connection between Migdal Tsebaya, Tarichaea and Magdala has made a lasting impression so that you will see the names of these places used interchangeably or in combination, with Migdal Nunya thrown in for good measure; and you will often read of the Roman destruction of Mary Magdalene's supposed home town because of its debauched reputation, which fits in nicely with the later image created of Mary Magdalene by the Church.

Religion has played havoc with identifying the site and the significance of Magdala and its association, if there is any, with Mary Magdalene. The problem began in the early Christian centuries and has been perpetuated and further confused by biblical archaeologists and New Testament scholars in modern days. Tying Mary Magdalene to some spot is like finding some bone, some rib or skull, and saying it is hers; places become relics for people who need that sort of thing.

CHAPTER TWO

The Kingdom of God

THOUGH LUKE TELLS US nothing about the nature of the
women's afflictions nor about Mary Magdalene's seven devils,
he is very specific that Mary Magdalene's travelling companion is
Joanna, the wife of Chuza, who was a steward of Herod's estates.
To know something about Mary Magdalene's devils and the
women's evil spirits and infirmities we need to look at the world of
Herod, that world from which Joanna, Mary Magdalene and Jesus
himself were struggling to escape – that world that had just cut off
the head of John the Baptist.

Herod and Hellenism

Herod Antipas was the son of Herod the Great, infamous in the
Bible for the massacre of the innocents after the birth of Jesus.
According to the gospel of Matthew 2:1-16, the magi tell Herod
of the birth of a child who would become king of the Jews, and
fearing for his throne Herod orders the death of all the newborn
children at Bethlehem.

> Now when Jesus was born in Bethlehem of Judaea in the days of Herod the king, behold, there came wise men from the east to Jerusalem, Saying, Where is he that is born King of the Jews? for we have seen his star in the east, and are come to worship him. ...

> Then Herod ... slew all the children that were in Bethlehem, and in all the coasts thereof, from two years old and under.

The story allows Matthew to have the Holy Family flee into Egypt from where they will eventually return after the death of Herod, so fulfilling the prophesy of Hosea 11:1, 'Out of Egypt have I called my son'. But Matthew's Flight into Egypt is directly contradicted by Luke 2:22 and 2:39 who has the Holy Family, forty days after Mary's purification following the birth of Jesus, peacefully returning home from Bethlehem to Nazareth via Jerusalem. For that reason and because there is no evidence that any such massacre ever occurred, most scholars doubt the historical reality of the event.

But the story does contain a truth, that Herod, a Jew who owed his throne to the Romans and promoted Graeco-Roman culture over strict Jewish tradition, was suspicious of Jewish threats to his rule.

Herod the Great was a product of a new cosmopolitan civilisation that arose in the wake of the conquests of Alexander the Great in the 330s BC. Hellenistic culture – that compound of Greek culture with local elements – was a brilliant and liberating civilisation that permeated western Asia and the Eastern Mediterranean, offering new discoveries and opportunities in philosophy, education, theatre, religion, technology, trade, government and law, and above all it provided a shared language, koine Greek, a simplified version of Greek that became the lingua franca.

Aramaic, the old common language of the Middle East, continued to be spoken for everyday needs, and for Jews Hebrew was the language of ritual and prayer. But in Palestine, as elsewhere,

The Temple at Jerusalem, enlarged and embellished by Herod the Great in the first century BC, as reconstructed by the painter James Tissot, 1894. A grandiose promoter of Hellenism, Herod employed Greek, Roman and Egyptian architects to build his Temple which became the largest religious complex in the ancient world.

Greek became the written language for every educated person and anyone of rank, while if anything Hellenisation was reinforced by the Romans who succeeded the Greeks as masters in the East in the first century BC; the Roman governing class spoke Greek and they supported practices and trends in religion, philosophy, drama and architecture that owed their origins to the Greeks. The gospels themselves and the whole of the New Testament were first written in Greek.

Herod the Great, who had ruled Judaea from 37 to 4 BC as a Roman client king, was a grandiose promoter of Hellenisation. He built the new port city of Caesarea on the Mediterranean and in Jerusalem he constructed the Temple Mount, a vast platform over a natural hill to give support to his gigantic Temple built in 25-10 BC. Herod's new Temple was something more than just an enlargement of the Second Temple that had been built centuries earlier on the site of Solomon's original Temple; planned by Roman, Greek and Egyptian architects all in white marble and in classical style, Herod's Temple dwarfed the Parthenon and became the largest religious complex in the ancient world.

At Herod's death in 4 BC his kingdom was divided between his four sons, though Judaea, the central area extending from Jerusalem in the Judaean highlands to Caesarea on the Mediterranean, soon fell under the direct rule of a Roman prefect. Herod Antipas, the youngest of the sons, was made tetrarch, meaning ruler of a quarter, and was given Galilee in the north and Perea on the east bank of the river Jordan.

Herod Antipas, like his father, was a great builder; in AD 19 he built Tiberias, his completely new capital on the western shore of the Sea of Galilee, its plan and architecture in the Greek and Roman tradition, which he named for his master, the Roman emperor Tiberius.

But Herod Antipas was not alone in being thoroughly Hellenised and Romanised; significant elements of Jewish society were Hellenised too, especially the Jewish upper class. The Sadducees, the aristocratic Jewish families, dominated affairs; from their number came the Temple priests, including the high priest.

Power over Jewish religious affairs was vested in the Sanhedrin, a council of leading and learned figures, including Sadducees and their rivals the Pharisees which were socio-political and religious parties or sects. The Sadducees based their authority on the Temple and the written Torah with its depiction of the priesthood, while the Pharisees did not fill Temple positions and gave authority to both the written and the developing oral Torah. While the Sadducees were the old landowning aristocracy and were comfortable with Hellenisation, the Pharisees were scholars and teachers who ran the schools and saw Hellenism, with its lure of assimilation, as threatening the social, moral and religious fabric of the nation.

But the vast number of Jews were neither Sadducees nor Pharisees. The Roman-Jewish historian Flavius Josephus, himself a Pharisee, says that there were no more than about six thousand

Pharisees in Palestine in the AD 60s; the Sadducees were fewer still. Josephus does say, however, that the Pharisees were popular among ordinary Jews. The Essenes, another sect, were ascetics who withdrew from everyday life and lived by the Dead Sea where the Dead Sea Scrolls were discovered; but though the scrolls were part of their library it is not known if the Essenes were their authors. John the Baptist is sometimes described as having been a member of the Essenes or influenced by them but there is no evidence for this.

Jesus is often depicted in the gospels as disputing with the Pharisees, who are sometimes presented as his enemies, plotting with the Herodians against him; in fact Jesus and the Pharisees had much in common in that both were popular among the common people, both (unlike the Sadducees) believed in the afterlife, and both upheld the Torah over the Temple. But Jesus, for whom God's love was paramount, found the Pharisees excessive and rigid in their views on the law and called them hypocrites and flaunted

A coin from the reign of Herod Antipas, ruler of Galilee in the time of Jesus. Unlike his father Herod the Great and other members of the Herodian dynasty, Antipas publicly observed the Jewish prohibition of images of himself in sculpture and on coins. We therefore have no knowledge of how he looked. This coin is typical in using simple plant motifs. On one side it says, in Greek letters, 'Tiberias', the name of Antipas' new capital city on the shore of the Sea of Galilee, while on the other side it says 'Herodou Tetrarchou', Herod the Tetrarch.

his fellowship with tax collectors and women on the margins of society. This, however, was merely the sort of infighting that occurs between factions who otherwise share very similar values.

But while Hellenism was having a pervasive effect on local culture, the impress of Roman rule was only lightly felt; though Judaea was under the direct rule of a Roman prefect based at Caesarea, traditional Jewish institutions, legal, educational and religious, were left in local hands, and Rome's military presence was slight. Generally the Romans went out of their way to respect Jewish sensibilities; the local coinage, for example, was minted without images, and Roman soldiers were advised not to take their image-bearing ensigns with them when entering Jerusalem.

In Galilee, governed by Herod Antipas who had his own army of Jews and gentile mercenaries, there was not a single Roman fortress nor a Roman soldier. (The famous scene in Matthew 8:5-13 and Luke 7:1-10 of Jesus' exchange with a centurion in Capernaum says nothing about the officer being a Roman, only a gentile; the Greek word used in the gospels was commonly applied to both Roman and non-Roman officers, and this 'centurion' was most likely an officer in the service of Herod Antipas whose father was known to have had Gauls, Germans and Thracians in his bodyguard.)

Apart from an uprising in AD 6 in reaction to the Roman imposition of a census for tax purposes, Galilee, Jerusalem and the rest of the Jewish lands were calm throughout the whole of Jesus' life.

The uprising came as a warning, however, for it had quickly taken on a fundamentalist religious character – its leaders said a census was an offence to God and called for a theocracy, a republic based on Jewish law and recognising only God as king. And though the Romans crushed the revolt, tensions between Hellenistic and Jewish traditions continued to simmer beneath the surface.

In Galilee Herod Antipas was nervous that religious opinion would be stirred up against his rule, while in Judaea the priestly party, the Sadducees, who controlled the Temple at Jerusalem, shared Herod's anxieties – as did nearly everyone who was Hellenised and had made an accommodation with the Romans.

But for all that Hellenisation opened up Palestine to the opportunities and benefits of the larger Mediterranean world, it was also seen by some – and not only by the Pharisees, but perhaps even by those Jews who were Hellenised – as eating away at their very identity. For some Jews there was no question about it, no compromise was possible; Hellenism was an affliction, a contamination that stood in the way of reestablishing purified Judaism in the world and becoming closer to God.

In barely more than a generation after those days when Mary Magdalene joined Jesus as he preached the kingdom of God across the hills and villages of Galilee, the Jews rose in revolt against Roman rule. The savage Roman-Jewish War began in AD 66 and lasted for seven years; by the time it was over tens of thousands were dead and the Temple at Jerusalem was destroyed.

Reborn in the River Jordan

John the Baptist is a thoroughly historical figure. He is mentioned in all four gospels, Matthew, Mark, Luke and John, which are generally thought to have been written between AD 65 and AD 110. He is also recorded in *The Antiquities of the Jews* written in about AD 94 by the historian Flavius Josephus who describes John's practice of baptism as the culmination of living life virtuously. 'John, that was called the Baptist, ... was a good man, and commanded the Jews to exercise virtue, both as to righteousness towards one another, and piety towards God, and so to come to baptism.'

Jesus, who was baptised by John, and who according to Luke 1:36 was John's cousin, made John's message fundamental to his own teachings. 'Thou shalt love the Lord thy God with all thy heart, and with all thy soul, and with all thy mind', Jesus says in Matthew 22:37-40, echoing the Baptist. 'This is the first and great commandment. And the second is like unto it, Thou shalt love thy neighbour as thyself. On these two commandments hang all the law and the prophets.'

John was not founding a new religion, but his rite of baptism, the immersion in water, was something wholly new to Judaism. John

The Baptism of Christ by Giotto, 1305, in the Scrovegni Chapel, Padua.

was saying that descent from Abraham, the founding figure of the Jewish people, was not enough to guarantee salvation. Instead, just as God had called the Jews out of Egypt and led them across the river Jordan into the Promised Land, so Jews now had to become a new people by immersing themselves in the waters of baptism in that same river.

Bypassing the rituals of the Temple in Jerusalem and its priests who were widely seen as substituting religiosity for an authentic relationship with God, baptism meant a new start, a rebirth. Baptism was simple and made salvation accessible to *all* – the gospels stressing that word, as when Mark 1:5 recounts the vast numbers who journeyed far into the wilderness seeking John, 'And there went out unto him all the land of Judaea, and they of Jerusalem, and were all baptised of him in the river of Jordan, confessing their sins'. Those who were baptised by John emerged from the waters as newly born, or they were like people who had been dead and buried but had risen, people who had made the journey from death to life.

In particular, this simple act of immersion made salvation accessible to women who in male-oriented Judaism stood outside the traditional covenant between man and God – because women were not circumcised. Circumcision goes back to the first book of the Old Testament, to Genesis 17:10, where God speaks to Abraham, the founding figure of the Jewish people: 'This is my covenant, which ye shall keep, between me and you and thy seed after thee; Every man child among you shall be circumcised'. Whether women could therefore be part of the covenant between man and God was a question asked then and is still asked now; at best they enjoy a covenant with God only through men. But John's baptism rite provided a radical answer and opened the way to direct salvation for everyone, so that he attracted *all*, as the gospels say.

The Head of John the Baptist

Many in those days believed that the moment of judgement was near, and John's message of salvation stirred excitement and expectation throughout the land. Josephus records how many 'came in crowds about him, for they were very greatly moved by hearing his words'. The hunger for purity, but innocent of fanaticism and political insurrection, was expressed by those who sought salvation at the hands of John the Baptist in the river Jordan. But Josephus also tells how the appeal of John's message led directly to his death. 'Herod, who feared lest the great influence John had over the people might put it into his power and inclination to raise a rebellion, for they seemed ready to do any thing he should advise, thought it best, by putting him to death, to prevent any mischief he might cause.'

The gospels say more about John the Baptist's death. Herod Antipas had married his brother Philip's wife, Herodias, contrary to Leviticus 20:21 which says, 'If a man shall take his brother's wife, it is an unclean thing'. As Mark 6:18-24 relates the story, John repeated this to Herod, saying 'It is not lawful for thee to have thy brother's wife', at which Herodias, the wife of the two brothers, flew into a rage and would have killed the Baptist, but Herod, fearing the popular support enjoyed by John, stopped short of taking

The dance of Salome at the birthday feast of Herod Antipas as imagined by the French painter Gustave Moreau, 1876. An apparition of John the Baptist's head hovers before her.

his life and imprisoned him instead. But then 'Herod on his birthday made a supper to his lords, high captains, and chief estates of Galilee; And when the daughter of the said Herodias came in, and danced, and pleased Herod and them that sat with him, the king said unto the damsel, Ask of me whatsoever thou wilt, and I will give it thee. And he sware unto her, Whatsoever thou shalt ask of me, I will give it thee, unto the half of my kingdom. And she went forth, and said unto her mother, What shall I ask? And she said, The head of John the Baptist'.

The girl whose dance cost the life of John the Baptist has been famously known as Salome in legend and in music and paintings for nearly two thousand years. The gospels tell the story of the dance but do not name the girl; on the other hand Josephus, who says nothing of the dance, reports that Herodias had a daughter called Salome who married and had three sons. Rightly or wrongly popular imagination has combined the two and has eroticised her dance as the Dance of the Seven Veils so that Salome lives forever as the ultimate femme fatale.

Dancing girl apart, both Josephus and Mark are telling essentially the same story (and the gospel of Matthew which here parallels Mark); in condemning Herod's marriage to his brother's wife, John was accusing him of not being a good Jew, which would have undermined what authority Herod had as a Jew ruling over Jews on behalf of his Roman masters. And then John might have whipped up popular outrage against Herod Antipas, threatening his throne. One way or another Herod might think it would make good sense to eliminate John the Baptist.

The gospel of Mark provides a revealing detail in its account of the dinner at which Herodias' daughter danced for Herod and demanded the head of John the Baptist, for Mark tells us that the guests included the 'lords, high captains, and chief estates of Galilee'. That means Chuza was most likely a witness to the scene, Chuza, the steward of Herod's estates, mentioned in Luke as the husband of Joanna, Joanna who was the companion of Mary Magdalene. Was Joanna herself at this gruesome dinner?

Not that John the Baptist's head was brought to the dinner itself. According to Josephus, the Baptist was imprisoned and executed at the remote rocky hilltop fortress of Machaerus in Parea, that part of Herod Antipas' tetrarchy that lay in the desert to the east of the Dead Sea. But as the dinner guests were notables of Galilee the famous dance would not have taken place in a fortress difficult of access far away across the Dead Sea but in Herod's luxurious palace at Tiberias on the shores of the Sea of Galilee. But wherever it happened, the beheading of John the Baptist was a traumatic event, infamous enough for Josephus to write about it, disturbing even to Herod who was never sure he wanted the Baptist dead, and appalling to Joanna and others who sympathised with John's vision of renewal for the Jewish people.

The news of the death of John the Baptist came immediately to Jesus. The gospels of Mark and Matthew record that when John's disciples heard of his death they came and laid his body in a tomb, with Matthew 14:12 adding that 'his disciples came, and took up the body, and buried it, and went and told Jesus'. In fact John's arrest, followed by his death, may have been the events that changed the entire nature of Jesus' calling, for as John 3: 23-24 explains, Jesus had only recently been sharing with John the work of baptising in the river Jordan: 'After these things came Jesus and his disciples into the land of Judaea; and there he tarried with them, and baptized. And John also was baptizing in Aenon near to Salim, because there was much water there: and they came, and were baptized. For John was not yet cast into prison'. This passage has Jesus baptising away from his familiar ground; he is in the south, in Judaea, close to John who is in Parea on the east bank of the Jordan. It is as though the two cousins were sharing a single mission and a single vision.

If until now Jesus was content to baptise, the arrest and death of John the Baptist created an urgency, and Jesus threw himself into a campaign which drew a great multitude of people from the villages and cities round the Sea of Galilee, as the multitudes had once come to hear John. So many came from so wide and far that Jesus commanded his disciples to feed them with all they had, five loaves

Titus Flavius Josephus, the first-century AD Jewish Roman historian who mentions among others Herod Antipas, Pontius Pilate, John the Baptist and Jesus in his *The Antiquities of the Jews*.

and two fishes that he blessed and multiplied so that they fed five thousand men and numerous more women and children.

The gospel of John 1:35-42 tells how Andrew and another who is unnamed had been followers of John but after his imprisonment they decided to follow Jesus and persuaded Andrew's brother, Simon Peter, to join them too.

Those women who Luke says were travelling with Jesus as 'he went throughout every city and village, preaching and shewing the glad tidings of the kingdom of God', among them Joanna, wife of Chuza, and Mary Magdalene – in the beginning they too may have been John the Baptist's followers, drawn to him by his rite of baptism which bypassed the traditional covenant with God expressed by male circumcision and which instead offered salvation to men and women alike, to everyone. But now after Herod's brutal response to the Baptist's message of rebirth, Mary Magdalene and her companions understood the danger they all faced, for as Mark 3:6 writes of plots against Jesus, 'And the Pharisees went forth, and straightway took counsel with the Herodians against him, how they might destroy him.' But if this was a dangerous time, it was also the end of time; there was no more waiting now, for as Jesus proclaimed, the kingdom of God was at hand.

Galilee

In contrast to the desolation described by travellers as recently as the nineteenth and early twentieth centuries, in the lifetime of Mary Magdalene the country round the Sea of Galilee was bountiful and beautiful. Plants as diverse as walnuts and palms, figs and olives, all flourished here; 'one may call it the ambition of nature', said Josephus, speaking of the way the rich soil and varied climate 'forces those plants that are naturally enemies to one another to agree together; it is a happy contention of the seasons, as if every one of them laid claim to this country'.

Josephus, who was governor of Galilee a generation after the death of Jesus, knew the country well. 'The whole area is excellent for crops and cattle and rich in forests of all kinds, so that by its adaptability it invites even those least inclined to work on the land. Consequently every inch has been cultivated by the inhabitants and not a corner goes to waste. It is thickly studded with towns, and thanks to the natural abundance the innumerable villages are so densely populated that the smallest has more than 15,000 inhabitants'. Josephus was right about the abundance of Galilee but he grossly exaggerated its population; village sizes were far smaller, in the hundreds not the thousands.

Josephus also reported that the waters of the lake supported a thriving fishing industry, including a fleet of 230 fishing boats. Four of Jesus' disciples were fishermen and shared in the prosperity of Galilee, a prosperity underlined by the archaeological evidence of comfortable and substantial houses at Capernaum, the base of Jesus' ministry and home to Peter.

Galilee lay on a main trading route between Egypt and Syria; roads ran everywhere; it enjoyed commercial links with the Decapolis, the coast of Palestine and Syria, with Asia Minor and Cyprus. The Greeks, Hasmoneans, Romans and Herodians all built cities here – the Hasmoneans developed the place now called Migdal or Magdala on the western shore of the lake, making it the most important port on the Sea of Galilee, and Herod Antipas founded Tiberias just to the south and made it his capital. The population of Galilee, which numbered about two hundred thousand in the first century AD, was quite mixed and included Greeks, Canaanites, Egyptians and Nabataeans, though the majority were Jews. For all these reasons Galilee was a more outward-looking place than Jerusalem.

Much of the ministry of Jesus occurred on the shores of the Sea of Galilee. He gave the Sermon on the Mount just to the north of Capernaum; and he performed miracles at the lake, walking on its waters, calming the storm, filling his disciples' boats with a great catch of fish, and feeding the five thousand.

Marriage and Miracle at Cana in Galilee

Jesus performed his first miracle at Cana in Galilee. This is the marriage feast to which Jesus and his mother and the disciples are invited, but the wine runs out and after being nagged by his mother Jesus turns the water into wine. The event is described in John 2:1-5.

> And the third day there was a marriage in Cana of Galilee; and the mother of Jesus was there: And both Jesus was called, and his disciples, to the marriage. And when they wanted wine, the mother of Jesus saith unto him, They have no wine. Jesus saith unto her, Woman, what have I to

do with thee? mine hour is not yet come. His mother saith unto the servants, Whatsoever he saith unto you, do it.

Jesus then had the servants fill six jars with water; when it was tasted by the chief steward or governor of the feast, who knew nothing of what Jesus had done, the steward complemented the bridegroom saying, 'Every man at the beginning doth set forth good wine; and when men have well drunk, then that which is worse: but thou hast kept the good wine until now' (John 2:10).

The Wedding at Cana, Jesus turning water into wine. German, early 18th century. But whose wedding was it?

The symbolism lies in Jesus transforming the water used in the old Jewish rituals of purification into the wine of a new faith. But the scene is strange, as though it recalls a once significant event, now forgotten or edited out. After all, as Jesus says, it is no concern of his to make good a shortage in the wine; he and his mother and the disciples are only guests. Or are they?

Mary addresses Jesus in a tone of expectation and she tells the servants to follow whatever orders he gives them. This is the behaviour not of guests but of people who are hosting a wedding feast. Some Bible commentators have suggested that the wedding might have been that of a close relative of Mary's, but beyond that they will not venture; they name no names.

But according to the late fourth-century historian and theologian St Jerome, who spent the last decades of his life in Bethlehem – or at least according to Domenico Cavalca, a fourteenth-century Franciscan who wrote a *Life* of Mary Magdalene and attributes his information to Jerome – the marriage was between Mary Magdalene and John the Evangelist, the author of the fourth gospel, who immediately abandoned his bride and joined Jesus in heralding the kingdom of God.

This story has been imaginatively recreated by Marguerite Yourcenar, author of *The Memoirs of Hadrian*, in her collection of stories about women in love called *Fires*. Mary Magdalene is abandoned by John on their wedding night when he lets himself out the window to join Jesus in preaching the imminent kingdom. John's desertion and Mary's shame turn her into a prostitute. Later she meets and falls in love with Jesus but he is then crucified; when she goes to his tomb to anoint him she finds that he has risen: 'For the second time in my life, I was standing in front of a deserted bed'.

But there are clues in John's gospel that suggest the bridegroom was Jesus himself and that we are witnessing his marriage to Mary Magdalene. The marriage at Cana happens on 'the third day', says the gospel of John. The phrase 'the third day' appears fourteen times in the gospels, thirteen of those times referring to the

The marriage of Mary Magdalene to John the Evangelist, an illustration from a manuscript of *Der Saelden Hort*, a late-13th-century Swiss verse romance. The poem draws on the tradition that the feast at Cana was a celebration of the marriage of John, author of the fourth gospel, and Mary Magdalene.

resurrection when Mary Magdalene goes to the tomb and finds that Jesus has risen. The phrase occurs only one other time: 'And the third day there was a marriage in Cana of Galilee'.

Several of Jesus' disciples were married, including Peter (Matthew 8.14-17; Mark 1.29-31; Luke 4.38), and there is nothing in the New Testament that says Jesus was not married. In fact it would have been unusual for a man of Jesus' age not to have been married. Jesus was no ascetic like John the Baptist or the Essenes; he was relaxed about ritual washing and diet; he caricatured himself as 'a glutton and a drunkard' (Matthew 11.19; Luke 7.34); he loved food and drink and good talk; he was witty and sharp; he was at ease with women; and he was self-deprecating but had an intensity and aura about him that was very attractive. Were Jesus and Mary Magdalene married that would explain the intimacy between them, her constant companionship, her appearance at the crucifixion, and above all her visit to the tomb on the third day bearing spices to anoint his naked body, a task undertaken by a wife.

It would also help explain her name. Mary the Magdalene, the Watchtower of the Messiah, the Bride of Christ.

The Kingdom of God

When Jesus heard that John the Baptist had been thrown into prison he began gathering disciples and he started to preach. He travelled all about Galilee, teaching in the synagogues, healing the sick and the possessed and preaching the kingdom of God. 'And they brought unto him all sick people that were taken with divers diseases and torments, and those which were possessed with devils, and those which were lunatick, and those that had the palsy; and he healed them' (Matthew 4:24). Multitudes came to him from Galilee, Jerusalem, Judaea and from beyond the river Jordan and also from the Decapolis, ten cities founded by the Greeks or otherwise entirely Hellenised, including Damascus to the north, all with primarily gentile populations and large numbers of Hellenised Jews.

But gentiles were of no concern to Jesus. His three public activities were curing the sick, delivering people from demonic possession, and preaching, and all these were directed towards his fellow Jews. Nothing Jesus said or did suggests any political view; though paying taxes to Rome was considered the ultimate betrayal by Jewish radicals, Jesus said, 'Render to Caesar the things that are Caesar's, and to God the things that are God's' (Mark 12:17). He occasionally healed gentiles but he declared that his message was strictly for 'the lost sheep of the house of Israel' (Matthew 15:24), and he spoke harshly to and about gentiles, comparing them to dogs and pigs (Mark 7:27, Matthew 7:6, 15:26). Jesus explicitly directed his disciples to address only Jews and he forbade them to approach

Mary Magdalene with John the Baptist (not to be confused with John the Evangelist), by Angelo Puccinelli, mid-14th century. Mary Magdalene might first have been a follower of the Baptist, attracted by his message of salvation addressed to women as much as men.

gentiles. 'The only logical inference that can be drawn from these premises is that Jesus was conerned only with Jews, because in his view citizenship of the Kingdom of God was reserved for them alone', writes the leading Jesus scholar Geza Vermes in *The Authentic Gospel of Jesus*, adding that 'Jesus was not exactly the gentle, sugary, meek and mild figure of pious Christian imagination'.

Jesus certainly did not see himself as a saviour, least of all a universal saviour. He never spoke of himself as the messiah or the Son of God; he never claimed to rule, rather he said he had come to serve. He sought the lost lamb; he cherished repentant sinners and tax collectors, one of whom was his disciple Matthew (also known as Levi), and he loved children. Jesus was clear about what he was doing; when the scribes and Pharisees demanded to know why he ate and drank with tax collectors and sinners, he said to them, 'They that are whole have no need of the physician, but they that are sick: I came not to call the righteous, but sinners to repentance' (Mark 2:16-17).

This was the way of God, and to illustrate what he meant Jesus told the parable of the profligate son (Luke 15:11-32) – about the younger son who claims his inheritance from his father, goes into a far country and wastes everything in riotous living. When he has nothing and is on the point of starving he returns to his father and says, 'I have sinned against heaven, and in thy sight, and am no more worthy to be called thy son'. But his father, far from rebuking his younger son, has compassion and embraces him and kisses him and calls out to his servants, 'Bring forth the best robe, and put it on him; and put a ring on his hand, and shoes on his feet: And bring hither the fatted calf, and kill it; and let us eat, and be merry'.

The older brother, when he hears this, is angry and says to his father, 'Lo, these many years do I serve thee, neither transgressed I at any time thy commandment: and yet thou never gavest me a kid, that I might make merry with my friends. But as soon as this thy son was come, which hath devoured thy living with harlots, thou has killed for him the fatted calf'. The father answered him, saying, 'Son, thou art ever with me, and all that I have is thine'. But he explained

Jesus exorcises two men possessed by demons. Jesus drives the demons into a herd of pigs who rush into the Sea of Galilee and are drowned. French, early 17th century.

that it was right 'that we should make merry, and be glad: for this thy brother was dead, and is alive again; and was lost, and is found'.

God yearns, and his yearning is not so much for the righteous as for the sinners. And that is a reminder, preached Jesus, that no matter how much a man may follow the law, it is not man but God who decides.

Jesus rejected the charge that he was violating the Torah, that is the Jewish law. 'Think not that I am come to destroy the law, or the prophets: I am not come to destroy, but to fulfill' (Matthew 5:17). But Jesus also preached that to enter the kingdom of God one had not only to fulfill the law but go beyond it. Observing rituals and a moral system was not enough; one had to submit absolutely to God, a God who could be incomprehensible in the seemingly arbitrary and indiscriminate ways he chooses to love.

Jesus spoke of this in his Sermon on the Mount (Matthew 5:44, 45, 48).

> Love your enemies, bless them that curse you, do good to them that hate you, and pray for them which despitefully use you, and persecute you;
>
> That ye may be the children of your Father which is in heaven: for he maketh his sun to rise on the evil and on the good, and sendeth rain on the just and on the unjust. ...
>
> Be ye therefore perfect, even as your Father which is in heaven is perfect.

In the original Greek the word for 'perfect' is *teleios*, which can also be translated as entire or complete. The God of Jesus' teachings pours out his love on all. And just as God the father is entire and complete through his embrace of everyone in his love, so man should imitate God by loving absolutely.

Jesus' teaching appealed to the poor, the oppressed, the distressed and those on the margins; and this, combined with his powers as a healer and an exorcist, made him immensely popular among the crowds of Galilee.

The kingdom of God is coming, said Jesus, during his Sermon on the Mount as he taught his disciples how to pray to God the father. 'Our father which art in heaven, Hallowed be thy name. Thy kingdom come. Thy will be done in earth, as it is in heaven' (Matthew 6:9). In fact the kingdom of God is all about us, waiting for us to enter if we know how. 'The time is fulfilled, and the kingdom of God is at hand' (Mark 1:15).

The Ghost of John the Baptist

Mary Magdalene and the other women, and the twelve disciples, were taking a serious risk when they joined Jesus, for it was the arrest of John the Baptist by Herod Antipas that spurred Jesus into action. Most of John the Baptist's ministry had taken place on the east bank of the Jordan in Herod's territory of Parea; after John's imprisonment Jesus began his ministry in Herod's territory of Galilee. Herod Antipas took it as a challenge.

Herod's rule, as he saw it, offered a stable and peaceful and united world, sharing a common culture, a paradise on earth. And not only Greeks and Romans but many Jews had adopted Hellenistic ways.

But Herod feared that Jesus' kingdom would be seen by people as in conflict with his own and with the Romans'. When Herod heard about Jesus preaching throughout Galilee he said that 'John the Baptist was risen from the dead, and therefore mighty works do shew forth themselves in him. ... It is John, whom I beheaded: he is risen from the dead' (Mark 6:14,16).

CHAPTER THREE

On The Road With Jesus

JESUS IS SOMETIMES DESCRIBED as a radical for his attitude towards women. He included women in his entourage. And in mixing with women during his preachings and his healings, he did not observe the taboos. He did not feel himself polluted, for example, in the story told by Matthew and Luke of the woman who had suffered twelve years from an issue of blood; she had spent all her money on doctors to no avail but now among a throng of people she reached out and touched Jesus on the hem of his garment. 'And Jesus said, Who touched me? ... She came trembling, and falling down before him, she declared unto him before all the people for what cause she had touched him, and how she was healed immediately.' Where custom and belief would have caused other Jewish men to shrink from her and feel themselves defiled, Jesus said to her, 'Daughter, be of good comfort: thy faith hath made thee whole; go in peace' (Luke 8:44-48).

Women with Jesus

Jesus had an inclusive view of the twelve disciples and the women travelling with him round Galilee. When Luke 8:1-2 writes that 'the twelve were with him, and certain women', the women are not set apart; men and women are all 'with him'. Furthermore the women, like the men, are there throughout his ministry. 'The women that followed him from Galilee' are at the crucifixion, writes Luke 23:49; and on the third day when the women discover the empty tomb, two men in shining garments appeared among them, saying 'He is not here, but is risen: remember how he spake unto you when he was yet in Galilee. Saying, The Son of man must be delivered into the hands of sinful men, and be crucified, and the third day rise again. And they remembered his words' (Luke 24:6-8). Luke is being emphatic; from those early days in Galilee to the last days in Jerusalem, and for all the days in between, Jesus is accompanied by his close circle of women and by his twelve male disciples. Both the women and the men have shared in his teachings and have received his intimate revelations.

But the real radical was not Jesus. The radicals were the women. Jesus may have been unusual and inclusive in his outlook, but there was no question of having women in his movement unless – against almost all the laws and customs of Jewish society in Palestine – these women could live independently of family ties. The women in Jesus' entourage were not performing the conventional female roles of cooking meals and washing clothes, or if they were Luke does not say so, but what he does say is that neither Jesus nor any of his followers, women or men, were engaged in economically productive work. Just as the men have given up their employment to follow Jesus, Mary Magdalene and the other women exercised their independence and used their financial means to make the mission possible.

Yet if anything restrictions on Jewish women in Palestine were most severe at the time of Mary Magdalene, the moment when Judaism was most fiercely engaged in the struggle to preserve its identity against the influences of Hellenistic culture. While women

'Thy faith hath made thee whole', Jesus says to the woman with an issue of blood who touches the hem of his garment. The wall painting was discovered in the 3rd-century Catacombs of Marcellinus and Peter in Rome.

belonging to the Hellenistic world, from Italy through Greece and to Egypt, enjoyed increasing independence and financial opportunities, Jewish women of Judaea and Galilee were subjected to ever stricter interpetations of the Torah and yet more elaborate regulations.

In the traditional Jewish cultural environment of Palestine one woman of independent means can be an exception, but Luke's gospel tells us that Jesus was accompanied by Mary Magdalene 'and many others, which ministered unto him of their substance' (or 'provided for them out of their own resources' as the phrase is translated in the *New English Bible*). How did Mary Magdalene and her female companions come by their money? How had they preserved their independence from the men in their families? The gospels do not say.

Follow Me

According to Luke's gospel, John the Baptist began his mission in the fifteenth year of the reign of the emperor Tiberius, that is AD 29. John's mission did not last long; he was soon imprisoned and then beheaded, probably in that same year, which was also the year he baptised Jesus. As the gospel of Matthew 4:12-17 explains, Jesus had been forty days in the wilderness resisting the temptations of the devil, but 'now when Jesus had heard that John was cast into prison, he departed into Galilee; and leaving Nazareth, he came and dwelt in Capernaum ... From that time Jesus began to preach, and to say, Repent: for the kingdom of heaven is at hand'.

Follow me. Jesus calls the fishermen of Bethsaida and Capernaum to him, telling them that they will become fishers of men. German, early-16th century.

The first of the twelve disciples chosen by Jesus were Peter and Andrew, brothers and fishermen from Bethsaida, close by the River Jordan where it runs into the fresh waters of the Sea of Galilee. He said to them, 'Follow me, and I will make you fishers of men'. And as Matthew's gospel 4:18-24 says, 'They straightway left their nets, and followed him'. Continuing along the shore at Bethsaida, Jesus saw another two brothers, James and John, who were in a ship with their father Zebedee, mending their nets, and he called to them. 'And they immediately left the ship and their father, and followed him.'

Bethsaida was a fishing village close by the town of Capernaum on the north shore of the great freshwater lake. When Jesus then came into Capernaum and saw Matthew, a tax collector there, sitting at his work, he said, 'Follow me. And he arose, and followed him' (Matthew 9:9).

And so it went with all the twelve disciples, Simon (whom Jesus called Peter) and his brother Andrew; the brothers James and John, the sons of Zebedee; Matthew (also called Levi); Philip; Bartholomew (Nathanael); Thomas; James, the son of Alphaeus; Thaddaeus (also called Judas or Jude); Simon and Judas Iscariot. Jesus called, 'Follow me', and they left their work and they followed him.

Jesus taught in the synagogues and he healed all manner of sickness among the people, those afflicted with torments and diseases, the insane and those possessed with devils or trembling with palsy; and all the while he preached the kingdom of God. His mission took him all round Galilee and attracted Jews from Syria and beyond the Jordan and from Jerusalem; he led an army of healing and salvation, with camp followers and crowds of people eager to hear, to be healed and to be saved – a great campaign moving through the villages and towns of Galilee – that somebody had to pay for.

But there were even more than Jesus and the twelve to support, for the disciples sometimes travelled with women, who Paul's letter, 1 Corinthians 9:5, describes as their 'sisters and wives', and most likely they travelled with their children too. Or if they left them behind, these women and children still had to be supported, and the rest of the disciples' families as well; Peter, for one, was married and had a mother-in-law too; how did Peter's wife and mother-in-law survive?

Food, shelter and clothing for thirteen people for a year, possibly three years according to some estimates of the length of Jesus' mission, and for their dependents too. Also on at least one occasion Jesus sent out seventy people to prepare the way for his mission round the towns of Galilee: 'After these things the Lord appointed other seventy also, and sent them two and two before his face into every city and place, whither he himself would come' (Luke 10:1).

Paying for Jesus

Jesus himself in Mark 10:28-30 remarked on the scale of his undertaking and the sacrifices and costs involved.

> Then Peter began to say unto him, Lo, we have left all, and have followed thee. And Jesus answered and said, Verily I say unto you, There is no man that hath left house, or brethren, or sisters, or father, or mother, or wife, or children, or lands, for my sake, and the gospel's, But he shall receive an hundredfold now in this time, houses, and brethren, and sisters, and mothers, and children, and lands, with persecutions; and in the world to come eternal life.

But though Jesus talks of the spiritual reward, there was a financial cost as well. Who had the money to finance such major undertakings?

The gospel of Luke 8:1-3 gives the answer: Mary Magdalene, Joanna and Susanna and 'many others' (all women, for the original Greek of 'many others' is plural feminine) provided for Jesus and the twelve disciples out of their own resources. In other words Mary Magdalene and the other women were socially and financially independent and had sufficient means to help keep Jesus and his twelve disciples on the road, and to help maintain an unknown number of wives, children, aged parents and other dependent relatives left behind when the disciples 'followed him'.

Capernaum was Jesus' headquarters in Galilee. This aerial view shows the results of excavations and restoration works. On the right is a fourth-century AD synagogue which stands on the site of an earlier synagogue where Jesus would have taught. The structure on the left is a Franciscan church. The octagonal shape is owed to the foundations of an early Byzantine church which turned out to be built over an earlier house; the supposition is that Early Christians believed the house to be that of Peter whose walls can be seen by visitors today who enter into the heart of the church.

But how can that be? Luke's statement that Mary Magdalene and the other women were providing for Jesus and the disciples out of their resources is remarkable and strange considering that there were few economic activities open to Jewish women in Palestine and little opportunity for women to lead independent lives. In fact Jewish society in first-century AD Palestine was one of the most male-dominated and conservative societies in the ancient world and women's lives were tightly restricted and controlled.

The Old Testament mentions some exceptional cases, for example Deborah who in earliest history, at least as far back as the twelfth century BC, served as a judge and a military commander in battle against the Canaanites, and other women who in later times were prophets, sages and sorceresses, but from the end of the Babylonian exile in 538 BC Jewish women in Palestine were confined to domestic duties and tasks.

A woman who needed to earn an income could extend her domestic activities into the market place where she could sell clothing, farm produce and bread (though bakers were men), or she could be an innkeeper, letting out rooms in her house. Hairdresser, midwife and professional mourner were traditional occupations for women. But a woman's earnings were for the benefit of her family; she was not free to dispose of her money herself.

In Judaism women were legally the property of men. Before marriage girls were the property of their fathers; after marriage a woman became the property of her husband. Widows were placed under the authority of their fathers, sons, uncles or brothers-in-law. A woman achieved a measure of social standing by becoming the mother of a son, but if she remained childless for ten years her husband was obliged to divorce her. Men could initiate divorce at will; women were bound to remain married and faithful.

Women were not permitted to receive an education. Such religious instruction as they received at home was given by men. Women were not free to become followers of a teacher or rabbi and they certainly could not travel with one. They did not count among the necessary quorum of Jews required for worship – only men mattered. A woman's testimony was not accepted as evidence in a court of law.

Generally Jewish women were almost entirely dependent on men economically. They did not own property except in the rare case of inheriting land from a father who had no sons, and even then they were required to remarry within the tribe so as not to reduce its land holdings.

The first-century AD Roman-Jewish historian Josephus, writing of the Torah, summed matters up: 'The woman, says the Law, is in all things inferior to the man. Let her accordingly be submissive, not for her humiliation, but that she may be directed; for the authority has been given by God to the man.'

Independent Women

But the gospels tell us otherwise, about women who are not submissive, who are not under the authority of men; about women who are socially and financially independent. How to account for this? In speaking of Joanna, Luke gives us some clues. He says that Joanna was the wife of Chuza, who as Herod's steward was his minister of finance, or at the very least the steward of one of Herod's estates and in any case an important man. By mentioning Chuza, Luke emphasises Joanna's association with the rich and powerful; he shows the range of Jesus' appeal, to the poor and the marginal but also to those at the pinnacle of society; and he tells us that Joanna was a major financial contributor to Jesus' movement.

Joanna was probably from an aristocratic Galilean landowning family and one of those Herodian women known to have supported and financed the Pharisees who in turn opposed the Graeco-Roman culture promoted by the Herodian dynasty. It is not such a contradiction as it sounds. Herod Antipas made allies among the Pharisees in order to limit the power of the Sadducees, the old Judaean aristocracy who controlled the priesthood and Temple at Jerusalem; his ambition was to become king as his father Herod the Great had been, and the first step, with the support of the Pharisees, was to place himself at the centre of Jewish religious life by gaining authority over the Temple priesthood. But for Joanna to finance Pharisees was one thing and to follow Jesus was another matter; she may have been attracted to the message of John the Baptist and at his execution by Herod was drawn to Jesus. Not that Luke necessarily means that Joanna was still in a state of marriage; indeed it is hard to see her husband at the court of Herod allowing her to roam with Jesus and his followers. Instead, Chuza might have been dead, or he might have divorced Joanna.

Mary Magdalene by Sebastiano del Piombo, church of San Giovanni Crisostomo, Venice, 1510. Sebastiano has captured a Mary Magdalene more true to the gospels than the usually simpering, repentant, reclusive, passive, self-abasing Magdalene of Church mythology; instead here she is portrayed as a bold and superior woman, mysterious and powerful. 'This face and figure', said the novelist Henry James, 'are almost unique among the beautiful things of Venice'. She is 'a strange, a dangerous' woman, he said, 'she walks like a goddess. ... This magnificent creature is so strong and secure that she is gentle. ... But for all this there are depths of possible disorder in her light-coloured eye'.

Divorce and widowhood were the most likely ways in which a woman could find herself independent of men's control and also become financially independent, and this was particularly so if she belonged to an upper-class family.

A bride's father paid a dowry to her husband which he was free to use during the course of his marriage but if he divorced his wife or predeceased her the dowry was paid to her. In the case of wealthy families this could be a considerable sum. In addition there might be her ketubba, originally a bride price paid by a husband to the father of his bride as compensation for the loss of her domestic labours, but by the first century AD this had become a promise against the value of the husband's estate to provide for his divorced or widowed wife. Like the dowry, the value of the ketubba agreed among wealthy families could be very great.

Jewish law worked against the likelihood of women gaining from inheritance. The Torah prescribed that a woman could inherit her husband's entire estate only if the marriage and his previous marriages were childless. And a daughter could only inherit from her father if he had no sons or grandsons.

But Judaism's patriarchal system was not always as rigid as it seemed. A practice arose in upper class families for a father, husband, mother, brother or other relative to make a gift of property or other forms of wealth to a daughter, wife or sister. By speaking of gift rather than inheritance, disobedience to the Torah was avoided. This allowed women to acquire, own and dispose of property independently of men.

Hellenised Jews

The position of Hellenised women, including Hellenised Jewish women, was very different to women constrained by strict Jewish tradition. In the Jewish diaspora, in Syria, in Asia Minor, in Egypt, where Greek values and Roman law were the norm, Jewish women enjoyed more rights and autonomy; they could take oaths, be witnesses in court, initiate divorce, own property and engage in business. In Palestine the obstacles to the independence of Jewish women remained formidable, but upper-class women of powerful families were able to bend the rules, while Hellenised families and their women could ignore them altogether.

Hellenisation had spread in various degrees into all levels of Jewish Palestinian society, not least into the priestly class. Tellingly, the inscription at the Temple at Jerusalem warning strangers not to advance beyond a certain point was in Greek, and the Temple coffers into which the faithful put their contributions were also marked in Greek. Hebrew was all but a dead language except for liturgical use and almost all Jews spoke Aramaic or Greek; the Temple signs in Greek conceded the reality of Hellenised Jews and Jews of the diaspora, those of Syria and Asia Minor and Egypt, whose common language was Greek.

Jews were among the greatest beneficiaries of Hellenisation. Large numbers of Jews had long since left their homeland and lived as far afield as Mesopotamia and Egypt, Syria, Asia Minor and Greece; there were far more Jews in the diaspora than in Palestine and to a greater or lesser degree they had become Hellenised.

In Alexandria in Egypt, for example, founded by Alexander and the greatest of Hellenistic cities, where Jews numbered about two-fifths of the population, they had so lost their knowledge of Hebrew that the Torah and the rest of the Jewish Bible had to be translated into Greek as the Septuagint. When the New Testament, which was written in Greek, quoted the Old Testament, it did so not from the original Hebrew but directly from the Alexandrian Greek of the Septuagint.

The Septuagint was produced at the command of Ptolemy II Philadelphus. The Ptolemies, the dynastic successors to Alexander the Great, who ruled Egypt for three hundred years, concluding with the reign of the famous Cleopatra, strongly favoured the Jews. Ptolemy I Soter, the founder of the dynasty, introduced 30,000 Jewish colonists to Egypt at the beginning of the third century BC. A great wave of Jews left Palestine in the second century BC propelled by the 160s BC Maccabean revolt against the Seleucids, who like the Ptolemies were dynastic successors of Alexander and ruled over

So prevalent was the use of Greek among Jews of the diaspora, most of whom would have known no Hebrew or Aramaic at all, that the Temple authorities in Jerusalem had to set up this warning in Greek. 'No foreigner may enter within the balustrade around the sanctuary and the enclosure. Whoever is caught, on himself shall he put blame for the death which will ensue.' By foreigner the inscription means any non-Jew.

much of the Middle East. This new influx of Jews joined their already Hellenised compatriots in the Delta and the Fayyum and in Alexandria, and many rose to high positions; during the reign of Ptolemy IV, in the mid-second century BC, the control of Egypt's armed forces was entrusted to Onias IV, the emigrant son of the high priest at the Temple in Jerusalem.

Hellenised names became very common among Jews and their adoption of the Greek language was practically universal – the gospel writers called the rabbi Joshua, or Yeshua, by his Hellenised name, Jesus. The use of Greek encouraged Jews to adapt themselves in externals to the pattern of life around them to a remarkable degree, while preserving their distinct beliefs and practices. There are numerous examples of Jews in Egypt choosing to use Greek law and Greek courts despite the availability of their own independent and protected Jewish legal institutions. Jews also swore oaths by pagan deities. Jewish synagogue dedications read

The great lighthouse of Alexandria and the Greek version of the Jewish Bible were born at the same time, in the same city, on the same island of Pharos. The Jews of Egypt had so completely lost their knowledge of Hebrew that Ptolemy II Philadelphus, who was king from 283 to 246 BC, commissioned a Greek version of the Jewish Bible, called the Septuagint. This was the Bible commonly known not only to Hellenised Jews throughout the diaspora but to educated Jews in Palestine. When the New Testamant writers quote the Old Testament, they are quoting the Alexandrian Greek of the Septuagint. Septuagint means seventy in Greek and refers to the legend that Ptolemy II employed seventy Jewish scholars to translate the Hebrew to Greek. Each man was housed separately on the island of Pharos where Ptolemy had also constructed Alexandria's towering lighthouse, one of the Seven Wonders of the Ancient World, which took its name, the Pharos, from the island. When the work of translation was finished the seventy versions were compared and all were found to be identical.

just like pagan dedications to accommodate with Ptolemaic and Roman rule, but unlike pagan temples no statues were permitted in synagogues. Generally Jews accommodated themselves with the pagan world while maintaining the exclusive nature of their faith.

Second only to Egypt, Hellenic influence was strongest along the eastern shore of the Mediterranean, that is all along the coast of Palestine and Syria. Hellenism also took a firm hold in eastern Palestine; the cities of the Decapolis to the east and north of the Sea of Galilee were centres of Greek influence. In greater or lesser degree Hellenism made itself felt throughout Palestine and among all classes and in every area of life.

Greek-speaking Jews to some degree adapted belief and practice to Greek ways. This would have been especially true at Tiberias, but there were other major centres of Hellenism in Galilee too – Magadan, for instance, the city that centuries later a Byzantine scribe decided to call Magdala. Magadan was founded by the Jewish Hasmonean dynasty, who themselves were Hellenised and who – as the recent excavations show – built their city along Hellenistic lines. Morevoer, despite the Jewish prohibition on depicting living creatures, a Hellenistic-style first-century AD mosaic depicting a boat and fish has been unearthed at Magadan. Perhaps Mary Magdalene really did come from the city we now call Magdala, but whether from Magadan or Tiberias or some other place in Galilee or even from Jerusalem or elsewhere in Palestine, or from somewhere in the Jewish diaspora, her independence suggests that she was used to moving in a Hellenised world.

The Populations of Palestine and the Diaspora

Estimates for the size of populations in the ancient world based on the evidence of ancient authors themselves are almost always exaggerations and often demographically impossible. For example Josephus claims that 1.1 million people were killed during the Roman siege of Jerusalem in AD 70, but it is enough to know the area of the city enclosed by its walls to realise that this figure can have no basis in reality.

Scholars therefore have sought more reliable ways of determining population size. In the case of Palestine the most generally accepted method is to use the grain-growing capacity of the land which has remained constant until fairly recent times. There is good information available on grain consumption in the ancient world, in cities and towns and villages right round the Eastern Mediterranean from Greece to Egypt, and this compares closely to consumption in the same areas right up to the early twentieth century, including Palestine. Moreover there is good data from the ancient world telling the annual grain requirements of a labourer, a family, a soldier and so on. Average annual consumption can therefore be fairly accurately determined and when this information is correlated with grain growing capacity we arrive at the sustainable population size.

On this basis the first-century AD population of Palestine stood at about one million. But not all of these were Jews. There were Greeks, Canaanites and others living in Palestine at the time. For example, the Jewish Hasmonean dynasty began by controlling a fairly homogeneous Jewish population immediately round Jerusalem, numbering about a hundred thousand, but by the early first century BC the Hasmonean high priest, who was also the king, had greatly extended his boundaries to all of Palestine and also the Decapolis and ruled over an ethnically and culturally diverse population of nearly a million, doing so by means of an ethnically diverse administration drawn from powerful families of the subject districts.

Late in the first century BC the Hasmoneans were overthrown by the Romans and replaced by the dynasty of Herod the Great. The population was as mixed as ever and the Jewish element is not thought to have been much greater than half. At the time of Jesus, therefore, in the first century AD, the total population of Palestine stood at about one million and its Jewish population just over five hundred thousand.

But the Jews of Palestine were only a small proportion of the Jews throughout the ancient world, a dispersion that had been going on since at least the sixth century BC when the Persians conquered

Palestine. Even then Greeks were already settling and trading and serving as mercenaries throughout the East, but with the defeat of the Persians by Alexander the Great in the late fourth century BC all of the lands round the Eastern Mediterranean became influenced by Hellenism. The great Hellenistic cities were Alexandria in Egypt and Antioch in Syria, precisely the cities and the countries where the greatest numbers of Jews were to be found.

One ancient author who is thought to give reliable figures is the first-century AD Jewish philospher Philo, a citizen of Alexandria, who said there were one million Jews in Egypt out of a total population of about eight million. The Egyptians kept accurate population figures for taxation purposes, so Philo's number is unlikely to be fanciful. Jews were particularly concentrated in Alexandria. Piecing together written evidence, it is thought that the city's population was at least half a million, of which two thirds were said to be Jews; so something over 200,000 Jews lived in Alexandria in the first century AD.

Syria was also home to many Jews and there was a particular concentration of Jews in Antioch. Jews were numerous also in Asia Minor, Greece and Rome.

Whatever their precise accuracy, the figures demonstrate that by far the greater number of Jews in the ancient world lived outside Palestine. They paid their annual tribute to the Temple in Jerusalem and came to pray and sacrifice there when they could, but culturally they were Hellenised Jews of the diaspora.

Even within Palestine itself the Jews were part of a heterogeneous population that was likewise largely Hellenised, and many of these would have been Hellenised Jews.

CHAPTER FOUR

The Abomination of Desolation

W E KNOW WHAT JOANNA was doing in Tiberias. She was the wife of Chuza, steward to Herod Antipas, and Herod had his court at Tiberias. Herod had only recently, in AD 19, built his gleaming new capital on the Sea of Galilee; he named it after his benefactor the Roman emperor Tiberius and he gave it the appearance of a Graeco-Roman city. A wealthy woman, independent and free to follow her own inclinations, would have been at home in Tiberias, delightful for its lake breezes, for its shops and entertainments and luxurious spas, and for its easy ways. A woman like Joanna, and maybe a woman like Mary Magdalene.

Herod's New Capital

Tiberias was built as an open city – powerful walls were added only later in the century – and it was laid out to a Hellenistic plan, the colonnaded cardo maximus forming a north-south spine with a grid

Tiberias from the air sometime between 1910 and 1920. Like the ancient city built by Herod Antipas, this recent Tiberias is a long narrow strip along the shore of the Sea of Galilee, hemmed in by mountains behind. Though delightful for its lake breezes, when they were not blowing the atmosphere of the city could be close and feverish.

pattern of streets running off on either side. The cardo was lined with shops and statues, its surface patterned with basalt paving stones, and beneath it were pipes that distributed water to homes and fountains throughout the city, drawn by an aqueduct from springs to the east.

There were temples to Diana, Mars and Apollo; naked statues of Venus celebrated the goddess in the city baths; and a luxurious spa was fed from hot springs nearby. A great oval stadium gratified the Greek passion for sports and games and the Roman taste for gladiators and wild animals engaged in deadly combat, while a semi-circular theatre entertained audiences of seven thousand with

Herod Antipas built a complete Roman-style city here on the shores of the Sea of Galilee, including an amphitheatre seating seven thousand for plays and other entertainments.

lectures and plays. Herod also built himself a magnificent palace at Tiberias, its walls richly decorated with scenes of painted or carved animals. The fertility of the surrounding farmland was proverbial and the city's position by the teeming lake provided a handsome living for fishermen.

But though Herod founded Tiberias in the lifetime of Jesus, it is mentioned only once in the New Testament, and then only to say that some boats from the city had carried people across the lake to hear Jesus give a sermon on the far shore (John 6:23). Perhaps once upon a time Mary Magdalene had made that crossing with Joanna to join the multitudes gathering to hear Jesus. But this time, as the boats sailed across the lake from Tiberias, Mary Magdalene was already on the far shore standing with Jesus and his disciples as he gave his last great sermon.

Loaves and Fishes

The events surrounding that sermon, including the miracle of the loaves and fishes, would mark the climax of Jesus' ministry in Galilee and lead directly to his crucifixion.

Herod, who had recently executed John the Baptist, began receiving reports of Jesus' preachings. Luke 9:7-9 describes their unnerving effect. 'Now Herod the tetrarch heard of all that was done by [Jesus]: and he was perplexed, because that it was said of some, that John was risen from the dead. ... And Herod said, John have I beheaded: but who is this, of whom I hear such things? And he desired to see him.'

Jesus instead withdrew into a remote place near Bethsaida where he was followed by a great multitude wanting him to speak to them of the kingdom of God and to heal those who needed healing. 'And when the day began to wear away', reports Luke 9:12-14, 'then came the twelve, and said unto him, Send the multitude away, that they may go into the towns and country round about, and lodge, and get victuals: for we are here in a desert place'. There were five thousand men to feed and great numbers of women and children too, but 'we have no more but five loaves and two fishes'. The miracle that followed, when Jesus said 'Give ye them to eat', and there was food enough for everyone, is one of only two miracles that is recorded in all four gospels – the other being the resurrection.

Afterwards Jesus prayed with his disciples, among them Mary Magdalene, and he asked them, 'Whom say the people that I am? They answering said, John the Baptist; but some say, Elias [Elijah]; and others say, that one of the old prophets is risen again. He said unto them, But whom say ye that I am? Peter answering said, The Christ of God.' This was the moment, according to Luke, that Jesus was recognised as the messiah. But 'he straitly charged them, and commanded them to tell no man that thing; Saying, The Son of man must suffer many things, and be rejected of the elders and chief priests and scribes, and be slain, and be raised the third day' (Luke 9:18-22).

Across the Sea of Galilee near Capernaum and Bethsaida Jesus heals the
sick and feeds the multitude. Jean LeClerc, French, early 17th century.

Jesus' mission in Galilee was at an end and now he turned
towards Jerusalem, to that momentous passion week concluding
with his crucifixion, his burial and his resurrection. 'And it came
to pass, when the time was come that he should be received up, he
stedfastly set his face to go to Jerusalem' (Luke 9:51).

Mary Magdalene was later reminded of those moments that
had taken place on the far shore of the Sea of Galilee when after
the crucifixion and after she discovered the empty tomb, two men
in shining garments appeared to her, saying, 'Why seek ye the living among the dead? He is not here, but is risen: remember how
he spake unto you when he was yet in Galilee. Saying, The Son of
man must be delivered into the hands of sinful men, and be crucified, and the third day rise again' (Luke 24:6-8).

Spiritual Pollution

The contrast between those two shores of the Sea of Galilee, the region to the north round Bethsaida and Capernaum which Jesus made the centre of his mission, and Herod's capital to the southwest at Tiberias could not have been greater. In the north people in their thousands followed Jesus and listened to his words about the kingdom of God. Across the water Herod's Tiberias was a spiritually polluted city, the abomination of desolation. Jesus appears to have avoided going to Tiberias; the gospels make no mention of him ever going there. But Mary Magdalene, companion of Joanna, wife of Chuza, may have known Tiberias all too well.

While Tiberias was a monument to Greek and Roman values it was a monumental desecration of Jewish beliefs, a standing testimony to Herod and his court's dismissive attitude to the prescriptions of the Torah. Not only had Herod married his brother's wife, for which John the Baptist charged him with breaching sacred law, but he also lavishly decorated his new palace with representations of animals, again in violation of the Torah. But worst of all, Herod had built his new city on a Jewish cemetery, knowing that corpse impurity was the worst kind of spiritual pollution. No devout Jew wanted to live there.

Josephus describes how Herod had to resort to grants of land and free housing to induce people to settle in Tiberias, how he admitted the poor and granted freedom to slaves if they would live in the city and even forced well-to-do Galileans to settle there. Relying on the lure of the court and the promise of prosperity, Herod also drew gentiles and foreigners to Tiberias.

> Strangers came and inhabited this city; a great number
> of the inhabitants were Galileans also; and many were
> necessitated by Herod to come thither out of the coun-
> try belonging to him, and were by force compelled to be
> its inhabitants; some of them were persons of condition.
> He also admitted poor people, such as those that were

collected from all parts, to dwell in it. Nay, some of them were not quite free-men, and these he was benefactor to, and made them free in great numbers; but obliged them not to forsake the city, by building them very good houses at his own expense, and by giving them land also; for he was sensible that to make this place a habitation was to transgress the Jewish ancient laws, because many sepulchres were to be here taken away, in order to make room for the city.

Sorceresses and Devils

When Jesus went about Galilee preaching the kingdom of God, says Luke 8:1-3, he was accompanied by 'certain women, which had been healed of evil spirits and infirmities', among them 'Mary called Magdalene, out of whom went seven devils, And Joanna the wife of Chuza, Herod's steward, and Susanna, and many others, which ministered unto him of their substance'. Mary Magdalene is mentioned first and she is also the worst afflicted; she has been tormented by seven devils.

There is a popular misconception, which was first promoted by the Church in the early medieval period, that Mary Magdalene's condition had something to do with sin. But this is plainly not true. Wherever Jesus is driving out devils the gospels are clear that he is healing people of their illnesses, mental and physical. 'And they brought unto him all sick people', says Matthew 4:24, 'that were taken with divers diseases and torments, and those which were possessed with devils, and those which were lunatick, and those that had the palsy; and he healed them.' Jesus heals blindness, deafness, paralysis, epilepsy and madness by driving out devils. 'Then was brought unto him one possessed with a devil, blind, and dumb: and he healed him' (Matthew 12:22). 'And it came to pass, when the devil was gone out, the dumb spake' (Luke 11:14). Jesus taught his disciples to do the same: 'Then he called his twelve disciples together, and gave them power and authority over all devils, and

66

Mary Magdalene is exorcised by Jesus who drives out seven devils in this
Early Christian wall painting.

to cure diseases' (Luke 9:1); and his disciples 'cast out many devils,
and anointed with oil many that were sick, and healed them' (Mark
6:13). Nowhere in the gospels does Jesus' healing campaign mean
driving out devils to rid people of sin, least of all does it mean
cleansing people of lust.

So Mary Magdalene is tormented by seven devils. But it is not
the word devils that makes Mary Magdalene the worst afflicted.
The word for devils in the original Greek of Luke is daimonia
which different editions of the Bible translate as devils or demons
but the meaning is the same. The other women suffer from evil
spirits, pneumaton poneton in the original Greek, which is simply another way of saying demon or devil. All the women, Mary
Magdalene, Joanna, Susanna and the rest suffer from spirits that
are evil.

What distinguishes Mary Magdalene's affliction is the number
seven. In the numerologies of ancient Egypt, Babylon and Persia
and in ancient Hebrew the number seven symbolised totality or
completion, so that in Genesis God made the heaven and the earth
and rested on the seventh day when creation was complete; while
in Revelation, the last book of the New Testament, there are seven

churches, seven stars, seven angels, seven spirits of God, seven seals, seven trumpets, seven thunders, seven heads, seven plagues, seven cups, seven mountains and seven kings – again expressing completeness or totality. The other women with Jesus had been afflicted and possessed, but Mary Magdalene's possession had been complete; she had been totally possessed by demons.

All these women, Mary Magdalene, Joanna and Susannah and the many others, are afflicted as though all of them are tormented by a shared spiritual condition. Joanna came from Herod's spiritually polluted capital of Tiberias and perhaps all the other women did too; like the city itself the women would have been made unclean by the evil spirits.

But though Tiberias was a centre for Herod's Hellenistic disregard for a strict adherence to Jewish beliefs and traditions, the problem was extensive and profound. Thoughout the towns and villages of Galilee Jesus was exorcising demons from people who came from far beyond, even from Jerusalem itself, the site of the Temple, Judaism's holiest shrine. 'And a great multitude from Galilee followed him', says Mark 3: 7-11, 'and from Judaea, And from Jerusalem, and from Idumaea, and from beyond Jordan; and they about Tyre and Sidon, a great multitude, when they had heard what great things he did, came unto him ... And unclean spirits, when they saw him, fell down before him, and cried, saying, Thou art the Son of God'. At a time when traditional beliefs were being undermined, the widespread sense of pollution and fear of demons became the disease of the age.

The Pharisees presented their version of the cure; ever closer observance of the Torah. But for women, who lived on the margins of Jewish ritual activity from which they were largely excluded, there was another answer: many turned to sorcery. This was an attempt by women to draw upon sacred forces and wisdom to combat afflictions or otherwise gain control over their lives and to promote for themselves and others health, knowledge, power or success. But it brought them dangerously close to the afflictions and demons they sought to cure or control; moreover, because female sorcery challenged the patriarchal structure of Judaism they were often condemned as themselves being agents of demons. Sorcery, or witchcraft, was powerfully condemned throughout the Old Testament, as in Exodus 22:18 'Though shalt not suffer a witch to live', a dictum that justified the hanging and burning of witches right up to modern times in Europe and America. But the legal prohibitions on sorcery and strong attacks on it in the Old Testament show that it was a persistent activity, part of the popular religion of Israel.

That so many women companions of Jesus were afflicted by evil spirits suggests that they had all shared the same experience, had all sensed acutely the spiritual ills of the age. All may have undergone renewal at the hands of John the Baptist, and all may have turned to some form of healing, but at his arrest and his death they looked for a new source of cleansing and found it in Jesus. The most spiritually sensitive of these women, the most aware and open to the kingdom of God, the one who most entirely immersed herself in battling demons – so that she was possessed by seven devils – was Mary Magdalene.

At the Court of Herod

Mary Magdalene and Joanna, the wife of Chuza, travelled together round Galilee with Jesus and his other followers. Joanna, as we know, was part of Herod's court at Tiberias. We can learn a lot more about Joanna and about the circumstances of Jesus' ministry – and about Mary Magdalene too – if we take a close look at Herod's unusual court.

Herod's capital was thoroughly Hellenised and mixed, and his court was mixed too. Joanna was Jewish, probably of an aristocratic landowning Galilean family, but her husband Chuza was an Arab. Chuza is a Nabatean name; Nabatea was an Arab kingdom with its capital at Petra in present-day Jordan. Herod Antipas' first wife, Phasaelis, was also Nabatean, that is his wife before he married his brother's wife Herodias for which he was denounced by John the Baptist. Chuza, who was likely high born, may well have come to the court at the time of Herod's first marriage; in marrying Joanna the pressure of Jewish tradition would probably have demanded that Chuza convert to Judaism, but as far as external proof was concerned he could have passed as a Jew because as an Arab he may already have been circumcised, and it is quite possible that privately he remained a polytheistic pagan. Even if he had genuinely converted he may well have worn his Judaism lightly.

It was suggested in an earlier chapter that it would be hard to imagine Chuza, a high ranking official at Herod's court, allowing his wife Joanna to roam with Jesus and his followers, and that perhaps he had divorced her or was dead. But at one point Herod himself was drawn to what John the Baptist and Jesus had to say; as Mark 6:20 tells us, Herod was much taken by John the Baptist and 'heard him gladly', and also he was keen to hear about Jesus' remarkable healings: 'Herod said, "... who is this man about whom I hear such things?" And he kept trying to see Him' (Luke 9:9). Initially, it seems, there was a certain tolerance and curiosity towards John the Baptist and Jesus. But that was before Herod gave way to the hatred and schemes of his new wife Herodias who demanded John the Baptist's head on a platter, at which Jesus took himself away to a remote place.

The closer we look at Herod's court the more we discover its contradictions, on the one hand how Herod himself and several closest to him were attracted to the preachings of John the Baptist and Jesus about the kingdom of God, on the other the fear that the kingdom of God would undermine the kingdom of Herod and could only be met in the most ruthless way. Chuza and Joanna would have experienced this volatile atmosphere at first hand, perhaps even witnessing Salome's infamous dance – and Manaen would have too.

No one was closer to the heart of the court than Manaen, Herod's childhood companion, his foster-brother and his closest advisor – yet he would become one of the founders of the Christian church at Antioch in Syria, the very place where the followers of Jesus were first called Christians, and there he would mentor Paul

Herod Antipas first ruled from Sepphoris, which he rebuilt, in the words of Josephus, as 'the ornament of Galilee'. Jesus grew up in Nazareth only four miles to the northwest and could hardly have escaped the atmosphere of Hellenism that pervaded Galilee. Even after Antipas transferred his capital to Tiberias, Sepphoris continued to flourish as witnessed by this beautiful floor mosaic dating from the end of the second century AD. Popularly known as 'the Mona Lisa of Galilee' she suffers not from devils but from love, if she suffers at all. But this was the world rejected by Jesus and the reformist Jews of his time.

and send him with Barnabas on his first great missionary journey. 'Now there were in the church that was at Antioch certain prophets and teachers; as Barnabas, and Simeon that was called Niger, and Lucius of Cyrene, and Manaen, which had been brought up with Herod the tetrarch, and Saul' (Acts 13:1).

Here 'brought up with' is the translation of syntrophos, the original Greek word used by Luke when writing Acts. Syntrophos means 'brought up with', 'reared up together', 'foster-brother', 'fed from the same breast'. In the Hellenistic kingdoms of the East syntrophos was a title designating a courtier as the intimate friend of the king. From boyhood to manhood Manaen was a trusted member of Herod Antipas' innermost circle.

Manean went from Herod's inner circle to being a founding father of the Christian Church. Herod was educated at Rome and we can assume that Manaen was too; he was probably the first of Jesus' followers to have lived in the imperial city and it may have been by his guidance that Paul directed his life towards Rome. He was a man who knew Paul; many scholars think he must also have been known by Luke, who is thought to have been from Antioch, and that this accounts for the numerous references to Herod Antipas in Luke's gospel, far more than in any other gospel.

Joanna is thought to have been one of Luke's sources too, further accounting for Luke's knowledge of Herod's court and for the large number of references to women in his gospel. Joanna and Manaen would also have provided their own eyewitness testimony to the accounts in Mark and Matthew of the circumstances surrounding John the Baptist's death.

Like Manaen, Joanna had an afterlife, that is after the crucifixion of Jesus, for according to some scholars she is the Junia who appears in Paul's epistle to the Romans 16:7 where he speaks of being in jail with fellow Christians in Rome. 'Salute Andronicus and Junia, my kinsmen, and my fellow prisoners, who are of note among the apostles, who also were in Christ before me.' Hellenised Jews would have two names, one their Jewish name. To boy children their parents also gave a Greek name and to their girl children they gave a Roman name. Junia is thought to be Joanna's Roman name. And Andronicus might possibly be Chuza; if he became a follower of Jesus and went to Rome he may well have taken this Greek name. Or Chuza might have died and Junia was remarried.

However it was, it is striking that Paul calls Junia and Andronicus 'apostles, who also were in Christ before me'. For Matthew, Mark and Luke an apostle is one of the twelve disciples; an apostle has to be a companion of Jesus and a witness to the resurrection. For Paul, who did not know Jesus in his lifetime, an apostle was one who was called by an appearance of the risen Jesus, which according to his epistle 1 Corinthians 15:5-9 included hundreds of people, including himself because he had seen Jesus in a vision; and Paul also counted as an apostle any man or woman who was delegated by a church, such as that at Antioch, to promote the word, which again included himself.

One way or another Junia and Andronicus were apostles and they became so before Paul's conversion (they 'were in Christ before me'), which very much makes it look that Junia knew Jesus in his lifetime and therefore could well be Joanna and as if to have been a witness of everything from the time of Jesus' baptism by John.

Circle of Familiarity

Many of the characters of the gospel story – Herod and Joanna and Menaen and John the Baptist and Jesus – lived within a circle of familiarity. The mood of spiritual renewal engaged them all, and their backgrounds were less dissimilar than we might first think.

John the Baptist's family may also have been part of the Hellenistic elite; John's father Zechariah had been a priest at the Temple in Jerusalem, a position he owed to Herod Antipas' father, Herod the Great, acting on behalf of the Romans who had the final word in appointing the priests.

And if Luke 1:36 is correct in saying Jesus was the cousin of John the Baptist, that would at the very least place Jesus on the fringe of that Hellenised elite. No gospel says that Jesus is a carpenter; instead in one gospel the question is raised whether Jesus is the son of Joseph the carpenter while in another the question is whether Jesus himself is a carpenter. The original Greek word tekton, used in the gospels, can mean builder, also a creator, or a master in some field, for example a master in medicine or in literary composition, and in turn it may have been a translation of the Aramaic naggar, which can mean scholar.

Matthew 13:55 says only that Joseph was a carpenter, not Jesus: 'Is not this the carpenter's son? is not his mother called Mary? and his brethren, James, and Joses, and Simon, and Judas?'

Mark 6:3 describes the same incident and in this case Jesus is claimed to be a carpenter: 'Is not this the carpenter, the son of

Mary, the brother of James, and Joses, and of Juda, and Simon? and are not his sisters here with us? And they were offended at him'. But this is a question, not a statement of fact; the local people are offended that Jesus has given a lesson at the synagogue on the sabbath, meaning he has delivered the sermon; they are offended because they do not realise that he is a rabbi. But the synagogue authorities do know that Jesus is a rabbi, otherwise he would not have been allowed to give the sermon. They do not look on him as a carpenter. The people are offended, but also they are mistaken; Jesus is a rabbi.

For that matter Joseph may not have been a carpenter either. Tekton is the word used to describe both Jesus and Joseph, and the word means master, in the way that rabbi means master. Jesus is called rabbi or rabboni nine times in the New Testament, and John 1:38 makes it clear that rabbi also means master: 'Then Jesus turned, and saw them following, and saith unto them, What seek ye? They said unto him, Rabbi, (which is to say, being interpreted, Master,) where dwellest thou?' Rabbi is a Hebrew and Aramaic word, so for the benefit of his Hellenised readers John is here translating the unfamiliar word into Greek as didaskale, which means teacher or master – just as tekton means master.

Nowhere in the gospels does Jesus call himself a carpenter. Instead people approach Jesus asking him to heal the sick, cast out devils or discuss his teachings. They know he is a rabbi; he calls himself a teacher and rabbi; teaching and healing and exorcising is the sort of thing that rabbis do.

The one scene in all the gospels that we are given of Jesus in his childhood (Luke 2:41-5) shows him not at work in a carpenter's shop but as a twelve-year old prodigy in discussion with the elders at the Temple in Jerusalem – clearly literate and highly educated; a scholar.

Which does not mean that Jesus could not have been a carpenter as well; he might well have combined scholarship with artisanry. Be that as it may, the indications are that Jesus and his family moved in prosperous social circles; witness the marriage at Cana where the

Early Christians saw Jesus in the simplest and most unadorned terms, as the Good Shepherd who looks after his flock, as in this 2nd-century fresco on the ceiling of the Catacombs of San Callisto in Rome. And in the lifetime of Jesus, Mary Magdalene was the Tower of the Flock. Only from the fourth century, reflecting the imperial pretensions of the Church, was Jesus depicted with long hair and a beard like a Roman emperor.

household has servants (John 2:1-5). Jesus also had powerful and influential friends such as Joseph of Arimathea, mentioned in all four gospels (Matthew 27:57-60; Mark 15:42-46 Luke 23:50-53; John 19:38), who is a member of the Sanhedrin and a rich but secret disciple with direct access to Pontius Pilate who grants him permission to lower Jesus' body from the cross, wrap it in fine linen and bury it in Joseph's own newly cut tomb, all before sundown that same day. And there was also Nicodemus, a Pharisee and another member of the Sanhedrin, also one of the richest men in Jerusalem, who would come to Jesus by night to listen to his teachings (John 3:1-3).

Nor was Nazareth, where Jesus grew up, a backwater, isolated from the Graeco-Roman world. Herod Antipas first ruled from Sepphoris, which he rebuilt, in the words of Josephus, as 'the ornament of Galilee'; Nazareth was only four miles to the northwest. With the construction of his new city of Tiberias Herod applied a further impress of Hellenism to Galilee that had long before begun when the Hasmonean dynasty helped build the city we call Magdala up the coast. Moreover, in countless every day ways the Jews of Palestine, and not only those in the big cities, were exposed to all sorts of Graeco-Roman practices and habits; for example Jews readily adopted Greek bathing practices, and bath houses proliferated throughout Galilee, and they decorated their homes with pagan symbols; these were the cultural imports that derived from the highly developed export trade in such products as dried fish which were prized as far away as Rome and brought prosperity to the fishermen of Bethsaida and Capernaum. To a greater or lesser extent everyone was affected by Hellenism, by their contact with the wider Graeco-Roman world.

But for some a reaction set in. If John the Baptist had any thoughts to follow in his father's footsteps he soon set himself apart, and rededicating himself to the Torah, he took up the life of an ascetic, living in the wilderness dressed in goat's hair and feeding himself on locusts and wild honey, and soon his cousin was baptising with him too, and teaching and healing and exorcising in expectation of the kingdom of God.

The Struggle for Jerusalem

Herod Antipas was popular among the Jews. In Jerusalem, according to Josephus and other Jewish writers, the people and the leading Jews would have preferred to have Herod Antipas as their king rather than be governed by Pontius Pilate on behalf of Rome. From time to time Pilate would cause offence through some inept display of Roman power as when he set up votive shields on the walls of his residence in Jerusalem bearing dedications to the divine cult of the emperor. It was a blasphemy in the eyes of the Jewish people who sent a delegation to Rome that included members of the Sanhedrin and also Herod Antipas. The votive shields were taken down.

Unlike his father and his older brother, Herod the Great and Herod's brief successor Archelaos, who were both involved in violent confrontations with the common people and the leading figures in Jerusalem, and also unlike Pontius Pilate, Herod Antipas was seen as mild and modest in his dealings with the Jews. Only two events troubled his rule as tetrarch of Galilee and Parea; one was the foundation of Tiberias on Jewish graves and the other was the execution of the popular and righteous John the Baptist, but neither caused any violent uproar.

The aim of Herod Antipas was to use his support in Jerusalem to persuade the Romans that he should become king of Judaea. This meant gaining the full support of the Sanhedrin, the ruling body of Jewish elders, which included members of two factions, the Sadducees and the Pharisees. The Sadducees were the old aristocracy who through long years of cooperation with the Hasmoneans and the Romans were comfortably Hellenised. The Pharisees who in many instances were as much exposed to Hellenism nevertheless promoted strict teaching of the Torah and a return to traditional Jewish values.

Herod was a thoroughly Hellenised ruler in Galilee and Parea and if he became king of Judaea his natural party, one would think, would have been the Sadducees. But their interest was to maintain control of the Temple and its priesthood, something they already enjoyed under Roman rule. The Pharisees, on the other hand, though not at all sympathetic to Herod's Hellenisation, were eager to further their influence in the land by reducing or eliminating the Sadducees' control over Jewish life.

And so in his project to become king, Herod found that he and the Pharisees, who otherwise seemed opposed to one another, had a shared interest. Both wanted power.

Jesus understood this very well as in Mark 8:15 where he warns his disciples against the leaven, or yeast, of the Pharisees and the leaven of Herod, by which he means their promise of the kingdom on earth. And again in Luke 12:1 Jesus tells his disciples, 'Beware ye of the leaven of the Pharisees, which is hypocrisy'. Both Herod and the Pharisees were set upon political power.

Into this complex situation John the Baptist had inserted himself and now Jesus. Neither was promoting a political programme; both wanted a renewed Judaism. But Jesus was opposed to the corruption and faithlessness of the Temple and therefore made himself unwelcome to the Sadducees. And of the Pharisees he said that following the law was not enough; one had to go beyond the law, and that angered many Pharisees against him. Herod saw Jesus as a threat because his preachings were about a higher power, an imminent kingdom that was awakening the multitudes, which undermined his own terrestrial ambitions.

And so the chase was on. Jesus learns of John the Baptist's execution and withdraws into the wilderness. Nine more times Jesus withdraws, always following a threat or some hostile act by Herod. And not just Jesus but the twelve disciples and Joanna and Susannah and all the other women and Mary Magdalene.

Herod was dangerous because of his indecisiveness, for how easily he was swayed. He had not wanted to kill John the Baptist. Or maybe he did, but he knew that the people loved John and he feared rousing them against his rule. To appease his wife Herod threw the Baptist into prison but did no more until trapped by his fateful promise to Herodias' daughter. Herod was 'a reed shaken with the wind', said Jesus, the complete opposite of John the Baptist, the indomitable prophet who drew the multitudes into the wilderness to hear him speak. 'What went ye out into the wilderness

to see?', Jesus told the multitudes. 'A reed shaken with the wind?
But what went ye out for to see? A man clothed in soft raiment?
behold, they that wear soft clothing are in kings' houses' (Matthew
11:7-8) – a pointed reference to Herod's court at Tiberias.

Herod was unpredictable, treacherous, always dangerous, and
towards Jesus he was ambivalent. Herod wanted to see him, hear
him, watch him perform miracles; Herod was fascinated by Jesus,
perhaps interested in what he had to say but also frightened of this
apparition and his powers; Jesus seemed like John the Baptist come
back to life.

Jesus called Herod Antipas 'that fox'. This was his answer to the
Pharisees who came to Jesus and warned him that he must leave
Galilee because Herod wanted to kill him. 'And he said unto them,
Go ye, and tell that fox, Behold, I cast out devils, and I do cures to
day and to morrow, and the third day I shall be perfected' (Luke
13:32). Jesus knew that even as the Pharisees were warning him
against Herod they themselves were laying in wait for him, 'seeking to catch something out of his mouth, that they might accuse
him' (Luke 11:54).

But Jesus had friends among the Pharisees in Jerusalem and it
may be that through them he hoped to win the city over. There
was Joseph of Arimathea and Nicodemus, both members of the
Sanhedrin. Both men would honour Jesus after his death, Joseph
by placing his body into his own fresh-cut tomb, Nicodemus by
bringing ointments to anoint the corpse, one of several things
about Nicodemus that links him to Mary Magdalene. For all the
importance of Joanna in Tiberias, it is always Mary Magdalene
whose name is placed first, as Jerusalem is more important than
Tiberias; Jerusalem, the holy city and pilgrims' goal, a venture
in which Nicodemus had considerable interests.

Now, as Passover was approaching, Jesus went up to Jerusalem
with his disciples and the women and Mary Magdalene.

Nevertheless I must walk to day, and to morrow, and the
day following: for it cannot be that a prophet perish out

of Jerusalem. O Jerusalem, Jerusalem, which killest the prophets, and stonest them that are sent unto thee; how often would I have gathered thy children together, as a hen doth gather her brood under her wings, and ye would not! Behold, your house is left unto you desolate: and verily I say unto you, Ye shall not see me, until the time come when ye shall say, Blessed is he that cometh in the name of the Lord. (Luke 13:33-35).

CHAPTER FIVE

Strange Days at Bethany

THE GOSPELS TELL OF Jesus' parables, his sermons and his healings as he takes his ministry round Galilee but this is presented as hardly more than a preamble to the last week of his life – his Passion in Jerusalem which takes up a quarter of Matthew and Luke, a third of Mark and John. Jesus enters Jerusalem in triumph, cheered by the multitudes. But the atmosphere is heavy with warnings as triumph turns to dread and a mysterious conspiracy unfolds. And then suddenly in the space of a single night and day Jesus is arrested and tried, he is beaten, taunted and humiliated, the multitudes shout for his destruction, and he is nailed to a cross until he is dead.

Until this last moment when Jesus is dying on the cross Mary Magdalene is nowhere to be seen in the gospels except in those three brief verses of Luke 8:1-3. But at the height of the Christian drama as Jesus dies, is buried and rises from his tomb Mary Magdalene plays a central role. Finally at the heart of the Christian mystery there are only two people; this is the mystery of Jesus and Mary Magdalene.

The Triumphal Entry into Jerusalem

John the Baptist had been beheaded by Herod just the year before; now Mary Magdalene was with Jesus as he journeyed the two hundred miles from Galilee to Jerusalem along with the disciples and the other women. They crossed over to the east bank of the river Jordan and revisited the spot where John had baptised Jesus and had proclaimed, 'He that cometh after me is mightier than I' (Matthew 3.11). Jesus knew the road well because as Luke 2:41 tells us, 'his parents went to Jerusalem every year at the feast of the passover'; a hard tortuous road that climbed up through the barren Judaean steppe, an ancient pilgrimage route leading to Jerusalem and its Temple. Jesus had walked this road from childhood to man; now Mary Magdalene was with Jesus as he walked it for the last time.

The travellers came to the village of Bethany; beyond it rose the Mount of Olives overlooking Jerusalem. Over the coming days strange things would happen here at Bethany and Jerusalem, among them events of great significance in shaping the identity and meaning of Mary Magdalene.

As Jesus approached Bethany – all the synoptic gospels tell this story, Matthew 21:1-7, Mark 11:1-2 and Luke 19:29-35 – he sent two of his disciples ahead to bring him a colt, the usual biblical name for the foal of a donkey or an ass. This was the donkey on which Jesus would make his triumphal entry into Jerusalem.

> And it came to pass, when he was come nigh to Bethphage and Bethany, at the mount called the mount of Olives, he sent two of his disciples, Saying, Go ye into the village over against you; in the which at your entering ye shall find a colt tied, whereon yet never man sat: loose him, and bring him hither. And if any man ask you, Why do ye loose him? thus shall ye say unto him, Because the Lord hath need of him. And they that were sent went their way, and found even as he had said unto them. And as they were loosing the colt, the owners thereof said unto them, Why loose ye

the colt? And they said, The Lord hath need of him. And
they brought him to Jesus. [Luke 19:29-35]

Jesus knew about the donkey but the disciples did not; Jesus had
made the arrangement for the donkey in advance with the help of
someone he knew at Bethany – someone who was helping Jesus
stage his triumphal entry into Jerusalem, who would also announce
his coming and rouse the multitudes too. 'And the multitudes that
went before, and that followed, cried, saying, Hosanna to the Son of
David: Blessed is he that cometh in the name of the Lord; Hosanna
in the highest. And when he was come into Jerusalem, all the city
was moved' (Matthew 21:9-10).

This triumphal entry into Jerusalem had been carefully arranged
so that Jesus would be seen to fulfill a prophecy. 'All this was done',
says Matthew 21:4-5, 'that it might be fulfilled which was spoken by

During Passover week Jesus and his followers stayed at Bethany, a two-
mile walk over the Mount of Olives to Jerusalem. Photograph by Félix
Bonfils in 1875.

Jesus' triumphal entry into Jerusalem, fresco by Giotto, 1305, in the Scrovegni Chapel, Padua.

the prophet, saying, Tell ye the daughter of Sion, Behold, thy King cometh unto thee, meek, and sitting upon an ass'.

Matthew is quoting from the Old Testament book of Zechariah 9:9: 'Rejoice greatly, O daughter of Zion; shout, O daughter of Jerusalem: behold, thy King cometh unto thee: he is just, and having salvation; lowly, and riding upon an ass'. In accordance with the prophecy, Jesus came not as a conquering warrior on a horse but as a humble man of peace.

A man of peace but a king all the same, who comes to the daughter of Zion. We have met the daughter of Zion before; she is there in the prophecy of Micah 4:8: 'And thou, O tower of the flock, the strong hold of the daughter of Zion, unto thee shall it come, even the first dominion; the kingdom shall come to the daughter of Jerusalem'.

The triumphal entry into Jerusalem, arranged as though a ceremonial ritual, is the enacting of prophecies, and Jesus is not acting alone. These are the Last Days; they are marked by the appearance of the messiah, the descendant of King David, who like a shepherd gathers in the dispersed, the afflicted and the lost. When Jesus enters Jerusalem he is delivering the kingdom to the daughter of Zion; she is the holy city of Jerusalem, she is the people of Israel, she is the tower of the flock, she is the migdal, the name Jesus gave to Mary Magdalene.

Cleansing the Temple

Jesus entered Jerusalem as hundreds of thousands of pilgrims poured into the city from all over Palestine and the diaspora, for this was the feast of the Passover in early April, which celebrates the Exodus from Egypt as well as the beginning of the spring planting season, and all were making their way to the Temple for sacrifices and prayers.

Though Judaea was a Roman province, Jerusalem was policed by Jewish troops under the authority of the Temple high priest with the support of the Sanhedrin, that is the council of Jewish elders. It was not the task of the Roman army to patrol the streets.

Pontius Pilate, the Roman governor, was based at Caesarea, the provincial capital on the coast where he kept four cohorts, each cohort numbering about 480 men, and some cavalry. The Romans also kept a cohort at Jerusalem to defend the Antonia fortress and its arsenal at the northwest corner of the Temple Mount, but when the governor came to Jerusalem for major feasts like Passover he would bring soldiers from Caesarea and quarter them in the Praesidium, the governor's palace, which some identify with Herod the Great's former palace to the west. So as not to offend Jewish religious sensibilities, the Romans had learnt to come to Jerusalem without their battle standards and their shrines to their pagan gods.

Pilate himself had learnt the strength of Jewish feeling about images when he once sent troops from Caesarea to take up winter quarters in Jerusalem and allowed them to set up their ensigns there. They did so at night so that no one would notice but the people found out and multitudes went to Pilate at Caesarea and implored that he remove them. As Josephus tells the story, Pilate ordered the protesters to disperse but they fell on the ground and bared their necks, saying they would willingly die rather than accept the violation of their laws about images, 'upon which Pilate was deeply affected with their firm resolution to keep their laws inviolable, and presently commanded the images to be carried back from Jerusalem to Caesarea'.

What mattered to Jesus was not Roman rule but the practices at the Temple and the behaviour of its priesthood. According to the three synoptic gospels, Jesus straightway went to the Temple where he cast out the moneychangers and others who were selling there; they had turned this 'house of prayer', said Jesus, into a 'den of thieves' (Matthew 21-12-13). Jesus went about the cleansing of the Temple with some violence, overturning the changers' tables and throwing their money to the ground, while according to John 2:15-16, who places the event earlier in Jesus' career, he lashed out at the traders with a whip.

> And when he had made a scourge of small cords, he drove them all out of the temple, and the sheep, and the oxen; and poured out the changers' money, and overthrew the tables; And said unto them that sold doves, Take these things hence; make not my Father's house an house of merchandise.

Each pilgrim would wish to sacrifice a lamb, a goat, a dove or some other animal; tens of thousands of animals each day were sacrificed during Passover week. Suitable animals were raised on Temple-owned lands such as the fields near Bethlehem, at Migdal Eder, the Tower of the Flock, where lambs were specially raised for the sacrifice. The Temple was a vast abattoir where the pilgrim or a priest cut the animal's throat and priests captured the spilling blood in bowls of silver or gold and splashed it against the corners of the altar. Unless it was a bird the animal

Jesus attacks the moneychangers and sellers of sacrificial animals, driving them from the Temple with a whip. By Alexandre Bida, French, 1870s.

was flayed and the skin kept by the priests, while the fatty portions of the animal were put on the altar fire and burnt until they were reduced to ash.

Each animal cost money but it had to be paid for with the Temple's own sacred shekels, not the impure currency of the Romans stamped with a profane image such as the head of the emperor or a pagan motif, hence the moneychangers.

When Jesus drove the moneychangers from the Temple and the sellers of doves and other sacrificial animals he was attacking the whole process of sacrifice which kept the priesthood and their auxiliaries in business; he was threatening the very economy of Jerusalem which depended almost entirely on its status as the cultic capital of Judaism.

After his symbolic cleansing of the Temple, Jesus taught there daily, but 'the chief priests and the scribes and the chief of the people sought to destroy him, And could not find what they might do: for all the people were very attentive to hear him' (Luke 19:47-48). By what authority did he teach, the priests wanted to know, but Jesus turned the tables on them, asking, 'The baptism of John, was it from heaven, or of men?' The catch, they understood, was that 'If we shall say, From heaven; he will say, Why then believed ye him not? But and if we say, Of men; all the people will stone us: for they be persuaded that John was a prophet'. So they answered Jesus, saying they could not tell whether John's baptism was from heaven or of men, 'And Jesus said unto them, Neither tell I you by what authority I do these things' (Luke 20:4-8).

Without actually saying so Jesus was declaring that John's authority and his own came directly from heaven; he was asserting direct communion with God, a free worship of the heart unmediated by the priesthood and their rituals. He was talking of that vision of the divine that he shared with Mary Magdalene, the woman he had named the migdal, the tower, the beacon, the saving light in the darkness. And again the gospels tell us that 'the chief priests and the scribes the same hour sought to lay hands on him' (Luke 20:19) and 'sought how they might kill him' (Luke 22:2).

Strange Days in Bethany

Every evening after teaching at the Temple during Passover week Jesus and his disciples would return the two miles over the Mount of Olives to their lodgings in Bethany. There while Jesus was at the house of Simon the leper 'came unto him a woman having an alabaster box of very precious ointment, and poured it on his head, as he sat at meat' (Matthew 26:7). Simon must have been a cured leper as otherwise his leprosy would have excluded him from social occasions. The gospel of Mark 14:3 describes the same event: 'And being in Bethany in the house of Simon the leper, as he sat at meat, there came a woman having an alabaster box of ointment of spikenard very precious; and she brake the box, and poured it on his head'.

In each case the woman is nameless; she comes and she goes. And yet when his disciples protest at the extravagance of the act,

Jesus answers them, saying, 'For in that she hath poured this ointment on my body, she did it for my burial. Verily I say unto you, Wheresoever this gospel shall be preached in the whole world, there shall also this, that this woman hath done, be told for a memorial of her' (Matthew 26:12-13; Mark 14:8-9 says the same thing).

But though Jesus tells us that this woman will be remembered throughout the world for what she has done, Mark and Matthew do not allow us to remember her; they conceal her name.

Further confusion sets in with Luke 7:37-38 who describes an anointing of Jesus by an unnamed woman in the house of Simon,

The anointing of Jesus at Bethany. *Mary Magdalene* is the title of this wood engraving by Eric Gill in 1926.

but this Simon is a Pharisee, not a leper, and the event takes place at Capernaum during Jesus' ministry in Galilee.

> And, behold, a woman in the city, which was a sinner, when she knew that Jesus sat at meat in the Pharisee's house, brought an alabaster box of ointment, And stood at his feet behind him weeping, and began to wash his feet with tears, and did wipe them with the hairs of her head, and kissed his feet, and anointed them with the ointment.

The fourth gospel, that is the gospel of John, returns us to the eastern slope of the Mount of Olives and also gives a name to the woman who anoints Jesus. Here in Bethany, says John 12:2-3, Jesus sat at supper not with Simon the leper nor the Pharisee but with Lazarus and his two sisters Martha and Mary. 'Then took Mary a pound of ointment of spikenard, very costly, and anointed the feet of Jesus, and wiped his feet with her hair: and the house was filled with the odour of the ointment.' On this occasion it is Judas Iscariot who complains at the expense while Jesus again connects the ointment to his death: 'Then said Jesus, Let her alone: against the day of my burying hath she kept this' (John 12:7).

Both John and Mark place a measurable value on the precious ointment, giving its cost as more than three hundred denarion in the original Greek (three hundred pence in the King James translation) at a time when a denarius was a day's wages (see Matthew 20:2), so that Jesus was anointed to the value of a man's labour for a year. The source of this considerable wealth is left unexplained. How did this woman of the anointing, this nameless woman of Mark and Matthew, or this Mary the sister of Lazarus in John, possess such very precious ointment, and what allowed her to feel free to use it on Jesus? The gospels do not say.

One might try to explain this confusion by saying these are separate anointings at Bethany on different days. Mark and Matthew say the anointing dinners were 'two days' before the Passover meal while John gives the impression that it was on the same day as Jesus' arrival at Bethany, 'six days' before the Passover meal. But in essence it is always the same event, for each gospel remarks on the costliness of the anointing, the protest against the expense and Jesus' remark that it is done against his own death and burial.

Some of this confusion might otherwise be explained by the nature of Bethany itself. Bethany was a place where pilgrims stayed while visiting the Temple at Jerusalem during the feasts. Galileans, who had to travel especially far from the north, had established something of a colony at Bethany, taking in guests or otherwise providing for others and being provided for. There were also hospices and almshouses there for the sick and poor. That might explain why Lazarus and his sisters were at Bethany and also Simon the leper; Jesus might have stayed or dined with one and then another or they might all have been together at the same house. Simon the leper was perhaps the father of Lazarus, Martha and Mary.

Bethany was a headquarters for Jesus and his followers, not only during this Passover visit to Jerusalem but during earlier visits too. Jesus had friends living in Bethany and knew the place well enough to make arrangements for the donkey to be awaiting his Passover arrival, and the multitudes who greeted his entry into Jerusalem would have been told in advance by his followers in Bethany that he was coming. Sometime before this last Passover visit to the city his friends Martha and Mary, whom he had known in Galilee (Luke 10:38-39), desperately called him to Bethany where he performed his most spectacular miracle when he raised their brother Lazarus from the dead (John 11:1-45).

In none of these stories is Mary Magdalene mentioned at all and yet amid the strange and confusing events that take place at Bethany, and the things left unsaid, there is a strong sense that Mary Magdalene is there.

The week of Jesus' passion begins with his anointing in Bethany and ends with Mary Magdalene coming to anoint him in the tomb. Jesus himself makes the connection between the two events when

The Raising of Lazarus, fresco by Giotto, 1305, in the Scrovegni Chapel, Padua.

he tells his disciples at Bethany that the nameless woman of Mark and Matthew or the woman whom the gospel of John names as Mary, sister of Martha, has anointed him in preparation for his death. 'For in that she hath poured this ointment on my body, she did it for my burial' (Matthew 26:12; Mark and John are similar).

The resurrection of Jesus is the defining event of Christian belief; Jesus says the woman who anoints him at Bethany will forever be remembered, and Mary Magdalene comes to anoint him at the tomb, yet the gospels themselves cannot remember or get it straight between them who anointed Jesus.

The Plot Against Jesus

At Jesus' earlier visit to Bethany – the one some months before Passover – a crowd of neighbours and onlookers had gathered round Mary's house when he answered her plea and raised her brother Lazarus from the dead. Jesus himself required no proof of God's love; his faith in his Father was absolute. But now as he called for Lazarus to rise he lifted his eyes to God and said, 'I knew that thou hearest me always: but because of the people which stand by I said it, that they may believe that thou has sent me' (John 11:42).

Jesus was right; many of those who witnessed the miracle now believed that God was working through him. And some went to the Temple and told the priests and the Pharisees what they had seen. 'What do we? for this man doeth many miracles', the priests and Pharisees said in alarm. 'If we let him thus alone, all men will believe on him: and the Romans shall come and take away both our place and nation' (John 11:47-48). The Temple priests and the Pharisees saw Jesus' ability to demonstrate his direct relationship with God as a threat to the institutionalised rituals of the Temple and the authority of the Sanhedrin on which their very existence depended and, in their view, their authority as political intermediaries between the Romans and the Jewish people. Jesus was saying that anyone who believed could have a direct relationship with God; the priests and Pharisees were saying that bypassing their authority would result in direct rule by the Romans.

The high priest Caiaphas spoke to the assembled religious hierarchy and put it to them succinctly, 'that it is expedient for us, that one man should die for the people, and that the whole nation perish not'. The assembly agreed that Jesus should be a sacrifice, the Passover lamb, and 'from that day forth they took counsel together for to put him to death' (John 11:50, 53).

Jesus' triumphal entry into Jerusalem on a donkey was a challenge as was his cleansing of the Temple; now the day of the Passover was approaching and he was about to enter the city again.

Believers and Friends

As Jesus had challenged Herod in Galilee, so now he was engaged in a dangerous contest against the high priest and the Jewish elders in Jerusalem. But Jesus had reason to believe that he could win

The Pool of Siloam which was supplied from the Gihon Spring, Jerusalem's only source of water. When Jesus sent his disciples to meet a water carrier who would lead them to the Upper Room, site of the Last Supper, they would have met with the man near here. Archaeological excavations show that at the time of Jesus this was a quarter of large and luxurious houses; most likely Nicodemus would have lived here.

over the support of key members of the Sanhedrin. 'Among the chief rulers', records John 12:42-3, 'also many believed on him; but because of the Pharisees they did not confess him, lest they should be put out of the synagogue: For they loved the praise of men more than the praise of God'.

Yet it was precisely among the Pharisees that Jesus had significant support, and two of these are mentioned in the gospels by name, Joseph of Arimathea and Nicodemus. Both men sat on the Sanhedrin, the ruling council of seventy-one members which assembled on the Temple Mount where it acted as legislature and court in controlling all aspects of Jewish religious and political life. Joseph of Arimathea was a secret follower of Jesus while Nicodemus was at least sympathetic to him; Nicodemus would come to Jesus at night and talk about spiritual rebirth.

> There was a man of the Pharisees, named Nicodemus, a ruler of the Jews: The same came to Jesus by night, and said unto him, Rabbi, we know that thou art a teacher come from God: for no man can do these miracles that thou doest, except God be with him. Jesus answered and said unto him, Verily, verily, I say unto thee, Except a man be born again, he cannot see the kingdom of God. Nicodemus saith unto him, How can a man be born when he is old? can he enter the second time into his mother's womb, and be born? Jesus answered, Verily, verily, I say unto thee, Except a man be born of water and of the Spirit, he cannot enter into the kingdom of God. (John 3:1-5)

Born of water and of the spirit, says Jesus, meaning the water of baptism but also Jesus is making an allusion to Nicodemus himself who, if he is the same man known in the Talmud as Nicodemus Ben Gurion, was one of the three or four wealthiest men in Jerusalem and controlled the water supply for the religious ablutions of the tens of thousands of pilgrims who came to the city at festival times. The Talmud also tells us that the Gurion family estates were at Ruma in Galilee, six miles north of Nazareth.

The Water Carrier

In the same way that Jesus had foreknowledge about the donkey on which he would make his triumphal entry into Jerusalem, so he also had foreknowledge of the arrangements for what would turn out to be the Last Supper. In Luke 22:8-12 Jesus tells his disciples Peter and John to enter the city and 'there shall a man meet you, bearing a pitcher of water; follow him into the house where he entereth in'. At the time of the feast it was expected that residents of Jerusalem would make spare rooms available to visitors to take their Passover meal and so, as Jesus has already secretly arranged, the owner of the house will lead them to 'a large upper room furnished: there make ready'.

The story is retold in Matthew 26:18 where Jesus tells his disciples to 'Go into the city to such a man', a man not identified in the gospel but clearly a man whom Jesus knows. In Mark 14:13-15 the story is repeated: 'And he sendeth forth two of his disciples, and saith unto them, Go ye into the city, and there shall meet you a man bearing a pitcher of water: follow him'. Once again there will be a man waiting; the disciples do not have to find the man, the man will make himself known to the disciples. And again he is a water carrier.

The man was a water carrier, or he was disguised as one, because he likely came as a messenger from Nicodemus. The gospels do not say so, but the likelihood fits.

The traditional site of the Last Supper is marked by the Cenacle, a large rectangular hall, its vaulted ceiling supported by columns with gothic capitals. This was built in the twelfth century as the southern gallery in the upper level of the Church of St Mary of Zion which in turn stood on earlier structures that at the time of Jesus stood within the walls at the southwest corner of Jerusalem. The tradition that this is the site of the Last Supper is very old for the spot is identified on a mid-sixth-century map and it was visited by the Bordeaux Pilgrim already in 333 and by the redoubtable Egeria from the Iberian peninsula in 384.

This neighbourhood was close to the Pool of Siloam to which water was diverted by Hezekiah's tunnel from the Gihon Spring, Jerusalem's only source of water. The water carrier would have met the disciples at the pool and brought them to the Upper Room; archaeological excavations show that at the time of Jesus this was a quarter of large and luxurious houses. The scene of the Last Supper in the Upper Room may have been in or close by the home of Nicodemus.

The Last Supper

According to the gospels of Matthew, Mark and Luke the house to which the disciples were led by the mysterious man was the scene of Jesus' last meal before his arrest and trial and his crucifixion. It occurred towards the end of the week. During the meal Jesus predicts his betrayal by one of those present and foretells that before the cock crows Peter will have denied knowing him three times. In these same synoptic gospels Jesus breaks the bread and offers the wine, gives thanks for what he is about to eat, and says this is my body and my blood – this being counted by the Church as the first Eucharist, the word deriving from the Greek for thanksgiving.

The *Communion of the Apostles*, a fresco by Fra Angelico at the convent of San Marco at Florence, c.1440. The woman kneeling on the left is probably a donor to the convent not a diner at the Last Supper.

In each of the synoptic gospels Jesus shares the Last Supper with 'the twelve'; the gospel of John mentions the disciples without giving a number. In none of the gospels is there mention of anyone else being there, but there may have been more, and there would have been servants bringing the food and wine. There is no reason why women should not have been partaking of the dinner along with other followers of Jesus; this would be entirely normal for a Passover seder at which women would be expected to play the same role as men and additionally light the candles.

The disciples would have been reclining on couches or carpets and pillows arranged round a table as was the habit of the time. Christian art has since given us a different impression of the Last Supper with the men sitting at a table, often circular or semi-circular, but this meant that some of the disciples showed only their backs.

During the Italian Renaissance the convention developed for the disciples to be arranged in such a way that they could be seen full face or in profile, as in the *Communion of the Apostles*, the fresco by Fra Angelico that he did in the convent of San Marco at Florence in about 1440. Here there are two tables set at right angles, the seated disciples looking at Jesus who stands at the centre of the room giving the Eucharist to four disciples who are kneeling before him to the right. This is the occasion in the synoptic gospels when Jesus offers bread to his disciples and says 'Take, eat: this is my body', and offers them wine, saying, 'This is my blood' (Mark 14:22-24; Matthew and Luke are similar).

Intriguingly in the fresco a woman kneels at the left, but this is almost certainly not a suggestion by Fra Angelico that a woman was actually present at the Last Supper; as a Dominican he would have stayed strictly within the accepted interpretation of the scriptures. Fra Angelico did sometimes introduce Mary the mother of Jesus to his frescos where he places her off to one side so that she can witness the events in her son's life. Or the woman in this fresco is a donor; she has given to San Marco and this is her acknowledgement. Fra Angelico did include Mary Magdalene in his frescos where called for by the gospels, most famously in his *Noli Me Tangere*, his depiction of

Leonardo Da Vinci's *Last Supper* which he painted from 1494 to 1498 on the refectory wall of the Convent of Santa Maria delle Grazie in Milan. There has been much speculation over the identity of the young androgynous figure to the left of Jesus. Curiously all the identifications in some way relate to Mary Magdalene; the figure is variously Mary Magdalene herself, or John the Evangelist, who some say was Mary Magdalene's groom at the marriage of Cana, or Lazarus, who may have been Mary Magdalene's brother.

the resurrection (see p.2), but her hair is always uncovered, at least partly, and it is always red, which is not the case here.

The windows above the table give a view across the courtyard to the opposite wing of the convent, identifying the world of San Marco in Florence with the built-up landscape of urban Jerusalem as seen from the Upper Room. And at the far right of the fresco is a well. Symbolically this recalls Isaiah 12:3: 'Therefore with joy shall ye draw water out of the wells of salvation'. But the well also literally recalls the water carrier who brought the disciples to this place somewhere in the city.

The most famous depiction of the scene, however, is Leonardo Da Vinci's *Last Supper* which he painted from 1494 to 1498 on the refectory wall of the Convent of Santa Maria delle Grazie in Milan.

Here all the disciples sit along one side of a long table, their faces in plain view. Like Fra Angelico, Leonardo looks to the gospel text, but his subject is not the Eucharist, rather the moment when Jesus announces that one among them will be his betrayer. All the gospels mention this, but Leonardo's painting specifically captures the moment described at John 13:21-26 when Jesus suddenly says, 'One of you shall betray me'. The disciples are shocked; we see them fearfully wondering who it could be, questioning one another, demanding an answer from Jesus, who tells them, 'He it is, to whom I shall give a sop, when I have dipped it'. And we see Jesus reaching out his hand to the bread which he will dip in the wine and give to Judas Iscariot.

To the left of Jesus, that is sitting on his right, is a young beardless and rather androgynous figure who in recent years has become the subject of popular fascination thanks to Dan Brown and *The Da Vinci Code* which refers to the figure's 'flowing red hair, delicate folded hands, and the hint of a bosom', and declares that this is Mary Magdalene, her presence in the painting part of an elaborate code by Leonardo to conceal but yet transmit the truth suppressed by the Church that Mary Magdalene and Jesus were married and had a child.

The putative Magdalene figure in Leonardo's *Last Supper*.

The beardless youth, however, is entirely familiar and frequently repeated in Christian art where he is recognised as John, the youngest of the disciples, who is usually identified as the one referred to in the gospel of John as the Beloved Disciple. The Church Fathers consider him the same person as John the Evangelist and John of Patmos, author of Revelation. He is conventionally depicted as dreamy, he is always placed to the immediate left or right of Jesus, and he is often leaning against him or even asleep in his lap.

But there is another identification, as we shall later see, that the Beloved Disciple might be Lazarus and that Lazarus might be the brother of Mary Magdalene.

Uniquely in the gospel of John, and immediately before Jesus announces that he will be betrayed, Jesus pours water into a basin and begins to wash the disciples' feet. Peter protests; 'Thou shall never wash my feet', he says, but Jesus says, 'Ye are not all clean' – not Judas who will betray him nor even Peter who will deny him three times before the cock crows. But Jesus means more than that. 'Know ye what I have done to you?', Jesus asks the disciples. 'Ye call me Master and Lord: and ye say well; for so I am', but as Jesus explains, he is the servant of God, as all the disciples are the servants of God; 'The servant is not greater than his lord' (John 13:5-16).

By washing the feet of his disciples Jesus is demonstrating that all are the servants of God.

After the Last Supper, as all the gospels relate, Jesus went with his disciples to the garden of Gethsemane to pray. He feared that the final confrontation with the Sanhedrin and the Temple had come and he put himself into the hands of God. 'Father, if thou be willing, remove this cup from me: nevertheless not my will, but thine, be done ... And being in an agony he prayed more earnestly: and his sweat was as it were great drops of blood falling down to the ground' (Luke 22:42-44).

Soon the Temple soldiers came with the chief priest, the captain of the Temple and several members of the Sanhedrin, and Jesus challenged them, asking why do you come with swords and staves as though you have come to take a thief? 'When I was daily with you in the temple, ye stretched forth no hands against me: but this is your hour,

The English poet and painter and mystic William Blake had his own
ideas about who was at the Last Supper which he painted in 1799.
Various disciples are on the left and right; Adam and Eve are sitting
naked facing Jesus; next to them is Judas counting his money; and sitting
with Jesus at the head of the table is an unidentified young woman.

and the power of darkness' (Luke 22: 53). At this moment Jesus' disciples ran away. 'And they all forsook him, and fled'. But one man
remained, 'a certain young man, having a linen cloth cast about his
naked body'; the militia laid hold of him, but the young man 'left
the linen cloth, and fled from them naked' (Mark 14:50-52).

Over the Mount of Olives in Bethany they waited for Jesus to
return, there in the house of Lazarus where Mary had 'anointed the
feet of Jesus, and wiped his feet with her hair' (John 12:3). Anointing
the feet or the head was symbolic of anointing the whole body. Dry-
ing Jesus' feet with her hair is adopting the role of servant; masters
dried themselves on their servant's hair. Mary of Bethany (or whoever
she and the other nameless woman at Bethany were) was prescient in
anointing Jesus before his death; she had foreseen what was to come
and shared with him the agony of Gethsemane.

CHAPTER SIX

The Trial and Death
of Jesus

T HE GOSPELS TELL HOW Caiaphas, the high priest, laid
plans for the arrest and killing of Jesus during Passover week
in Jerusalem.

> Then assembled together the chief priests, and the scribes,
> and the elders of the people, unto the palace of the high
> priest, who was called Caiaphas, And consulted that they
> might take Jesus by subtilty, and kill him. But they said,
> Not on the feast day, lest there be an uproar among the
> people. (Matthew 26:3-5)

But now in the darkness the moment had come. Jesus was taken
by night from the Garden of Gethsemane to the palace of the high
priest Caiaphas 'where the scribes and the elders were assembled'
(Matthew 26:57).

The Sanhedrin Interrogates Jesus

Caiaphas who was a wealthy and leading member of the aristocratic Sadducees had been appointed high priest in AD 18 by Pontius Pilate's predecessor Valerius Gratus; his father-in-law Annas had been high priest before him; the position of high priest ran in families. The high priest led the ceremonies at the Temple acting as intermediary between God and the people of Israel. He was also head of the Sanhedrin, that assembly of priests and scribes and elders responsible for Jewish affairs, which had long been the intermediary between the Jewish people and Rome. These were the men before whom Jesus was brought for interrogation inside the walls of the city that night.

The Sadducees, the party of the aristocracy and the chief priests, the party that had most accommodated itself to the Romans, dominated the Sanhedrin, but a growing number of Pharisees filled its ranks. The Sanhedrin was comprised of twenty-three Temple priests, twenty-three scribes who were learned in the law and twenty-three elders who were heads of tribes and families and were leading men of affairs; with the high priest at their head they were seventy in all, though some accounts speak of a deputy head, making seventy-one. Members were men of age and experience, fully versed in the scriptures and the oral law; each was also married and had to be a father; when delivering judgements fathers were considered more merciful. Jesus knew a number of these men, perhaps all of them. He had debated with the priests and the scribes at the Temple and some among the elders were sympathetic to him; the gospels name two of these, Joseph of Arimathea and Nicodemus.

Joseph of Arimathea is known in all the gospels as the man who buried Jesus in his own freshly-cut tomb. He was probably a Pharisee, not all of whom shared the view of the Sadducees that Jesus was a threat who needed to be eliminated. 'He was a good man, and a just', says Luke of Joseph of Arimathea, adding that he had dissented from the Sanhedrin's verdict against Jesus; moreover Joseph 'himself waited for the kingdom of God' (Luke 23:50-51).

This medieval illumination depicts the events of Jesus' trial in three registers. At the top Jesus is brought before the high priest; in the middle register Peter denies Jesus; and at the bottom Pilate has Jesus scourged. Codex Egberti, Germany, c.980.

As for Nicodemus, 'who was a man of the Pharisees' (John 3:1), he knew of the plot among members of the Sanhedrin to kill Jesus and turned on them saying, 'Doth our law judge any man, before it hear him, and know what he doeth?' (John 7:51). To which they replied with a mixture of dismissiveness and menace, 'Art thou also of Galilee?', meaning nothing good comes from Galilee, certainly not Jesus, 'for out of Galilee ariseth no prophet' (John 7:52), but they also knew that Nicodemus had family lands in Galilee.

Nicodemus almost certainly told Jesus about the Sanhedrin plot; throughout Jesus' final days in Jerusalem and up to that night of agony in the Garden of Gethsemane he was filled with knowing and dread, but trusting in the father and the kingdom to come.

When Jesus was arrested and taken to the Sanhedrin Peter followed at a distance and even entered the palace where three times he was noticed but denied that he was one of the disciples.

> And when they had kindled a fire in the midst of the hall, and were set down together, Peter sat down among them. But a certain maid beheld him as he sat by the fire, and earnestly looked upon him, and said, This man was also with him. And he denied him, saying, Woman, I know him not. And after a little while another saw him, and said, Thou art also of them. And Peter said, Man, I am not. And about the space of one hour after another confidently affirmed, saying, Of a truth this fellow also was with him: for he is a Galilaean. And Peter said, Man, I know not what thou sayest. And immediately, while he yet spake, the cock crew. And the Lord turned, and looked upon Peter. And Peter remembered the word of the Lord, how he had said unto him, Before the cock crow, thou shalt deny me thrice. And Peter went out, and wept bitterly.' (Luke 22 55-62)

The account of Jesus before the Sanhedrin therefore does not come from Peter, or only partly; primarily it comes from 'another disciple: that disciple was known unto the high priest, and went in with Jesus into the palace of the high priest' (John 18:15). Some say that John the gospel writer was himself that disciple but he would have been as easily identifiable and intimidated as Peter; instead the disciple was known to Caiaphas who could not bar him from the proceedings because he was himself a member of the Sanhedrin; possibly he was Joseph of Arimathea or his name was Nicodemus, who appears only in John's gospel; but another possibility, as we shall later see, is that he is Lazarus of Bethany.

When Jesus was brought before the Sanhedrin he was mocked and blindfolded and struck about the face, shoved and spat upon and beaten in front of these priests, these scribes, these elders he knew. 'I spake openly to the world', Jesus told them; 'I ever taught in the synagogue, and in the temple, whither the Jews always resort; and in secret have I said nothing. ... If I have spoken evil, bear witness of the evil: but if well, why smitest thou me? (John 18:20-23).

In the face of his interrogators Jesus remained silent or turned their questions round. 'Answerest thou nothing?' demanded the high priest after false witnesses testified that Jesus had said 'I will destroy this temple that is made with hands, and within three days I will build another made without hands', whereas actually Jesus was repeating prophecies found in Jeremiah and Micah. 'But he held his peace, and answered nothing' (Mark 14:58-61).

When asked if he was 'the Son of God', Jesus answered, 'Thou has said' (Matthew 26:64) or 'Ye say that I am' (Luke 22:70). But his ambiguous replies were leapt on as admissions. In the version given by Mark 14:61-2 the high priest asks 'Art thou the Christ, the Son of the Blessed? And Jesus said, I am: and ye shall see the Son of man sitting on the right hand of power, and coming in the clouds of heaven', but to be a messiah (Christ is Greek for the Hebrew messiah) was not a blasphemy; many people claimed at one time or another to be the messiah and not one was ever accused of or tried for blasphemy. Nor was it blasphemous to be the Son of Man or even the Son of God, as all the people of Israel were the Sons of God – though mention of the name God was blasphemous, explaining why Jesus talks of the 'Son of man sitting on the right hand of power'; power, not God; he was being careful not to be blasphemous.

But in forgiving sin, as Jesus had done to the sinful woman who washed his feet with her tears in the house of the Pharisee at Capernaum, he could be seen as assuming a power of forgiveness that among Jews belonged to God alone. But whether in response to those words 'I am' in Mark or to the ambiguous answers that Jesus gives in the other gospels, including Matthew, the Sanhedrin delivered its judgement. 'Then the high priest rent his clothes, saying, He hath spoken blasphemy. ... What think ye? They answered and said, He is guilty of death' (Matthew 26:65-66).

Although the gospel accounts differ in detail, the synoptics agree that Caiaphas and the Sanhedrin condemned Jesus for blasphemy. But this may have been a misunderstanding by the gospel authors writing generations later; no longer as Jewish followers of Jesus but rather as Christians they saw the messiah as divine in the way Jews did not. But the gospel of John does not make this mistake; it tells a different story, that Jesus was questioned by the high priest but no trial or judgement took place.

All four gospels say, however, that Jesus was now bound and led away to Pontius Pilate. Addressing the Roman governor the Sanhedrin said nothing about the religious charge of blasphemy. They lacked authority to execute anyone; that power lay exclusively with the Romans; but Caiaphas and his followers wanted Jesus out of the way and therefore they presented his transgression as a political one threatening Roman rule. Nicodemus and Joseph of Arimathea and others sympathetic to Jesus had done what they could but this course had been set in advance by the high priest and his supporters who now told the Roman governor that Jesus, who had caused havoc at the Temple, who had entered Jerusalem in triumph, had proclaimed himself the King of the Jews.

Jesus Brought Before Pontius Pilate

As Judaea was a province of the Roman Empire any claim to be King of the Jews would be taken as rebellion and treason. But Jesus responded to the Roman governor Pontius Pilate in the same way as he had to the Sanhedrin.

> And Pilate asked him, Art thou the King of the Jews? And
> he answering said unto him, Thou sayest it. And the chief

priests accused him of many things: but he answered nothing. And Pilate asked him again, saying, Answerest thou nothing? behold how many things they witness against thee. But Jesus yet answered nothing; so that Pilate marvelled. (Mark 15:2-5)

The gospel of Luke adds the further information that when Pilate realised that Jesus was a Galilean he decided that he belonged to Herod's jurisdiction, and therefore he sent him to Herod who had come to Jerusalem for the Passover feast. But though the chief priests and the scribes stood before Herod and vehemently accused

'Ecce homo' – 'Behold the man' – Pontius Pilate says to the crowd as he shows them Jesus bound, scourged and crowned with thorns, to which they reply 'Crucify him!' A scene by Antonio Ciseri, Swiss, 1871.

Jesus, still he answered nothing, and after the tetrarch's soldiers ridi-
culed Jesus and mocked him, Herod returned him without charge
to Pilate. This was not the absolution it seemed, however; rather
in passing Jesus back and forth between them Pilate and Herod
were each acknowledging the authority of the other which gratified
them both, for as Luke goes on to say, 'And the same day Pilate and
Herod were made friends together: for before they were at enmity
between themselves' (Luke 23:12).

But there was still the Sanhedrin which Pilate hoped to appease
by giving Jesus a good beating. And so he called together the chief
priests and the elders and told them that he had 'found no fault
in this man touching those things whereof ye accuse him. ... I will
therefore chastise him, and release him' (Luke 23:14,16).

The release of a prisoner at the time of the feast was a custom
according to all four gospels. But the crowd that had gathered outside the governor's quarters were whipped up by the chief priests
and their supporters among the elders to cry out for the release
not of Jesus but of Barabbas, an insurrectionary, a robber and a
murderer. 'And Pilate answered and said again unto them, What
will ye then that I shall do unto him whom ye call the King of the
Jews? And they cried out again, Crucify him. Then Pilate said unto
them, Why, what evil hath he done? And they cried out the more
exceedingly, Crucify him' (Mark 15:12-14).

Pilate understood that behind this demonstration was the power
of the chief priests whose collaboration he required if Judaea was
to be governed with the least incident. And so Pilate 'released
Barabbas unto them, and delivered Jesus, when he had scourged
him, to be crucified.' (Mark 15:15)

A Woman from Nowhere

Mary Magdalene was there among the people as Pilate showed
them the scourged and bloody figure of Jesus, dressed in a robe
of royal colour, a crown of thorns pressed upon his head, and said
'Behold the man'. And when they answered 'Crucify him, crucify
him' (John 19:5-6) Mary Magdalene was there.

The Via Dolorosa is the route through Jerusalem that Jesus is traditionally believed to have taken after his conviction by Pontius Pilate to Golgotha, the place of his crucifixion.

Mary Magdalene pressed her way through the narrow streets as
Jesus was led to Golgotha, most likely the hill resembling the top
of a skull just outside today's Lion Gate opposite the Garden of
Gethsemane, with the Mount of Olives and Bethany beyond. Here
Jesus was stripped naked and Mary Magdalene heard the hammer
blows driving iron nails through his hands and feet. A sign was
placed at the top of the cross reading in Greek, Latin and Hebrew,
The King of the Jews, mocking his entry into Jerusalem on the back
of a donkey less than a week before.

Were it not for Luke 8:1-3 where he mentions those women who travelled with Jesus round Galilee and financed his ministry we would not yet have heard of Mary Magdalene. Even so she arrives on the scene as a surprise, the chief witness to the crucifixion of Jesus and to the events that follow. You would expect that a person who plays such a central role in the final drama would also have appeared elsewhere in the gospels, yet apart from that brief mention in Luke she is not there. She seems to have appeared out of nowhere. Or has she?

Has Mary Magdalene been there all along, the chief witness to the ministry of Jesus and his closest companion?

The theme of anointing runs through the gospels, of women anointing Jesus, in particular the women – or the woman – at Bethany. The gospels of Mark and Matthew do not mention her name which leaves open the possibility that she is Mary Magdalene. We will see that Mark talks of Mary Magdalene coming to anoint Jesus at the tomb.

But strangely the gospel of Luke makes no mention of an anointing at Bethany. Neither does Luke mention Mary Magdalene by name at the crucifixion nor as one of the women from Galilee who prepares spices and ointments to anoint Jesus at the tomb. But Luke does tell of a sinner woman who washes Jesus' feet and anoints him at Capernaum, and he does so in chapter 7 of his gospel immediately before introducing Mary Magdalene by name in chapter 8 as a woman possessed by seven devils, which might make you think that Luke was trying to draw invidious associations in your mind.

Luke is also the author of The Acts of the Apostles which nowhere acknowledges the existence of Mary Magdalene. Instead the function of Acts is to draw Paul into the story, Paul who never knew Jesus in his lifetime but proclaimed himself an apostle on the basis of having had a vision known only to himself; yet Paul's vision of the risen Jesus becomes the reality of Acts while Mary Magdalene's experience at the crucifixion, burial and resurrection is totally suppressed. For some reason the Evangelist Luke feels the need to manipulate his gospel and the Acts of the Apostles to diminish and even eliminate Mary Magdalene.

The author of John's gospel is seemingly more forthcoming. The woman who anoints Jesus at Bethany is identified as Mary, sister of Martha and Lazarus. And at the resurrection John's gospel will have Jesus appear to Mary Magdalene in an intimate and moving scene. But John will not have Mary Magdalene prepare spices and ointments nor bring them to the tomb to anoint Jesus; Nicodemus will have done that when the body of Jesus is placed in the tomb of Joseph of Arimathea – thereby breaking the link between Mary of Bethany and Mary Magdalene, or so it seems, for as we shall see John leaves us with other clues.

Anointing has two primary purposes in the Bible; it can be personal, to beautify and soothe the body, and sometimes it is a way of honouring a special guest. Or anointing can be performed as part of a religious rite. Kings and priests are anointed, and also the messiah. In the Bible anointing means imparting the Divine Spirit. Messiah is Hebrew for the anointed one; in Greek the word is Christ. If Mary Magdalene is anointing Jesus and imparting the Divine Spirit, what does that make Mary Magdalene?

You could be forgiven for thinking that the gospels have been edited so that that question does not occur to you. But the words of Jesus remain. 'She hath done what she could: she is come aforehand to anoint my body to the burying. Verily I say unto you, Wheresoever this gospel shall be preached throughout the whole world, this also that she hath done shall be spoken of for a memorial of her' (Mark 14:9; Matthew 26:13).

The Cross

'They crucified him', say Mark 15:25 and Luke 23:33, preferring the bare understatement of fact to any description of what crucifixion involved; and the other gospels are the same; they led Jesus away 'to crucify him' says Matthew 27:31, 'to be crucified' says John 19:16. But the Evangelists are conspicuous in saying next to nothing about the nature of Jesus' crucifixion. Historical records outside

Jesus is stripped naked before being nailed to the cross. The loin cloth shown in depictions of the crucifixion is for the sake of the viewers' modesty. But the Romans thought otherwise. Stripping the man naked, hanging him up in a public place and exposing his mutilated body to jeers and flies was all part of the Romans' purpose to inflict the greatest possible pain and humiliation on the condemned. Woodcut by Eric Gill, English, 1917.

the New Testament hardly say more; a vast silence hangs over the topic of crucifixion and with good reason. The humiliating and grotesque slow death of crucifixion was terrifying and repellant.

Decapitation by the sword, burning and crucifixion were the three common forms of Roman execution, but crucifixion was the worst, reserved for traitors, pirates, brigands and slaves; being put into the arena and torn apart by wild animals was considered a better death because it came more quickly.

The crucifixion of a Roman citizen was forbidden by law. Even the subject was avoided. 'The very word "cross"', said Cicero, the first-century BC statesman, 'should be far removed not only from the person of a Roman citizen but from his thoughts, his eyes and his ears.' Josephus called it as 'the most wretched of deaths'. Cicero described crucifixion as 'supplicium crudelissimum taeterrimumque', a disgusting and cruel punishment.

Roman executions were preceded by scourging, which meant that Jesus' back was torn open by the braided leather thongs of a whip at the end of which small iron balls and sharp pieces of sheep bone were sewn. The condemned was then made to carry his cross to the place of execution, and according to the gospel of John this is what happened; Jesus was made to carry his cross to Golgotha. But Matthew, Mark and Luke all say that a man in the crowd called Simon of Cyrene was made to carry the cross for him; his lacerated back meant that Jesus was almost certainly suffering from circulatory shock. An entire cross would have been too heavy to carry, let alone for a man who had just received the 'half death', as scourging was called, and so this would have been just the cross-piece, probably weighing fifty to a hundred pounds.

When Jesus was brought to the hill called Golgotha, the soldiers would have laid Jesus on the cross-piece, stretched out his arms, and then driven nails through his wrists or hands into the wood. The upright had already been set into the ground; now Jesus was hoisted up, the full weight of his body tearing at the nails, until the crosspiece was slotted over the top of the upright shaft. The soles of his feet were nailed flat against the shaft of the cross or nails were driven through his ankles so that his feet were attached to either side of the shaft.

The image of Jesus upon a high cross, suffering but strangely still and majestic does not accord with reality. The height of the assembled cross would have been about seven and a half feet; Jesus therefore would be suspended not much more than a foot or two above those looking on – almost face to face. Jesus was completely naked, no decorous loin cloth as in the familiar icons and paintings.

Crucifixion loosened the bladder and the bowels, and his body would be streaming with sweat and blood. The suspended weight of his body made it difficult to fill his lungs to breathe. Flexing his knees, he raised himself to fill his lungs but his pinioned feet suffered terrible pain. As his body rose and fell his scourged back rubbed against the rough cross adding to his torture.

Death by crucifixion was deliberately slow, to maximise the agony and draw the greatest crowd. Stripping the man naked, hanging him up in a public place and exposing his mutilated body to jeers and flies was all part of the Romans' purpose to inflict the greatest possible pain and humiliation on the condemned. Eventually death would come by suffocation or heart failure. Victims could take three days to die; their bodies were then left hanging on the cross until they rotted and fell off or were devoured by birds and scavenging dogs. In every sense, as Cicero said, crucifixion was 'disgusting'; the point of it was to demonstrate the absolute power of the state and the abject helplessness of the victim, his pain and degradation serving a terrifying public warning. The worst part of it, as one executioner said, was the screaming.

So it was with Jesus, writhing on the cross, crying out in agony and calling upon God. His executioners busied themselves dividing up his clothes, casting lots for who should get what. Passers-by came up close and jeered at Jesus to his face, for the cross was barely higher than a man. Among his tormentors were the chief priests, and some scribes and elders of the Sanhedrin who said, 'He trusted in God; let him deliver him now, if he will have him: for he said, I am the Son of God' (Matthew 27:43).

According to Mark and Matthew, all the men who had followed Jesus had fled; but watching from afar were women from Galilee, Mary Magdalene, Mary the mother of James the Less and Joses (Joseph), and Salome who was the wife of Zebedee and the mother of his sons the disciples James and John. Towards the end Jesus cried out in Aramaic, 'Eloi, Eloi, lama sabachthani? which is, being interpreted, My God, my God, why hast thou

The Romans probably crucified tens of thousands of people over the centuries; after the slave uprising led by Spartacus they crucified 6000 people in a day. Jesus is often depicted high upon a cross as in this illustration, but the reality was more ordinary and sordid. Gustave Doré, French, 1867.

forsaken me?' (Mark 15:34) As he raised himself to open his lungs bolts of pain shot through his hands and feet but lowering himself meant slow suffocation; suffering excruciating pain he raised himself again. Mark and Matthew report a final scream. At three in the afternoon Jesus was dead.

Thy Will Be Done

Onlookers heard Jesus cry from the cross. 'Eloi, Eloi, lama sabach-thani?' Some thought he was calling to Elijah to come down from heaven and release him. To others it might have seemed a cry of pain and despair, that God had abandoned Jesus, that his mission to bring about the kingdom of God had been betrayed by God himself. But Mary Magdalene understood. She knew that Jesus, speaking in the Aramaic vernacular, was bringing the Hebrew of Psalm 22 to the here and now.

'My God, my God, why hast thou forsaken me? why art thou so far from helping me, and from the words of my roaring?' So it begins. But the Psalm continues with declarations of God's reward for the trust placed in him. 'Our fathers trusted in thee: they trusted, and thou didst deliver them. They cried unto thee, and were deliv-ered: they trusted in thee, and were not confounded.'

Trust even as the sufferer is jeered like Jesus on the cross. 'All they that see me laugh me to scorn: they shoot out the lip, they shake the head, saying, He trusted on the Lord that he would deliver him: let him deliver him, seeing he delighted in him.'

The sufferer in Psalms undergoes pain and humiliation very much like that of the dying Jesus. 'I am poured out like water, and all my bones are out of joint: my heart is like wax; it is melted in the midst of my bowels. My strength is dried up like a potsherd; and my tongue cleaveth to my jaws; and thou hast brought me into the dust of death. For dogs have compassed me: the assembly of the wicked have inclosed me: they pierced my hands and my feet. I may tell all my bones: they look and stare upon me. They part my garments among them, and cast lots upon my vesture.'

But God intervenes and saves. 'He hath not despised nor abhorred the affliction of the afflicted; neither hath he hid his face from him; but when he cried unto him, he heard.'

The gospel of John recounts the crucifixion somewhat differ-ently. There Jesus' final words are 'It is finished' (John 19:30). The original Greek word in the gospel is tetelestai and appears only twice, the first time two verses earlier. 'After this, Jesus knowing that all things were now accomplished, that the scripture might be fulfilled, saith, I thirst.' And so his final words mean finished in the sense of accomplished. Dying on the cross was the supreme accomplishment; it was the final great act of trusting in and surrendering himself to the Father, the summation of everything Jesus ever taught in his parables and in his sermons about the kingdom of God – God's embrace of everyone in his love, as in the parable of the profligate son (Luke 15:11-32), and as in the Sermon on the Mount in which God 'maketh his sun to rise on the evil and on the good, and sendeth rain on the just and on the unjust' (Matthew 5:45) – so to enter the kingdom of God one had to submit absolutely to God, a God who could be incomprehensible in the seemingly arbitrary and indiscriminate ways he chooses to love.

Mary Magdalene knew the courage of Jesus, his inextinguishable faith, she knew his love, she knew he was not offering himself as a sacrifice, nor to redeem anyone's sins – no such notion as original sin ever entered his mind; for Jesus man was good and God was good. She knew that for Jesus his death was a pure act of acceptance and perfection of the Father's love.

The message is always the same, in John, in the Psalms, in the Sermon on the Mount, on the cross. 'Thy kingdom come. Thy will be done.'

They had destroyed his body but not his love. And not her love.

The Burial

Jesus died unusually quickly on the cross, in three hours according to the synoptic gospels, six hours says the gospel of John. More commonly the torment lasted two or three days. Nor even then were the bodies taken down; Roman practice was to leave corpses hanging on the cross until they were devoured as carrion or rotted and fell off. But the scourging given to Jesus must have been especially ferocious, making him die sooner.

Also the Romans would have been mindful of Jewish burial customs. For the day of Jesus' crucifixion was a Friday, the eve of the sabbath which would begin at sundown; Jewish custom was for the body to be buried on the day of death but never on Saturday the sabbath; so Jesus would have to be buried that day or be left on the cross, alive or dead, until Sunday.

To hasten death the crucified victim received a final merciful brutality; his legs were smashed below the knees with something like a sledgehammer. The shock itself might kill but in any case the victim could now no longer use his legs to raise himself; he died of asphyxiation or heart failure within minutes. This was done to the two men crucified on either side of Jesus. 'Then came the soldiers, and brake the legs of the first, and of the other which was crucified with him. But when they came to Jesus, and saw that he was dead already, they brake not his legs'.

But the Roman execution squad was taking no chances, and 'one of the soldiers with a spear pierced his side, and forthwith came there out blood and water' (John 19:32-34). The water suggests that Jesus had died of heart failure; the spear released the build-up of water round his heart and then pierced the heart itself.

The Sanhedrin took charge of the bodies of the two men crucified with Jesus; it maintained cemeteries for Jews who had been executed, then it retrieved their bones after a year and released them to their families in an ossuary. But Jesus received a private burial thanks to the intervention of Joseph of Arimathea, one of the elders of the Sanhedrin. 'When the even was come, there came a rich man of Arimathea, named Joseph, who also himself was Jesus' disciple' (Matthew 27:57). Joseph sought permission from Pontius Pilate to remove Jesus from the cross and place him in his own tomb which had recently been cut from the rock in a garden not far from Golgotha. There before sunset in this April afternoon Joseph of Arimathea hurriedly wrapped the bloody and mangled body in clean linen and laid it to rest until it could be properly washed and anointed after the sabbath.

In the gospels of Mark and Matthew, Mary Magdalene and 'the other Mary', the mother of Joses, watched to see where Jesus' body was laid. But Luke and John tell it differently.

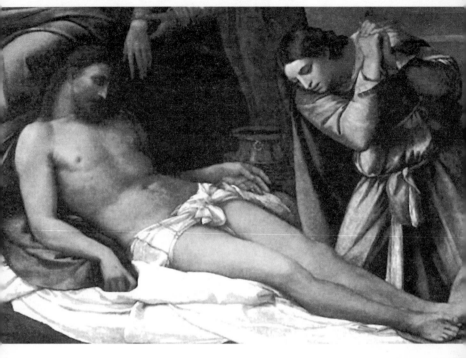

Mary Magdalene with Jesus after his body has been lowered from the cross. Detail of *The Deposition* by Sebastiano del Piombo, Italian, 1516.

Luke talks only of 'the women'; he mentions no names. 'And the women also, which came with him from Galilee, followed after, and beheld the sepulchre, and how his body was laid. And they returned, and prepared spices and ointments; and rested the sabbath day according to the commandment' (Luke 23:55-56). Likewise Luke had earlier avoided identifying those who witnessed the crucifixon, saying only that 'all his acquaintance, and the women that followed him from Galilee, stood afar off, beholding these things' (Luke 23:49). Nevertheless the three synoptic gospels are in agreement in having Mary Magdalene, or in Luke's case 'the women', witnessing the crucifixion standing afar off, and likewise the synoptics agree in having Mary Magdalene or 'the women' watching to see where Jesus is buried.

But the gospel of John gives an entirely different account of the witnesses to the crucifixion and also of the burial.

Instead of standing afar off as in the synoptic gospels, John has the witnesses to the crucifixion standing at the foot of the cross. 'Now there stood by the cross of Jesus his mother, and his mother's sister, Mary the wife of Cleophas, and Mary Magdalene', and they are joined there by the disciple 'whom he loved' (John 19:25-26). The Beloved Disciple appears six times in John's gospel but in none of the synoptics; he is never named.

As for the women, Mary Magdalene for once is mentioned last; John's gospel gives primacy to Mary the mother of Jesus. Her appearance here is her first since the early days of Jesus' ministry in Galilee when people began to think he was 'beside himself' and possessed by the devil. Together with Jesus' brothers, Mary came along to have a word with him and maybe take him away (Mark 3:31-35, Matthew 12:46-50, Luke 8:19-21). But Jesus dismissed his mother and brothers, saying that only those who do the will of God could count as his family. Now here in the gospel of John, at the foot of the cross, we are presented with a reconciliation. In later centuries the Church would seize on this moment in John's gospel to promote Mariology, the veneration of Mary as the Mother of God.

John also differs from the synoptics in his account of Jesus' burial. Joseph of Arimathea, 'a disciple of Jesus, but secretly' (John 19:38), goes to Pilate and obtains permission to take away the body. But with him is Nicodemus, a Pharisee and fellow member of the Sanhedrin, the man who used to come to talk with Jesus by night. Nicodemus brings with him 'a mixture of myrrh and aloes, about an hundred pound weight. Then took they the body of Jesus, and wound it in linen with the spices'.

This was not embalming, a practice all but unknown in Judaea, rather the spices were used to remove the odour; nor were coffins used in biblical times, the linen was sufficient. The practice was for the body to be left in the sepulchral chamber until it was reduced to a skeleton, then the bones were collected, wrapped in linen, and interred.

But the quantity of spices brought by Nicodemus is spectacular. In the version given by the gospel of John there could have been nothing discreet about removing Jesus' body from the cross, placing it in the sepulchre, and bringing so great a quantity of spices that several servants and perhaps a donkey or a cart must have been required, a small procession to the tomb. And the expense would have been enormous, but then Nicodemus was a very wealthy man, one of the wealthiest in Jerusalem.

All the gospels say that a great stone was rolled across the entrance to the sepulchre. But unlike the synoptic gospels John says nothing about Mary Magdalene or any other women looking on to see where Jesus was laid; in John there will be no need for Mary Magdalene to anoint Jesus after the sabbath as that service has already been performed by Nicodemus.

The day was over.

CHAPTER SEVEN

The Empty Tomb

'AND VERY EARLY IN the morning the first day of the week, they came unto the sepulchre at the rising of the sun.' This is Mark's gospel telling about Mary Magdalene visiting the tomb when the sabbath was past to anoint the body of Jesus. With Mary Magdalene are Mary the mother of James, and Salome. 'Who shall roll us away the stone from the door of the sepulchre?' But when they looked they saw that the stone was already rolled away.

Inside they saw a young man clothed in a long white garment and they were afraid. Do not be frightened, he said, 'Ye seek Jesus of Nazareth, which was crucified: he is risen; he is not here: behold the place where they laid him.' Tell Peter and the disciples, said the young man, that Jesus has gone to Galilee; there you will see him.

> And they went out quickly, and fled from the sepulchre;
> for they trembled and were amazed: neither said they any
> thing to any man; for they were afraid.

GLORIAM·VIDI·RESURGENTIS

Mary Magdalene discovers that the tomb is empty. *The Resurrection*, wood-cut 1917, by Eric Gill.

And there at Mark 16:8 is where the original version of Mark's gospel ends. The oldest of the canonical gospels ends with nobody seeing the risen Jesus; Mary Magdalene and her companions see only the empty tomb. That is the amazing and frightening event.

The Unseen Divine

But at some point the gospel was extended and twelve verses, Mark 16:9-20, were added; they seem to be borrowed and adapted from verses found towards the end of Matthew, Luke and John so that the ending of Mark would conform to the other gospels. This is the version of Mark found in Bibles today. After Mary Magdalene departs from the empty tomb, Jesus appears to her and she tells the others but they do not believe her; then Jesus appears to two followers along the road but they also are not believed; and finally Jesus shows himself to the eleven male disciples who are sitting at dinner and upbraids them for not having believed news of his resurrection.

The extended version of the gospel of Mark ends with Jesus telling the disciples to 'Go ye into all the world, and preach the gospel to every creature. He that believeth and is baptized shall be saved; but he that believeth not shall be damned. ... Then after the Lord had spoken unto them, he was received up into heaven, and sat on the right hand of God' (Mark 16:15-16, 19).

This command by the resurrected Jesus to go out and spread the gospel throughout the world is known as the Great Commission; it is the basis for the dispersal of the apostles from Jerusalem to found the apostolic sees and with it the principal of apostolic succession which is the fundamental building block of the hierarchy of the Church.

But the earliest Christians would not have found these verses in the original version of Mark nor in the oldest known complete texts of the New Testament, the Codex Sinaiticus and the Codex Vaticanus, both of the early fourth century AD. Although at least some of these additional verses are known to have been circulating as early as the end of the second century AD, the late fourth-century Church Father Jerome attested that verses 16:9-20 were absent from almost all Greek copies of Mark known to him. It is clear that at the time

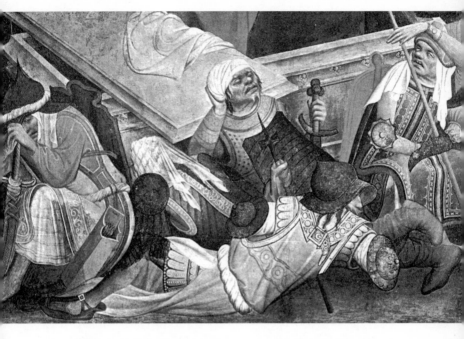

At the resurrection of Jesus the guards posted by the Sanhedrin 'did shake, and became as dead men', and afterwards, according to the gospel of Matthew, they were bribed to say that the disciples had taken the body away. Detail, *The Resurrection* by Meister Francke, German, 1424.

Mark's gospel was written, which is generally put at around AD 70, Mark himself and many early Christians accepted the empty tomb as a sufficient explanation of events.

For Mary Magdalene, in the original version of Mark, the amazement and fear she felt in the empty tomb was the awe one feels in the presence of the divine. The experience was comparable to entering the Holy of Holies of the Temple at Jerusalem, the inner sanctum where only the high priest could go and then only once a year. In every other temple in the ancient world the inner sanctum would contain the image of a god. But at the heart of the Temple in Jerusalem the Holy of Holies was empty – except as home for the unseen divine. And so it was for Mary Magdalene in the empty tomb. No appearance of Jesus, no palpable resurrection, no touching of wounds, no ascension into heaven, no sitting on the right hand of God, no

Church hierarchy nor threat of damnation was required. Jesus had said, and Mary Magdalene understood, that the kingdom of God is all round us; it is waiting for us to enter if we know how. 'The time is fulfilled, and the kingdom of God is at hand' (Mark 1:15).

Doubts About the Resurrection

The late addition to Mark which extends the text of that gospel beyond the discovery of the empty tomb goes on to promote the idea of a resurrected Jesus in the teeth of considerable doubt from the disciples themselves. The same is true in the gospels of Matthew, Luke and John. Each was written later than Mark, perhaps not much later but just enough to record the developing belief of a physically resurrected Jesus despite considerable doubts among those to whom the gospels were addressed, the early members of the Jesus movement.

Led by Mary Magdalene, the women go to the tomb on the third day. An engraving by Alexandre Bida, French, 1870s.

What we see in the gospels is a debate among early followers of Jesus over the credibility of the resurrection and also whether resurrection was supposed to take place physically – a raising of bodies – or spiritually. More fundamentally, for many followers of Jesus what mattered were his teachings of the Kingdom of God; notions of sin, resurrection and salvation were alien to them.

The Pharisees believed in the resurrection of the righteous with the coming of the messiah, but exactly in what form seems to have been evolving; for example Josephus in his earliest writings gives the impression that the Pharisees believed only in a spiritual resurrection, though later he is clear that the righteous who observe the Torah will enjoy bodily resurrection. But that was at the end of days; and the Pharisees neither believed that Jesus was the messiah nor in his immediate physical resurrection. Instead, as the following episode in the gospel of Matthew tells us, it was 'commonly reported among the Jews until this day', in other words decades after the crucifixion, that the empty tomb had more to do with bribery than resurrection.

Matthew reports that some members of the Sanhedrin anticipated that persons close to Jesus would steal the body to make it seem that he was raised from the dead, so they went to Pontius Pilate asking him to set a guard at the tomb. 'The chief priests and Pharisees came together unto Pilate, Saying, Sir, we remember that that deceiver said, while he was yet alive, After three days I will rise again. Command therefore that the sepulchre be made sure until the third day, lest his disciples come by night, and steal him away, and say unto the people, He is risen from the dead' (Matthew 27:62-64). Pilate had already satisfied himself that Jesus was dead; if the Jews were worried that some among them might think otherwise if the body disappeared, they should deal with the problem themselves, not with Roman soldiers but with the Temple's own militia. 'Pilate said unto them, Ye have a watch: go your way, make it as sure as ye can. So they went, and made the sepulchre sure, sealing the stone, and setting a watch' (Matthew 27:65-66). (Some commentators mistakenly assume that the guards were

Roman soldiers, but as Geza Vermes writes in his *Jesus*, when the Sanhedrin delegation asked Pilate to keep the tomb under military observation, '"Do it yourselves" seems to have been the governor's sharp reply'.)

But to no avail. 'In the end of the sabbath', continues the gospel of Matthew, 'as it began to dawn toward the first day of the week, came Mary Magdalene and the other Mary to see the sepulchre. And, behold, there was a great earthquake: for the angel of the Lord descended from heaven, and came and rolled back the stone from the door, and sat upon it. His countenance was like lightning, and his raiment white as snow: And for fear of him the keepers did shake, and became as dead men.'

Matthew attempts to counter scepticism about a resurrection with his story of a spectacular supernatural event, an earthquake and, instead of 'a young man sitting on the right side, clothed in a long white garment' as in Mark 16:5, an angel from on high which so terrifies the Jewish soldiers who had been keeping watch that they pass out on the spot. When they recover they go into the city and tell the chief priests what has happened. The chief priests then meet with the elders and decide to give 'large money unto the soldiers, Saying, Say ye, His disciples came by night, and stole him away while we slept. And if this come to the governor's ears, we will persuade him, and secure you. So they took the money, and did as they were taught: and this saying is commonly reported among the Jews until this day' (Matthew 28:13-15).

For Mary Magdalene, in Matthew as in Mark, the empty tomb was sufficient, and she 'departed quickly from the sepulchre with fear and great joy; and did run to bring his disciples word' (Matthew 28:8). But now Matthew goes beyond Mark and has Mary Magdalene running into the risen Jesus and holding him by the feet and worshipping him – a very physical encounter intended by Matthew to leave no doubt about a bodily resurrection. Jesus tells Mary Magdalene and her companion to 'go tell my brethren that they go into Galilee, and there shall they see me. Then the eleven disciples went away into Galilee, into a mountain where Jesus had

On the third day Mary Magdalene went to the tomb to anoint the body
of a naked man, something that no woman could do unless she was a
very close relative. *Nuptials of God* by Eric Gill, woodcut, 1922.

appointed them. And when they saw him, they worshipped him:
but some doubted' (Matthew 28:15-17) – face to face with Jesus on
a mountain in Galilee, yet still some of his disciples did not believe
in his resurrection.

The gospel of Luke tells the same story about the empty tomb and
of doubt about the resurrection. 'Now upon the first day of the week,
very early in the morning, they came unto the sepulchre, bringing
the spices which they had prepared, and certain others with them.
And they found the stone rolled away from the sepulchre. And they
entered in, and found not the body of the Lord Jesus' (Luke 24:1-3).

But Luke goes out of his way to avoid mentioning Mary Magdalene; instead he tells of 'the women'; for example on the evening of
the crucifixion 'the women also, which came with him from Galilee,
followed after, and beheld the sepulchre, and how his body was
laid' (Luke 23:55); and now after the sabbath 'they' have returned
to anoint the body.

This is the same Luke who says nothing of Jesus being anointed at Bethany but instead tells a story of a sinner woman wiping his feet at the home of a man called Simon in Capernaum.

Only after the women leave the sepulchre and tell the eleven disciples what they have seen does Luke trouble to tell us their names. 'It was Mary Magdalene and Joanna, and Mary the mother of James, and other women that were with them, which told these things unto the apostles. And their words seemed to them as idle tales, and they believed them not' (Luke 24:10-11).

Neither Mary Magdalene nor the women ever do see the risen Jesus in Luke's gospel. Instead later in Luke the disciples announce that 'The Lord is risen indeed, and hath appeared to Simon [Peter]' (Luke 24:34), though we are not told where or when.

Mary Magdalene and the Tradition of Visiting Family Tombs

Mary Magedalene, when she went to the tomb on the third day, was following an ancient Jewish tradition. The custom was for relatives of the deceased to visit the tomb in the first three days. This was to make sure that the body in the sepulchre was really dead. The practice of hurriedly entombing a person before sundown on the day of their death carried the risk of making a mistake through haste; there was the danger of burying people alive. Relatives came to see if the dead had come to life.

Also, according to the gospels of Mark and Luke, Mary Magdalene was there to anoint Jesus' body. The burial had been so rushed that there had not been time to wash and anoint his torn and bloody body on the first day, and the following day was the sabbath when nothing could be done.

Mary Magdalene is at the tomb in all four gospels. In Mark she is there with 'Mary the mother of James, and Salome'. In Matthew she is there with 'the other Mary'. In Luke she is there with 'Joanna, and Mary the mother of James, and other women'. Only in John is Mary Magdalene there alone but her experience of the resurrection is intimate and emphatic. The other women variously come and go; indeed their presence may have been invented to make the event more credible, taking into account the Torah's requirement for two or three witnesses: 'at the mouth of two witnesses, or at the mouth of three witnesses, shall the matter be established' (Deuteronomy 19:15). But Mary Magdalene is always there – which suggests that Mary Magdalene at the empty tomb was an event well known to followers of Jesus and to the earliest Christians; she was central to the story, though the truth of the story was obscured or lost, that Mary Magdalene and Mary Magdalene alone has a special relationship with Jesus.

On the third day Mary Magdalene went to the tomb to anoint the body of a naked man, something that no woman could do unless she was a very close relative. She also followed the tradition, practised by relatives of the deceased, of going to the tomb to ensure that Jesus was dead.

Jesus had a mother, he had sisters, he had other relatives, any of whom could have carried out these family duties. Yet it was Mary Magdalene who went to the tomb on the third day.

The Missing Body

In the gospel of John Mary Magdalene comes alone to the tomb early in the morning long before dawn. 'The first day of the week cometh Mary Magdalene early, when it was yet dark, unto the sepulchre, and seeth the stone taken away from the sepulchre.' She runs to Peter and to the beloved disciple and says, 'They have taken away the Lord out of the sepulchre, and we know not where they have laid him'.

Who does Mary Magdalene mean by 'they'? Did she mean the Sanhedrin? But according to Matthew the Sanhedrin posted guards to make sure Jesus' body was not taken from the tomb. Or did she mean the disciples, the people the Sanhedrin feared would take the body to make it seem that Jesus had risen? Yet the very first people she runs to are the disciples. Quite possibly Mary Magdalene had no one in mind at all. But those most likely to have removed Jesus from the tomb were those who put him there in the late afternoon of the crucifixion, Joseph of Arimathea and Nicodemus, who instead of burying Jesus might have used their great bulk of spices and the means needed to transport it to the tomb as a cover; instead of burying Jesus they could have taken him away. Or they came later and bribed the guards.

But that is not the Christian story which proclaims that Jesus was raised bodily from the dead, appeared to his disciples, and ascended to heaven to sit on the right hand of God, from where he will return in the end times to judge the living and the dead. But that Christian story took a long time to evolve. On the day Mary Magdalene went to the empty tomb it was not the story she knew.

Nicodemus and Jesus

We know that Nicodemus was a member of the Sanhedrin and a Pharisee. And we know he had got wind that Caiaphas was conspiring to arrest Jesus and he warned the Sanhedrin against condemning Jesus without hearing what he had to say. Nicodemus probably tipped off Jesus about his imminent arrest, leading to the agony at Gethsemane.

Nicodemus showed an interest in Jesus' teachings and came to him for discussions at night, that is after sunset. There was nothing secret about these meetings; there is no sense of secrecy in the gospel account; on the contrary, Nicodemus probably brought along his own disciples, including them in his use of the plural when he says to Jesus, 'Rabbi, we know that thou art a teacher come from God' (John 3:2). Jesus and Nicodemus had been teaching at the Temple during the day and now they have made the time to converse about spiritual rebirth in the coolness of the evening. Certainly Nicodemus did nothing to hide his sympathies on the day of the crucifixion when still in broad daylight he brought to the sepulchre a vast quantity of spices, enough to bury a king.

In those evening talks Jesus says to Nicodemus, 'I say unto thee, Except a man be born again, he cannot see the kingdom of God', to which Nicodemus replies, 'How can a man be born when he is old? can he enter the second time into his mother's womb, and be born?' There is something playful about this conversation; Nicodemus is a rabbi and he knows perfectly well about being born

Nicodemus with Jesus. Drawing attributed to Rembrandt, Dutch, 17th century.

again; the theme of rebirth runs throughout the Old Testament, as in Ezekiel 36:25-26: 'Then will I sprinkle clean water upon you, and ye shall be clean: from all your filthiness, and from all your idols, will I cleanse you. A new heart also will I give you, and a new spirit will I put within you: and I will take away the stony heart out of your flesh, and I will give you an heart of flesh'. The preachings of Jesus and others in the New Testament are a selective reworking of teachings in the Hebrew Bible. So Nicodemus, instead of being ignorant or naive, is drawing Jesus out, inviting him to expand and testing him, perhaps seeing if Jesus claims to be the messiah, for the Pharisees believed in the resurrection of the righteous at the coming of the messiah. When Nicodemus asks how a man can be reborn when he is old he is not saying that he himself is old; he is pressing Jesus to explain how anyone already born can be born again.

The Nicodemus Family of Jerusalem and Galilee

We do not know how old Nicodemus was but he might have been as young as Jesus, that is in his early thirties. Members of the Sanhedrin were highly educated in the Torah and in languages, mathematics and science, and therefore usually of a mature age, sufficient to reach the required level of accomplishment. But there was certainly room in the Sanhedrin for people of exceptional ability or standing in the community of any age from as young as eighteen. There is no need to assume that Nicodemus was more than about forty.

Nicodemus belonged to the Gurion dynasty, one of the very wealthy and well-known Pharisee families who comprised the Jewish governing elite in the period before the destruction of the Temple in AD 70. Nicodemus Ben Gurion is mentioned in the Talmud for famously securing Jerusalem's water supply when tens of thousands of pilgrims in the city were threatened with drought. His prayers to God were answered by a downpour which refilled twelve cisterns, earning him a reputation as a popular saint with miraculous powers.

During the First Jewish-Roman War, the rebellion of Jews in Judaea against Roman rule which broke out in AD 66, Nicodemus Ben Gurion was the wealthiest and most respected member of the peace party. He opposed the Zealots who were leading the revolt and he sought talks with the emperor Vespasian's son Titus, the general who was prosecuting the war. At the same time Nicodemus and his associates promised to supply Jerusalem for twenty-one years with all necessary provisions against a siege. The Zealots, however, burned all the provisions to force the people to fight to the death against the Romans; to which the historian Josephus adds that they also put to death Nicodemus' son who had been agitating for peace. In the event the Romans crushed the rebellion; in AD 70 Jerusalem fell and the Temple was destroyed.

Nicodemus' role in these events did nothing to harm his reputation in the rabbinic traditions where he is remembered entirely favourably and his charity and piety are praised. Nevertheless stories were told of the profligacy of Nicodemus' daughter Mary who was given a fabulous dowry of a million gold dinars and complained when she was allowed only four hundred dinars for unguents and perfumes on a particular day. But with the fall of Jerusalem, goes a story in the Talmud, Nicodemus lost all his wealth and his daughter was reduced to picking out barley corns from cattle dung.

As it happens there were two members of the Gurion family around this time called Nicodemus, an uncle and a nephew; so is this latter Nicodemus still the Nicodemus mentioned in the gospel of John? If he was young enough in the time of Jesus then it is possible that the Nicodemus who buried Jesus also witnessed the destruction of the Temple nearly forty years later. Or possibly the Nicodemus of AD 70 was the nephew of the first; in a sense it hardly matters; both were members of the powerful and rich Gurion dynasty of Pharisees whose religious, business and political affairs were centred on Jerusalem and whose lands were at Ruma, six miles north of Nazareth in Galilee. These were the Gurions known to Mary Magdalene.

Luke introduces us to Mary Magdalene in Galilee where she is travelling through the towns and villages with Jesus and supporting him and his mission from her own resources. But otherwise nothing necessarily attaches her exclusively to Galilee, least of all her name, for there was no such place as Magdala in Galilee. The synoptic gospels describe Mary Magdalene at the crucifixion and the burial as one of those women who had ministered to Jesus in Galilee which is not the same thing as her life being confined to Galilee, and the gospel of John does not connect her to Galilee at all. Nicodemus was very much a man of Jerusalem but his family lands were in Galilee. Perhaps the same was true of Mary Magdalene, a woman with connections to the court of Herod Antipas at Tiberias and to the aristocracy of Jerusalem. That Mary Magdalene was a woman associated with Jerusalem is suggested by her name, perhaps the name given her by Jesus; Migdal Eder was the tower of the flock spoken of, as noted earlier, in Micah 4:8.

> And thou, O tower of the flock, the strong hold of the daughter of Zion, unto thee shall it come, even the first dominion; the kingdom shall come to the daughter of Jerusalem.

Anointing and Burial

In the gospel of John the extravagance of the anointing at Bethany is repeated, as in no other gospel, by the extraordinary cost of the spices brought to the sepulchre by Nicodemus. The pound of nard with which Mary annointed Jesus at Bethany cost the equivalent of a man's wages for a year, and while a pound of myrrh was about half the price of a pound of the finest nard, a hundred pounds of myrrh would nevertheless have paid the wages of fifty men for a year. Using the spices as a measure, the house of Mary in Bethany was wealthy, a wealth of which we are reminded by the remarkable quantity of myrrh and aloes brought to the sepulchre by Nicodemus, a wealth in both cases set 'against the day of my burying' (John 12:7), as Jesus said of Mary at Bethany.

Jesus knew Bethany well and independently from his disciples from Galilee. Everything about his triumphal entry into Jerusalem, from obtaining the donkey to rousing the multitudes, was arranged with help from friends in Bethany; supper in the Upper Room in Jerusalem was also pre-arranged without his disciples knowing. From what we have seen at Cana (a stone's throw from Ruma of the Gurion family), where Jesus was a wedding guest at a household full of servants, and later at Bethany where he was lavishly anointed with a fortune's worth of spices, and at Jerusalem where he was honoured by Joseph of Armimathea and Nicodemus of the

Sanhedrin, Jesus had a number of wealthy and well-placed friends; his women followers were independent and wealthy and in the case of Joanna married to one of the most powerful figures in the court of Herod Antipas; and John the Baptist, Jesus' own cousin according to Luke, for all that he lived in the wilderness was born the son of a Temple priest.

That Jesus himself was a man of some substance is indicated by John 19:23-24 which describes how the soldiers at the crucifixion divided his clothes between them but threw lots for his tunic rather than rend it for it 'was without seam, woven from the top throughout'. Pope Benedict XVI in his book *Jesus of Nazareth* underscores this point when he writes that in the casting of lots for the seamless tunic 'we may detect an allusion to Jesus' high-priestly dignity', explaining that Josephus reports that the high priest of Israel wore just such a seamless garment.

A connection between Mary Magdalene and the Gurion dynasty of Nicodemus fits with what we can deduce of her life. She was an upper class Jewish woman, Hellenised, wealthy and independent, perhaps an aristocrat and linked to the priesthood. The name Nicodemus itself is Greek; Nicodemus means Conqueror of the People, perhaps an epithet earnt by an ancestor who was a successful general in the Hasmonean period – the family's estates in conquered Galilee, annexed to the Hasmonean Temple state, perhaps being a reward for distinguished military service. His Hebrew name was Buni, short for Benaiah, the name of a famous hero among King David's military commanders (which is why Israel's first prime minister adopted the name David Ben-Gurion; his name had been Grün); it was not unusual for an aristocratic Palestinian Jew also to bear a Greek name; in fact it is what one would expect of a Hellenising Jew who would oppose the fanatically nationalist Zealots and was prepared to talk peace with the Romans. Nicodemus was sympathetic to Jesus whose kingdom was not of this world; he was sympathetic to Mary Magdalene too. Moreover as one of the three or four richest men in Jerusalem, as a leading Pharisee and a member of the Sanhedrin, as a doer of good works and overseer of supplies for the various festivals and pilgrimages he would not be a man who could easily be slapped down by the high priest and his Temple coterie, though they tried with their sneering remark about no prophet arising from Nicodemus' native Galilee. A hundred pounds of spices for the burial of Jesus was Nicodemus' reply.

A Small and Intimate Circle

The numbers involved in the Jesus movement were very small. Though Jesus travelled about Galilee and occasionally gave sermons to thousands at a time and crowds welcomed him when he rode astride an ass from Bethany into Jerusalem, these were ephemeral gatherings. The Acts of the Apostles tells us that when his followers gathered at Pentecost, fifty days after Jesus' crucifixion, they numbered about a hundred and twenty in all (Acts 1:15).

These hundred and twenty, all of them Jews, would have known one another and many would have been related to one another; several were brothers and sisters and cousins of one another and of Jesus too. We are dealing with a very small and intimate circle of people.

The Bethany Connection

Bethany was on the pilgrimage route between Galilee and Jerusalem; it was a place where pilgrims stayed while visiting the Temple during the feasts and Galileans, who had to travel especially far from the north, established a colony in Bethany, taking in guests and providing hospices and almshouses for the sick and poor. Nicodemus himself, who had a reputation for good works and ensuring water for Jerusalem during pilgrimages, might well have been connected with Bethany, providing hostelries and hospices for pilgrims there. When Nicodemus talked one evening with Jesus about rebirth, that was when Jesus was staying in Bethany; perhaps Nicodemus also sometimes stayed in Bethany; possibly he had a home there. In fact are we looking at a family? Typically in first-century Palestine extended families lived together, communally using the same courtyards and doorless internal passages, an arrangement in which the movements of people could be quite fluid. Martha and Mary, unusual for apparently being unmarried, are both living in Bethany, both are well off; and they are living with their brother Lazarus. Were they all part of an extended family household?

And what about Mary Magdalene, to whom the gospels give no home, who goes to the tomb to anoint Jesus and finds it empty; and what about Mary who anoints Jesus at Bethany against his burial but then fails to appear at his crucifixion or at his tomb; are these two different women or are they one? Nowhere in the gospels is there a woman called 'Mary of Bethany'; she is only ever called Mary, and there are grounds for believing that in early tradition the Mary living in Bethany and Mary Magdalene were the same Mary.

The Secret Gospel of Mark

A controversial document called the *Secret Gospel of Mark* was discovered by Morton Smith, a professor of history at Columbia University, in 1958 at Mar Saba, a Greek Orthodox monastery clinging to the walls of the valley of the Kidron seven miles southeast of Jerusalem, one of the oldest continuously inhabited monasteries in the world and once famous for its ancient library. The document is a letter from the late second-century Church Father Clement of Alexandria which reproduces verses from a previously unknown gospel which reveal that Jesus practiced some form of initiation or ritual with a young man who came to him at night, scantily dressed, to be taught 'the mystery of the kingdom of God'. The young man is clearly Lazarus and the verses lead to the conclusion that Mary Magdalene is his sister.

Clement refers to these verses as part of the mystikon euangelion, literally the mystic gospel, to distinguish it from the ordinary canonical gospel of Mark in general circulation. The letter is addressed to Theodore who is concerned that the Secret Gospel is being distorted by the Carpocratians, a libertine gnostic sect, to justify their own licentious practices.

The *Secret Gospel of Mark* was discovered at the ancient monastery of Mar Saba which clings to the walls of the Kidron valley seven miles southeast of Jerusalem.

According to Clement's letter the Secret Gospel is a longer version of canonical Mark reserved for an initiated elite. Mark, he writes, while in Rome, 'wrote an account of the Lord's doings, not, however, declaring all of them, nor yet hinting at the secret ones, but selecting what he thought most useful for increasing the faith of those who were being instructed'. But later when Mark came to Alexandria he 'brought his own notes and those of Peter' and 'composed a more spiritual Gospel for the use of those who were being perfected', and at his death left these to the Alexandrian Church 'where it even yet is most carefully guarded, being read only to those who are being initiated into the great mysteries'.

But a copy of this *Secret Gospel of Mark* fell into the hands of the Carpocratians, who Clement says have wandered into 'a boundless abyss of the carnal and bodily sins'. Theodore has been combating their 'unspeakable teachings' but has written to Clement to learn exactly what is the true *Secret Gospel of Mark* and what has been corrupted by the Carpocratians. Clement's reply, in what survives of it, contains two sections of verse that he cites to Theodore as authentic, refuting the falsifications of the Carpocratians.

Morton Smith published Clement's letter in 1973 along with his exhaustive analysis and interpretation of the find. In Smith's own words the consequences of the find 'for the history of the early Christian Church and for New Testament criticism are revolutionary'.

The letter was immediately controversial. It upset many Christians because it meant that there was more than one version of Mark's gospel and also because the text struck some as homoerotic. Smith's interpretation also produced a reaction, independently of the contents of the letter, because it explained Jesus as a spiritually-inspired magus whose miracles were mystical visions; this went against the beliefs of those who saw the miracles as proof of divine power, but it also went against the thinking of those who prefer to see Jesus as a voice for social justice, a teacher of ethics. But also the letter was and remains controversial because of the nature of the discovery itself. Judging from the handwriting Clement's letter had been copied out

by an eighteenth-century monk in the endpapers of an 1646 printing of the works of Ignatius of Antioch – as though the monk was
preserving an earlier and deteriorating copy of the letter by trans-
ferring its contents to the book. But the authenticity of the letter's
provenance was questioned. Were these really the words of Clement
or had someone faked them, perhaps back in the earliest centuries
of Christianity or perhaps much later? Possibly Morton Smith had
faked the letter himself. But attempts to prove that the letter is a
fraud or a hoax have been less than convincing and its authenticity
is accepted by many distinguished scholars of Early Christianity at
Cambridge, Harvard and other universities. For many others, even
given their doubts, *Secret Mark*, as it is commonly called, cannot be
ignored and its authenticity is treated as a working hypothesis.

Resurrection Ritual at Bethany

The first and longest of the verses included in Clement's letter
concern the resurrection of a young man similar to the story of the
raising of Lazarus in the gospel of John. The story in *Secret Mark*
falls right after canonical Mark 10:34 in which Jesus tells the twelve
disciples the fate that will befall him in Jerusalem: 'And they shall
mock him, and shall scourge him, and shall spit upon him, and
shall kill him: and the third day he shall rise again'. The verse from
Secret Mark which is inserted here tells of a visit to Bethany where
in response to the plea of a woman Jesus rolls back the door of a
tomb and raises a rich young man from the dead. This young man,
neaniskos in Greek, looks upon Jesus, loves him and begs to be with
him. After six days Jesus commands the young man to come to him
at night which he does wearing only a linen garment, called a sindon in Greek, over his naked body. During the night Jesus instructs
the young man in the 'mystery of the kingdom of God'.

This is the entirety of the longer set of verses of *Secret Mark*
quoted by Clement in his letter.

> And they come into Bethany. And a certain woman whose
> brother had died was there. And, coming, she prostrated

herself before Jesus and says to him, "Son of David, have mercy on me." But the disciples rebuked her. And Jesus, being angered, went off with her into the garden where the tomb was, and straightway a great cry was heard from the tomb. And going near Jesus rolled away the stone from the door of the tomb. And straightway, going in where the youth was, he stretched forth his hand and raised him, seizing his hand. But the youth, looking upon him, loved him and began to beseech him that he might be with him. And going out of the tomb they came into the house of the youth, for he was rich. And after six days Jesus told him what to do and in the evening the youth comes to him, wearing a linen cloth over his naked body. And he remained with him that night, for Jesus taught him the mystery of the kingdom of God. And thence, arising, he returned to the other side of the Jordan.

Morton Smith concludes that the story in *Secret Mark*, though similar to the raising of Lazarus in the gospel of John, is not dependent on John nor is John dependent on *Secret Mark*; instead that it was a story in Aramaic that pre-existed both gospels, with each gospel drawing on the story in its own way. Smith believes that the initiation was a baptism, though not a baptism with water, rather with the spirit. In fact it looks like a ritual of rebirth, an enacting of death and resurrection, for the word sindon means a shroud, the same word used to describe the linen in which Joseph of Arimathea wrapped Jesus when he placed him in the sepulchre in Mark 15:46 and also the same word used to describe the cloth worn by the youth in the garden of Gethsemane in one of the strangest and otherwise inexplicable scenes in the gospels (Mark 14:51) – when the Temple militia burst into the garden to arrest Jesus, his disciples flee, and only a scantily dressed youth stays behind until the militia attempts to arrest him too, tearing the garment from his body, and he makes his escape naked into the night. In the gospel of Mark the naked youth in the garden has no context, no meaning, no explanation whatsoever; it reads like a memory fragment of a forgotten event.

The *Secret Gospel of Mark* provides an insight into one of the strangest scenes in the gospels, that moment when the Temple militia burst into the garden of Gethsemane to arrest Jesus and attempt to seize a youth who makes his escape, leaving his garment in their clutches and runs off naked into the night. Painting by Correggio, Italian, c.1522.

Likewise neaniskos, not the most usual word for a young man, is used to describe this young man in Gethsemane, and the young man, apparently a mortal, in the long white garment inside the empty tomb (Mark 16:5). Sindon and neaniskos are each used on only these two occasions in the canonical gospel of Mark, but they are also used to describe the appearance of the young man whom Jesus raises from the dead at Bethany in *Secret Mark*. Possibly it is always the same young man. What began as a ritual ends as history.

Nor is it just the repetition of a single word: the phrase 'a linen cloth cast about his naked body' is exactly the same when describing the initiation of the Bethany youth and the young man who flees from the garden of Gethsemane. These words and phrases amount to a signature linking the events and the people they describe.

Mary Magdalene and her Brother Lazarus

The second and shorter of the *Secret Mark* verses included by Clement in his letter to Theodore occurs further along in canonical Mark 10 where there is clearly a break in verse 46, as though something has been removed. As it stands it reads, 'And they came to Jericho: and as he went out of Jericho with his disciples and a great number of people, blind Bartimaeus, the son of Timaeus, sat by the highway side begging' – Jesus comes to Jericho and leaves Jericho, a completely pointless statement. Something happened in Jericho but canonical Mark does not say what. *Secret Mark* fills the gap, though obscurely; right after 'And they came to Jericho' it says,

> And the sister of the youth whom Jesus loved and his mother and Salome were there, and Jesus did not receive them.

Then canonical verse 46 resumes: 'and as he went out of Jericho with his disciples', etc. Clement is about to give 'the true explanation' and 'the true philosophy' of these interpolations, including the words 'and Jesus did not receive them', as opposed to what the Carpocratians have been making of them, when the manuscript of *Secret Mark* breaks off.

But the list of three women, 'the sister of the youth whom Jesus loved and his mother and Salome', does tell us something important. The word for youth here is again neaniskos, which identifies him with the young man at Bethany. And just as the young man at Bethany is clearly the same as the young man in the garden of Gethsemane, and both are therefore identified with Lazarus in the gospel of John, so we are being told the identity of 'the sister of the youth whom Jesus loved'; she is the sister of Lazarus. In the same way that neaniskos and sindon link events and characters together, so the naming of Salome serves the same purpose for she is mentioned only twice in the canonical gospel of Mark, at 15:40 where the women are at the crucifixion 'looking on afar off: among whom was Mary Magdalene, and Mary the mother of James the less and of Joses, and Salome'; and at 16:1 when on the morning after the sabbath the women came to the sepulchre, 'Mary Magdalene, and Mary the mother of James, and Salome, had bought sweet spices, that they might come and anoint him'.

In each case in canonical Mark Salome is last. Mary the mother of James and Jose is second; she is 'his mother', that is the mother of Jesus, who according to Mark 6:3 had four brothers, James, Joses, Juda and Simon, not to mention at least two sisters, a fact widely accepted in the first centuries of Christianity, at the time of the Church Fathers, until the fourth century when the invention of the doctrine of Mary's perpetual virginity began to gain ground, necessitating the identification of 'other' Marys to mother her children. And in first position in the list is 'the sister of the youth whom Jesus loved', that is the sister of Lazarus, who is Mary Magdalene.

The Bethany Family

We are presented with the story of a Bethany family linked across the gospels of John, Matthew, canonical Mark and *Secret Mark*. The family is wealthy and includes a brother and at least one sister who become prominent followers of Jesus, help finance his ministry, and offer their home in Bethany as a headquarters when he comes to Jerusalem. The brother is Lazarus and the sister is Mary Magdalene.

This early 20th-century photograph shows the church of Lazarus at Bethany which stands atop the traditional site of his tomb.

Lazarus was a wanted man. Whether he had actually been raised from the dead to life or had been engaged in a ritual of death and rebirth, the effect was so sensational that the Temple authorities not only conspired to kill Jesus but also Lazarus. When Jesus came to Bethany at Passover, people came from Jerusalem 'not for Jesus' sake only, but that they might see Lazarus also, whom he had raised from the dead. But the chief priests consulted that they might put Lazarus also to death' (John 12:9-10). And when Jesus made his triumphal entry to Jerusalem the people who gathered and shouted their hosannas were as much excited by Lazarus as by Jesus. 'On the next day much people that were come to the feast, when they heard that Jesus was coming to Jerusalem, Took branches of palm trees, and went forth to meet him, and cried, Hosanna: Blessed is the King of Israel that cometh in the name of the Lord. And

Jesus, when he had found a young ass, sat thereon; as it is written, Fear not, daughter of Sion: behold, thy King cometh, sitting on an ass's colt. ... The people therefore that was with him when he called Lazarus out of his grave, and raised him from the dead, bare record. For this cause the people also met him, for that they heard that he had done this miracle' (John 12:12-15, 17-18).

When Jesus went to the garden of Gethsemane he asked his disciples to 'Sit ye here, while I shall pray'. But going deeper into the garden he 'taketh with him Peter and James and John', saying 'My soul is exceeding sorrowful unto death: tarry ye here, and watch'. Watch what? If Jesus was not resisting his fate what was the purpose in standing guard? Had the disciples gathered in the garden of Gethsemane for a nighttime resurrection ritual enacted by Lazarus? Were Peter, James and John meant to be inducted? But the way the canonical version of Mark tells it, Peter, James and John are presumably meant to watch out for any approach by the Temple militia; instead they fall asleep and suddenly the garden is overrun by 'a great multitude with swords and staves, from the chief priests and the scribes and the elders' (Mark 14:34, 43). The disciples immediately run away. 'And they all forsook him, and fled'.

The disciples fled but one man remained, 'a certain young man, having a linen cloth cast about his naked body'. The militia laid hold of him, but the young man 'left the linen cloth, and fled from them naked' (Mark 14:50-52). Having already let the other disciples flee, Jesus alone would be handed over to the Romans. The attempt to grab Lazarus seems to have been half-hearted, possibly because his wealth and also perhaps connections with aristocratic and priestly families of the city dissuaded them from condemning him. (The name Lazarus, Eleizar in Hebrew, was very common in first-century AD Palestine, but it should be noted that it occurs in the lineage of the Gurion family and also in that of the family of the high priest Annas, father in law of Caiaphas. Some such connection with the elite might explain the identity of 'that disciple [who] was known unto the high priest, and went in with

Jesus into the palace of the high priest' (John 18:15); a now fully clothed Lazarus might have witnessed the trial of Jesus before the Sanhedrin.)

The disciples understood nothing of what was going on; only after the empty tomb did they begin to make sense of things; the ritual or actual rebirth of Lazarus from the dead, the anointing by Mary Magdalene of Jesus, finding the mysterious ass' colt, the triumphant entry into Jerusalem. 'These things understood not his disciples at the first: but when Jesus was glorified' – that is after his resurrection – 'then remembered they that these things were written of him' (John 12:16). While the disciples remained in ignorance, Jesus and his inner circle of followers, the ones with whom he had shared the mystery of death and rebirth, among them Lazarus and Mary Magdalene, had been arranging things over the Mount of Olives at Bethany – Jesus the magus and Mary Magdalene the sorceress.

Raising the Dead

On three occasions in the gospels Jesus seemingly raises someone from the dead. Jairus was the head of a synagogue in Galilee whose daughter falls ill; he begs Jesus to see what he can do, but as Jesus approaches the house onlookers pronounce that the girl has now died. The story is told in Mark 5:38-42, Matthew 9:23-25 and Luke 8:52-55, but in each of these gospel accounts Jesus announces that the daughter of Jairus is not really dead, only sleeping. As Mark tells it, Jesus takes the girl by the hand and in Aramaic says Talitha cumi, which means 'Damsel, I say unto thee, arise', and straightaway she arises and walks.

The second story is found only in the gospel of Luke and tells of the son of the widow of Nain whom Luke himself describes as dead. Jesus takes pity on the widow; as the body is being carried for burial outside the gate of the city Jesus touches the bier, 'And he said, Young man, I say unto thee, Arise. And he that was dead sat up, and began to speak' (Luke 7:14-15). Sceptics might easily have said that just as the daughter of Jairus was not really dead, so

The entrance to the tomb of Lazarus at Bethany, photographed in 1906.

neither was the son of the widow of Nain; the haste to bury the dead before the setting of the sun could lead to mistakes.

But the gospel of John, the last of the gospels to be written, intends to leave no doubt; over and over throughout chapter 11 it drives home the point that Lazarus really is dead.

Mary and Martha send word from Bethany to Jesus who is beyond the Jordan river that 'he whom thou lovest is sick', but Jesus does nothing and stays where he is for two days. After first telling his disciples that 'Our friend Lazarus sleepeth; but I go, that I may awake him out of sleep', suddenly his manner changes. 'Then said Jesus unto them plainly, Lazarus is dead'.

Only now does Jesus make the several days' journey to Bethany where he meets Martha waiting for him on the road and learns that Lazarus 'had lain in the grave four days already'. She says if only Jesus had come sooner her brother would not have died. 'Thy brother shall rise again', he says, 'I am the resurrection, and the life: he that believeth in me, though he were dead, yet shall he live: And whosoever liveth and believeth in me shall never die'.

Then Mary came and joined them, followed by mourners from the house, and the verses become more emphatic that Lazarus is dead. Mary reproaches Jesus as Martha had done. 'She fell down at his feet, saying unto him, Lord, if thou hadst been here, my brother had not died.' But here something strange happens; instead of telling Mary as he did Martha that he is the resurrection and the life, Jesus weeps. To Martha he must explain his divinity; to Mary he does not need to explain; she understands; he is free to be a man and to weep for his friend.

'Where have ye laid him?', he says, and being shown the tomb he asks the men to remove the stone. Martha protests. 'By this time he stinketh', she says. But Jesus 'cried with a loud voice, Lazarus, come forth. And he that was dead came forth, bound hand and foot with graveclothes: and his face was bound about with a napkin. Jesus saith unto them, Loose him, and let him go'.

Unlike the daughter of Jairus and the son of the widow of Nain, and unlike the young man in *Secret Mark* who, though buried in the tomb, let out 'a great cry', this Lazarus in the gospel of John had been four days in the tomb, stinking and dead. Nor was there any doubt that this was a bodily resurrection; Jesus said come forth and the dead man came forth, and Jesus said loose him from his graveclothes and let him go. Later this same Lazarus would sit at the table as Martha served and Mary anointed Jesus 'against the day of my burying' (John 12:7).

Yet though the raising of Lazarus was a bodily resurrection, nowhere in the synoptic gospels does Jesus give any indication that he believes in the resurrection of the body. For example the gospels of Matthew, Mark and Luke all tell the story about the Sadducees, who did not believe in any kind of resurrection, confronting Jesus at the Temple, giving him the example of the woman who according to Jewish law married the brother of her deceased husband, but after his death married in turn the next brother and so on until she had married seven brothers in all – so to whom was she married come the resurrection?

This is how Mark tells the story. 'Then come unto him the Sadducees, which say there is no resurrection; and they asked him,

THE QUEST FOR MARY MAGDALENE

saying, ... In the resurrection therefore, when they shall rise, whose wife shall she be of them? for the seven had her to wife' (Mark 12:18, 23). To which Jesus answers in Mark 12:25, 'when they shall rise from the dead, they neither marry, nor are given in marriage; but are as the angels which are in heaven'. In Matthew 22:30 Jesus says the same thing, they 'are as the angels of God in heaven'. And similarly in Luke 20:36, 'they are equal unto the angels'. These are not bodily resurrections; these 'angels' lack the needs and functions of flesh and blood. In the same way that the synoptic gospels present this as the view of Jesus so they are likely to have been the view of the generality of Jews in the first century AD.

But now, according to John's gospel, Jesus raises Lazarus bodily and he and his sisters all sit down and have dinner together at Bethany. 'In the beginning was the word'; this is how the gospel of John begins; 'and the word was God. ... And the Word was made flesh, and dwelt among us' (John 1:1, 14) In John there is a different understanding of resurrection at work in which Mary Magdalene must play her part.

Touch Me Not

> The first day of the week cometh Mary Magdalene early, when it was yet dark, unto the sepulchre, and seeth the stone taken away from the sepulchre. Then she runneth, and cometh to Simon Peter, and to the other disciple, whom Jesus loved, and saith unto them, They have taken away the Lord out of the sepulchre, and we know not where they have laid him.

This is how the resurrection scene begins in the gospel of John (20:1-2). Immediately Peter and the beloved disciple race to the tomb, but the beloved disciple, presumably being younger, 'did outrun Peter, and came first to the sepulchre. And he stooping down, and looking in, saw the linen clothes lying; yet went he not in'. Then Peter comes and goes into the sepulchre where he sees the napkin that had been about Jesus' head and the linen clothes. Now the beloved disciple comes in too 'and he saw, and believed' (John 20:4-5, 8). The race is like a contest for precedence; Peter, who enters the tomb first, will become leader of the Jesus movement, even the first pope in Rome; yet the beloved disciple arrived outside the tomb before Peter but he gave way, and when he finally went in he believed; perhaps he did not need to go into the sepulchre to believe; but we do not know if Peter believed. The matter ends

Recognising the risen Jesus in the garden, Mary Magdalene reaches out for the man who has returned to her. But nothing is the same. 'Touch me not; for I am not yet ascended to my Father.' *Noli Me Tangere* by Giotto, 1305, in the Scrovegni Chapel, Padua.

anticlimactically: 'Then the disciples went away again unto their own home' (John 20:10).

But not for Mary Magdalene who 'stood without at the sepulchre weeping'. And as she wept she stooped down and looked into the sepulchre and saw 'two angels in white sitting, the one at the head, and the other at the feet, where the body of Jesus had lain. And they say unto her, Woman, why weepest thou? She saith unto them, Because they have taken away my Lord, and I know not where they have laid him' (John 20:11-13).

This is only the second time that Mary Magdalene has spoken in the gospels. In Mark and Matthew and Luke she is given nothing to say. But in John she speaks and what she wants to know is what have 'they' done with Jesus' body. In Mark she does not ask, there is only silence; in Mark she knows all there is to know. But in John mystery is replaced by poetry.

Turning from the tomb, Mary Magdalene sees a man she thinks to be the gardener. 'Woman, why weepest thou? whom seekest thou?' And she says to him, 'Sir, if thou have borne him hence, tell me where thou hast laid him, and I will take him away'. 'Mary', Jesus says to her, and now she recognises him. 'Rabboni', she says, using the familiar Aramaic for master, and reaches out for the man who has returned to her. But nothing is the same. 'Touch me not; for I am not yet ascended to my Father.' (John 20:14-17)

It is a strange thing to say, for eight days later and ten verses on Jesus appears to Doubting Thomas. 'Then saith he to Thomas, Reach hither thy finger, and behold my hands; and reach hither thy hand, and thrust it into my side: and be not faithless, but believing. And Thomas answered and said unto him, My Lord and my God' (John 20:27-28).

So very different from the faith and vision of Mary. 'Go to my brethren', Jesus tells her, 'and say unto them, I ascend unto my Father, and your Father; and to my God, and your God'. According to John, Mary Magdalene did as she was told. 'Mary Magdalene came and told the disciples that she had seen the Lord, and that he had spoken these things unto her' (John 20:17-18).

And that is the last we hear of Mary Magdalene. Two decades or so later, in his first epistle to the Corinthians, Paul the self-appointed apostle to the gentiles told them how 'Christ died for our sins' and that 'he was buried, and that he rose again the third day', and that 'he was seen of Cephas [Peter], then of the twelve: After that, he was seen of above five hundred brethren at once; of whom the greater part remain unto this present, but some are fallen asleep. After that, he was seen of James; then of all the apostles. And last of all he was seen of me also' (1 Corinthians 15:3-8). But nowhere in his list is Mary Magdalene.

Yet Paul explains that those who have seen Jesus preach of his death and resurrection; 'so we preach, and so ye believed. Now if Christ be preached that he rose from the dead, how say some among you that there is no resurrection of the dead? But if there be no resurrection of the dead, then is Christ not risen: And if Christ be not risen, then is our preaching vain, and your faith is also vain' (1 Corinthians 15:11-14). But no Mary Magdalene.

Mary Magdalene called Jesus Rabboni but not my God. Could she have touched him? What did Mary Magdalene believe? Was it as in that sudden ending of the gospel of Mark; no appearance of Jesus, no palpable resurrection, no touching of wounds, no ascension into heaven, no sitting on the right hand of God, no Church hierarchy. Was it that she believed simply in the kingdom of God and the empty tomb?

One thing is certain. Nowhere in the canonical New Testament does anybody ever mention Mary Magdalene again.

CHAPTER EIGHT

The Disappearance of Mary Magdalene

MARY MAGDALENE DISAPPEARS FROM the Bible after her appearance at the crucifixion and resurrection in Matthew, Mark, Luke and John. She is not named in the Acts of the Apostles which was written by the same person who wrote the gospel of Luke – though perhaps we can assume she is there at Pentecost, seven weeks after the resurrection, where 'the women, and Mary the mother of Jesus' are gathered with the disciples and other followers, 'about an hundred and twenty' (Acts 1:14-15), in an upper room in Jerusalem where they are visited by the Holy Spirit.

The presence of the Holy Spirit is equivalent to the presence of Jesus himself; though Jesus has ascended to his Father and no longer walks among his followers, the faithful are filled with the Holy Spirit, invisible, inward and enduring, its truth to be spread by the disciples throughout the world.

Among 'the women' may have been Mary Magdalene, perhaps she at Bethany who had anointed Jesus with the Divine Spirit; but this is the last glimpse we have of her in the New Testament, anonymous now, lost among the crowd in an upper room.

Instead the Acts of the Apostles concentrates on Peter when it tells the story of the founding of the church in Jerusalem after Jesus' death, resurrection and ascension and increasingly on Paul when it tells how the new faith was spread throughout the Roman Empire – as intimated by the Holy Spirit which has those gathered in the upper room talking in tongues as though to the whole world.

This is no longer the world of Galilee nor the Jewish world of Palestine; this is the world of Paul, the Hellenised Jew – who will turn his back on the historical Jesus and ignore the existence of Mary Magdalene.

Paul the Hellenised Jew

Paul (which was his Hellenised name; Saul was his Hebrew name) was a Jew from Tarsus in Asia Minor (present-day Turkey). He described himself as 'a Pharisee, the son of a Pharisee' (Acts 23:6) but his wealthy family had also been granted Roman citizenship. By background, therefore, Paul was a man of several worlds. As well as speaking Aramaic and Hebrew, he also spoke Greek, for Asia Minor was part of the Greek world. The inhabitants of Tarsus were thoroughly Hellenised and Paul would have been familiar with Stoic philosophy of which the city was a great centre, the 'Athens of Asia Minor'.

Despite being well placed within the Graeco-Roman world, at first Paul chose to be narrowly sectarian. Jesus had already been crucified when Paul came to Jerusalem to study at the rabbinical school where in about AD 34 he approvingly witnessed the stoning of Stephen, the first Christian martyr.

Stephen belonged to a small circle of Jesus' followers, the Jerusalem church headed by Jesus' brother James, though it was no more than a Jewish sect, without rituals or holy places or a priesthood of its own. This was a Jewish movement; they faithfully followed the

Stephen proclaimed the divinity of Jesus and was stoned to death on orders of the Sanhedrin. An approving onlooker was Paul. Engraving by Gustave Doré, French, 1867.

Torah, they observed the dietary prohibitions and they insisted on circumcision. They also went into the Temple and prayed regularly, Luke 24:53 reporting that after Jesus' ascension his disciples 'were continually in the temple, praising and blessing God'. In time they might well have been reabsorbed into the mainstream of Judaism. But meanwhile they were observant Jews like Jesus himself who thought that the kingdom of God was at hand. And they spread this news to their fellow Jews.

But when Stephen told the Sanheddrin, 'Behold, I see the heavens opened, and the Son of man standing on the right hand of God', the Sanhedrin 'cried out with a loud voice, and stopped their ears, and ran upon him with one accord, and cast him out of the city, and stoned him: and the witnesses laid down their clothes at a young man's feet, whose name was Saul ... And Saul was consenting unto his death' (Acts 7:56-58; 8:1).

As is evident from his Greek name, Stephen was a Helleniser, his background probably not so different from Paul's. Stephen was born a Jew probably in the diaspora and his native tongue would have been Greek, and he preached to Jews from all over the Greek-speaking world, from Cyrenia in North Africa, and from Alexandria in Egypt, and also from Cilicia in Asia Minor, as told in Acts. Where the Jerusalem sect had stayed within traditional Jewish practice and belief, Stephen had loudly proclaimed the divinity of Jesus. The language of a man-god was intelligible in the Graeco-Roman world, but for the Sanhedrin, and for a man like Paul the Pharisee, Stephen had uttered a blasphemy.

Nor was the role of complicit bystander at the stoning of Stephen enough for Paul, who now 'made havoc of the church, entering into every house, and haling men and women committed them to prison' (Acts 8:3). Yet the way the story is told, the impression is given of a man driving himself towards fanaticism lest something within him gives way: Paul 'breathing out threatenings and slaughter against the disciples of the Lord, went unto the high priest, and desired of him letters to Damascus to the synagogues, that if he found any of this way, whether they were men or women, he might bring them bound unto Jerusalem' (this and the following from Acts 9:1-25).

'And as he journeyed, he came near Damascus: and suddenly there shined round about him a light from heaven: and he fell to the earth, and heard a voice saying unto him, Saul, Saul, why persecutest thou me? And he said, Who art thou, Lord? And the Lord said, I am Jesus whom thou persecutest.' Paul rose from the ground blinded by the vision and had to be led to a house in town, where for three days he neither saw nor ate nor drank. But on the third day a Jewish follower of Jesus called Ananias put his hands upon Paul, 'And immediately there fell from his eyes as it had been scales: and he received sight forthwith, and arose, and was baptised'. At once Paul rushed round the synagogues of Damascus preaching the very blasphemy that Jesus's followers in Jerusalem had hesitated to embrace, that Jesus was the living Son of God.

Paul himself however makes no mention of a vision on the road to Damascus; his epistle to the Galatians 1:11-16 says only that 'God revealed his Son to me'.

> But I certify you, brethren, that the gospel which was preached of me is not after man. For I neither received it of man, neither was I taught it, but by the revelation of Jesus Christ. For ye have heard of my conversation in time past in the Jews' religion, how that beyond measure I persecuted the church of God, and wasted it: And profited in the Jews' religion above many my equals in mine own nation, being more exceedingly zealous of the traditions of my fathers. But when it pleased God, who separated me from my mother's womb, and called me by his grace, To reveal his Son in me, that I might preach him among the heathen; immediately I conferred not with flesh and blood.

Note that Paul says that 'I conferred not with flesh and blood'. 'Not after man' did Paul learn about Jesus; no teaching brought him to an understanding of the kingdom of God; he did not come to Jesus like the disciples, like Mary Magdalene, by knowing the man; Paul received his authority directly and exclusively from his vision of a divinised Jesus, from the Christ.

In the instantaneousness of Paul's conversion, he dispensed with the doubts, the hesitations, the halfway houses that accompany argument and reflection, and became free to find radical solutions to the constraints of the Jesus cult. The very divinity of Jesus, the idea that a man could be a god, while utterly alien to Judaism, was in keeping with Hellenistic culture, even if the more sophisticated looked at it askance. As Paul himself said when he preached the divinity of

Jesus: 'For the Jews require a sign, and the Greeks seek after wisdom: But we preach Christ crucified, unto the Jews a stumbling block, and unto the Greeks foolishness' (1 Corinthians, 1:22-23).

Nevertheless to the gentiles of that Hellenistic culture Paul directed his mission, bypassing Jesus' followers in Jerusalem. They had known Jesus in his lifetime, as a Galilean, as a Jew, as a teacher

Paul's vision of Jesus on the way to Damascus led him to proclaim that he was a personal witness to the resurrection. Jesus was first seen by Peter, said Paul, 'And last of all he was seen of me also'. But Paul never mentioned Mary Magdalene. Engraving in the *Nuremberg Chronicle*, German, 1493.

who had tried to work within the particularity of his environment. But Paul's authority was his claim to have known Jesus through that vision on the road to Damascus according to Acts, to have known him as divine, as boundless and universal. Abandoning such Jewish shibboleths as dietary restrictions and circumcision, objectionable to the gentiles, while presenting his doctrines in the concepts and terms of Greek language and thought he had known at Tarsus, Paul embarked on a series of proselytising journeys that took him from Palestine to Asia Minor, Cyprus, Greece and ultimately to Rome itself, where according to tradition he was martyred in about AD 65.

Five years later, in AD 70, during the Jewish uprising against the Romans both Jerusalem and the Temple were destroyed. Josephus describes the scene.

> The slaughter within was even more dreadful than the spectacle from without. Men and women, old and young, insurgents and priests, those who fought and those who entreated mercy, were hewn down in indiscriminate carnage. The number of the slain exceeded that of the slayers. The legionaries had to clamber over heaps of dead to carry on the work of extermination.

The city, said Josephus, was 'so thoroughly laid even with the ground by those that dug it up to the foundation, that there was left nothing to make those that came thither believe it had ever been inhabited'. Great numbers of Jews fled throughout the Mediterranean. The Jesus movement in Jerusalem was dead.

The Disappearance of Mary Magdalene

What happened to Mary Magdalene in these years is a mystery. What is sometimes overlooked is that Paul's epistles and the Acts of the Apostles are the earliest Christian documents we have, yet she is missing from these; the gospels come much later and it is only in the gospels that we at last meet Mary Magdalene.

This relief on the Arch of Titus in Rome celebrates the fall of Jerusalem in AD 70. Legionaries triumphantly return home from the Jewish Revolt carrying a golden menorah and other sacred objects from the Temple.

The New Testament presents us with an order of events. First are the gospels, Matthew, Mark, Luke and John, which in their various ways describe the life of Jesus. Then comes the Acts of the Apostles which tells us of the early years of the Jesus movement. The remainder of the New Testament is largely taken up with the letters of Paul with their message that the death and resurrection of Jesus is the means to salvation. Epistles by other figures follow and finally the New Testament concludes with an apocalyptic work, Revelation.

But the order of composition of the New Testament was different. Before there were the gospels, before there was anything written about Jesus or Mary Magdalene, there was Paul. The letters of Paul, written in the AD 40s and 50s, are the earliest Christian works. The gospels follow quite a few years after, with Mark, the oldest, said to have been composed around AD 70 and John not earlier than AD 100. The Acts of the Apostles came almost last, after Revelation.

Therefore in a sense it is wrong to say that Mary Magdalene disappears from the New Testament after the gospels. The truth is that she is not there at the beginning; she is not there in the letters of Paul who specifically mentions meeting James and Peter and John in Jerusalem but makes no mention of Mary Magdalene. For example in his epistle to the Galatians 1:18-19 Paul writes that three years after his conversion he finally 'went up to Jerusalem to see Peter, and abode with him fifteen days. But other of the apostles saw I none, save James the Lord's brother'. Then in Galatians 2:9 he writes how fourteen years later he again went to Jerusalem where he met 'James, Cephas [Peter], and John, who seemed to be pillars'. But of Mary Magdalene Paul has nothing to say.

Paul has a reputation for misogyny but would this be enough for his failure to mention Mary Magdalene? At times he thinks women should sit still and keep quiet, 'Let your women keep silence in the churches: for it is not permitted unto them to speak; but they are commanded to be under obedience, as also saith the law. And if they will learn any thing, let them ask their husbands at home: for it is a shame for women to speak in the church' (1 Corinthians 14:34-35). As for relations between men and women, 'It is good for a man not to touch a woman ... But if they cannot contain, let them marry: for it is better to marry than to burn.' (1 Corinthians 7:1, 9). On the other hand Paul is entirely comfortable with women playing significant roles in the early movement; Priscilla, for example, who hosted congregations in her home; Phoebe, whom Paul describes as his patron; and Junia, the woman who may have been Joanna, the wife of Chuza, whom he calls 'of note among the apostles' (Romans 16:1-7).

It scarcely seems possible that during his visits to Jerusalem Paul did not meet Mary Magdalene or at least hear of her. James and Peter and John would have spoken of her. They would have told Peter how she was the first to discover the empty tomb.

And yet Paul says nothing about Mary Magdalene. But he makes no mention of Mary the mother of Jesus either. For that matter Paul has nothing to say about the living Jesus, nothing beyond two commonplace remarks, that he was 'made of a woman, made under the law' (Galatians 4:4) and was 'made of the seed of David according to the flesh' (Romans 1:3). Otherwise throughout all his letters Paul says nothing about the ministry of Jesus; nothing of his parables, nothing of his sermons, nothing of his healing, nothing of his teachings. For Paul Jesus exists simply as a crucified sacrifice; 'Christ died for our sins' (1 Corinthians 15:3) and to 'deliver us from this present evil world' (Galatians 1:4). Jesus was wasting his breath when delivering his Sermon on the Mount; Paul is not interested in what the living Jesus did or said, only that he gave his life to atone for our sins and was resurrected to free us from what Paul called this world of evil.

Only in the gospels, written generations after the events they describe, do we hear about the living Jesus and Mary Magdalene.

Peter and Paul etched into the wall of a fourth-century Roman catacomb. The two were said to have founded the first church in Rome and, according to legend, Peter became the first pope.

Paul Hijacks Jesus

In writing the Acts of the Apostles Luke creates a narrative bridge between the gospels, which relate Jesus' mission to his fellow Jews, and the rest of the New Testament, much of it taken up with the letters of Paul, which describe his journeys among the gentiles. In doing so, Acts makes it seem that Paul is an extension of the gospels – even the arrangement of the New Testament has Paul's epistles immediately following Matthew, Mark, Luke and John. Acts opens with Peter at Pentecost and the descent of the Holy Spirit, but a third of the way through its focus changes and it devotes itself overwhelmingly to Paul. Paul never knew Jesus and only came to Jerusalem after his crucifixion where he turned to persecuting Christians. Yet Paul is mentioned 155 times in Acts, while Peter, a prominent disciple of Jesus in all four gospels, is mentioned only fifty-six times. The entire final two-thirds of Acts is a narrative about Paul.

Nor is that the end of it. Paul has been credited with writing a large part of the New Testament; of its twenty-seven books fourteen have traditionally been assigned to Paul, though the authenticity of several is disputed by biblical scholars, with some thought to be pseudographia, that is written by followers in his name. There is general scholarly agreement, however, that Paul was the author of seven epistles – Romans, 1 Corinthians, 2 Corinthians, Galatians, Philippians, 1 Thessalonians and Philemon – and that these are authentic in whole. Whatever their authorship, all these books were seen fit to join the New Testament canon, and from the beginning of Acts to the end of Revelation, the last book of the New Testament, the ratio holds: Paul is mentioned three times as often as Peter. Apart from the gospels, the New Testament is essentially by and about Paul.

The faith preached by Paul was founded absolutely on the resurrection. 'And if Christ be not risen', Paul told the Corinthians, 'then is our preaching vain, and your faith is also vain' (1 Corinthians 15:14). 'I delivered unto you first of all that which I also received, how that Christ died for our sins according to the scriptures; And that he was buried, and that he rose again the third day according to the scriptures' – the scriptures being prophetic verses in the Old Testament such as Isaiah 53:5. Paul goes on to explain his own special place in the scheme of things. 'And that he [Jesus] was seen of Cephas [Peter], then of the twelve: After that, he was seen of above five hundred brethren at once; of whom the greater part remain unto this present, but some are fallen asleep. After that, he was seen of James; then of all the apostles. And last of all he was seen of me also, as of one born out of due time.'

So according to Paul the first person to see the risen Jesus is Peter, though that is not attested by any gospel. Then Jesus shows himself to the twelve disciples and appears to five hundred of the faithful before appearing before his brother James and all the other followers. 'And last of all he was seen of me also' (1 Corinthians 15:3-8), says Paul of his vision on the road to Damascus.

But Paul says nothing about the empty tomb and nothing about Mary Magdalene.

Paul's Journeys in the Footsteps of the Great Goddess

On his last journey, when Paul was sailing from Malta to Italy to stand trial in Rome, we are told in Acts 28:11 that he travelled with divine protection: 'And after three months we departed in a ship of Alexandria, which had wintered in the isle, whose sign was Castor and Pollux'. Known as the Dioscuri, 'sons of God', Castor and Pollux were the twin sons of Zeus, the god of thunder in the Greek pantheon.

The cult of the Dioscuri as saviour gods of sailors at sea was associated with the worship of Isis. Originally Egyptian but then Hellenised and universalised, Isis was the greatest of the pagan deities; the goddess of countless names, the all-embracing goddess.

The goddess in all her manifestations was no stranger to Paul. He would have heard, for it happened within living memory of his parents' generation, of Cleopatra's visit to Tarsus to meet Mark

The reverse of this silver tetradrachm minted in Alexandria in the early
first century AD shows Isis sailing towards the Pharos lighthouse. As Isis
Pelagia she was the protector of sailors and the goddess of the sea, and
as Isis Pharia she was goddess of lighthouses everywhere.

Antony; Cleopatra who in pharaonic tradition was the living incar-
nation of Isis, the saviour goddess of the ancient world, and Antony
her Osiris. The people of Tarsus were long familiar with the religion of Isis whose image even appeared on their coinage. Now even
as Paul was sailing to Rome the goddess travelled with him.

A temple of Isis stood at the base of the Pharos, the great lighthouse at Alexandria, one of the seven wonders of the world. An
annual procession in the city celebrated the cult of Isis Pharia, that
is Isis of the Pharos lighthouse, and the overflowing of the Nile
which sent Isis out of Egypt to roam the shores of the Mediterranean. As Isis Pelagia, that is Isis of the Sea, she was the protector

of sailors and the goddess of the sea, and as Isis Pharia she was goddess of lighthouses everywhere.

A first-century AD litany to Isis found on a papyrus at Oxyrhynchus in Egypt declares that her worship held sway all along the coasts of Palestine and Syria. She was worshipped at Caesarea, refounded as a great port along Hellenistic lines by Herod the Great in about 25 to 15 BC, where the cult temple to the goddess was associated with the lighthouse.

Isis was the sister-wife of the murdered Osiris whom she brought back to life long enough to get her with child; this was Horus with whom she is depicted seated on a throne, nursing the infant in her arms. She was the goddess of resurrection and new beginnings. The litany tells us that she made her son Horus the lord of the whole world; she created every day for joy; and she is the glory and the tender love of the female sex and has made 'the power of women equal to that of men'.

Her cult was in the ascendant during the lifetime of Jesus and Mary Magdalene in the first century AD. But long before then the influence of Hellenism had pressed inland from the coast and could be felt in the countryside and the villages, towns and cities all round the Sea of Galilee. The fishermen who ventured upon the waters of the lake at night were thankful for the towering beacons of Isis, the lighthouses that guided them safely back to their harbours in the hours before dawn – fishermen like those two disciples on whom Jesus bestows the name of Boanerges in the gospel of Mark 3:17: 'James the son of Zebedee, and John the brother of James; and he surnamed them Boanerges, which is, The sons of thunder'.

Many of Mark's readers or listeners, reading his gospel in its original Greek, would have associated 'sons of thunder' with the Dioscuri, Castor and Pollux, the twin sons of the thunder god Zeus. Just as readers of the gospels would know that one of the powers Jesus conferred on his disciples was to calm the storms in the Sea of Galilee, so they would know that the Dioscuri were the protecting gods of sailors and were invoked in times of storm when a sacrifice of white lambs was offered on the prow of a ship. The towering

Pharos lighthouse at Alexandria, home of the cult of Isis Pharia, was dedicated to Castor and Pollux and bore the inscription: 'To the Saviour Gods: for sailors'.

During Paul's first missionary journey he had met with antagonism from Jews when he attempted to preach the word of Jesus; he had done better at Antioch in Syria and at Salamis and Paphos in Cyprus, three places mentioned in consecutive lines of the Oxyrhynchus Litany as centres of Isis worship, and this resolved him to devote himself to spreading his doctrine of salvation among gentiles instead. Therefore on his second missionary journey he visited Tarsus, the Troad, Neapolis, Philippi, Amphipolis, Apollonia, Athens, Corinth and Ephesus, all known centres of Isis worship where Paul was preaching to pagans well familiar with sermons from priests on the saving powers of the goddess. Again he followed in the footsteps of Isis on his third missionary journey when he revisited many of the cities in Greece and Asia Minor that he had been to before.

Long before Paul was travelling round the Mediterranean, Isis had assimilated the worship and the stories of all the female goddesses of Egypt and also of Greece and Rome. Herodotus, the fifth-century BC Greek historian who travelled extensively in Egypt, said that Isis was the Greek goddess Demeter, that Osiris was Dionysus, that their children were the Greek gods Artemis and Apollo, and that Apollo was the Egyptian Horus. A century and a half later, after Alexander the Great conquered Egypt from the Persians and Alexander's successor Ptolemy I Soter initiated the Hellenisation of Egyptian culture, Isis became identified with goddesses from all round the Mediterranean, not only with Demeter, but with Persephone, Astarte, Aphrodite and with Artemis whom Herodotus had said was her daughter and also with Tyche, the Greek goddess of fortune, the Roman Fortuna.

Also already in the third century BC the Egyptian priest Manetho said that 'people often call Isis Athena'. The first-century AD Greek historian Plutarch echoed this when he observed that a statue of Athena in Egypt was identified with Isis and was inscribed, 'I am all that has been, and is, and shall be, and my robe no mortal has yet

The worship of Isis extended throughout the Roman Empire from Philae in Upper Egypt to Rome and London. This marble statue of Isis from the villa of the emperor Hadrian outside Rome stood at the very heart of imperial rule.

uncovered'. Plutarch added that Isis was sometimes called Sophia, the spiritual personification of wisdom, and described her as 'a goddess exceptionally wise and a lover of wisdom'.

By the time Paul reached Rome in about AD 60, the worship of Isis in the imperial capital was widespread, though it had been resisted for political reasons. Following the assassination of Julius Caesar in 44 BC, a temple in honour of Isis was decreed, probably with the encouragement of Cleopatra, the mother of Caesar's son, but the project was suspended by Augustus after his defeat of Cleopatra and Mark Antony in Egypt in 31 BC. Finally a temple

A temple to Isis was built in Rome in the AD 80s but nothing remains of it today, only this massive left foot from a colossal temple statue in the Via di Santo Stefano del Cacco; it was removed here in 1878 from the nearby thoroughfare which is still called Via di Piè di Marmo, the street of the Marble Foot. Several small obelisks that once belonged to the temple are distributed around Rome, one in front of the Pantheon close by.

was founded in Isis' honour in Rome by the emperor Domitian during the AD 80s.

But already in the reign of Claudius (AD 41-54) prayers were being offered to the emperor in conjunction with Isis; his predecessor Caligula (AD 37-41) had given state recognition to the Isis cult, had an Egyptian obelisk brought to Italy, and inaugurated the Navigum Isidis, an annual procession in honour of Isis held on 5 March, and according to the historian Josephus, Caligula himself took part in the masked parade dressed as a woman. In Italy the festival was suppressed by the Church in the early fifth century but in Egypt the Navigium Isidis was celebrated for a century longer – and in Catholic and Eastern Orthodox countries its successor is still celebrated today as carnival in the days before Lent.

Just as Paul sailed to Italy in a ship bearing the sign of the Dioscuri, so throughout his missionary journeys Paul was travelling in a world that put its faith in Isis and her companion gods. The very streets in which Paul wandered at Antioch, at Philippi, at Corinth and elsewhere, were thoroughfares for teachers and priests and devotees of Isis, and often he must have met them and talked to them there about the mysteries.

Paul's deified Jesus might have seemed to them as one more mystery cult to join the pantheon reigned over by Isis. But to Paul there could be no confusion and nothing shared, only salvation through the death and resurrection of Jesus Christ. Isis was the enemy of his new faith.

The Mysteries

The mysteries of the ancient world were religious practices, rituals and beliefs that were kept a fiercely guarded secret, known only to the initiated. 'Mysteries' comes from the Greek word mysteria, meaning secret. Isis and Osiris of Egypt, Cybele and Attis of Asia Minor, Aphrodite and Adonis of Lebanon, and Persephone and Demeter of Greece, these were the gods at the heart of the great pagan mysteries. What they all had in common was the story of life and death followed by rebirth. Their outer myths were well known. But their inner drama, the one undergone by their initiates, was a mystery.

The goddess was the essential life force in this ancient drama of death and rebirth. In the second century AD the Latin writer Apuleius, author of *The Golden Ass*, described his initiation into the Mysteries of Isis as a deeply moving spiritual experience in which he suffered a mystic death and resurrection, and felt bound to the goddess for the rest of his life.

Several Christian writers who heard something about the mysteries and felt no compunction about breaking the taboo of secrecy mentioned a ritual that sounds like ieros gamos, the Greek for holy sexual union or sacred marriage. In the second century AD, Clement of Alexandria referred to reports of a bridal chamber and crawling under a bed. Asterius, a fourth-century bishop of Amaseia in Asia Minor, expressed his horror at 'the descent into darkness, the venerated congress of the hierophant with the priestess'. And he went on to ask, 'Are not the torches extinguished and does not the vast and countless assemblage believe that in what is done by the two in the darkness is their salvation?'

Knowing whether this was actually a sexual act is less important than understanding its meaning. At the heart of the various mysteries was the story of death and life, or rather two types of life, for which the Greeks had two different words, zoe and bios. Isis and Aphrodite possessed zoe, eternal life. Osiris and Adonis possessed bios; they were creatures of the seasons who lived and died or were taken away to the land of the dead. All the mysteries involved descent into the underworld where the dead are regenerated, a regeneration that often requires healing from mutilation – Osiris cut to pieces, Adonis gored by a boar, Attis castrated. The sacred marriage was a healing and a resurrection; the individual whose life, bios, is lived within the rhythms of time was united with zoe, the life eternal.

The fundamental experience of these mysteries, which ritually enacted the initiate's death, may have been that death was an illusion. By submitting himself to death, the initiate was released from the conception of life and death as opposites; he entered into

The ieros gamos of the mysteries can be traced back to the most ancient beliefs. Here at the temple of Abydos in Egypt a relief from about 1285 BC shows Isis in the form of a bird copulating with her dead husband Osiris, regenerating him as lord of the underworld and bearing his son Horus.

union with the great processes of creation itself. The initiates had forgotten or lost this knowledge, but it was brought back to them by the rituals of the mysteries. Suggestive of such rituals were the anointings that took place between Jesus and the strange woman at Bethany, the woman whom John's gospel identified as Mary.

The story still retains its power. To this day people want to know if Jesus and Mary Magdalene were lovers, were married, had children; people want it to be so; it is the ancient and recurring story of death and love and rebirth.

The Jesus Mystery

Paul called Jesus the Christ, Christos in Greek, which is the translation used in the Septuagint for the Hebrew messiah, meaning the anointed one, the saviour or liberator of his people. But for Jews the messiah was a political figure who had nothing to do with resurrection nor with paying for people's sins. Paul lifted the concept of messiah from its Jewish context and presented his christos as a hero of the pagan mysteries whose suffering, death and resurrection are the means to salvation.

Paul spoke the same language as the pagan mystery cults. Just as followers of Isis participated in a ritual drama which led them through a symbolic experience of death to a new life, so in Romans 6:3-4 Paul offers a ritual death which leads to eternal life.

> Know ye not, that so many of us as were baptized into Jesus Christ were baptized into his death? Therefore we are buried with him by baptism into death: that like as Christ was raised up from the dead by the glory of the Father, even so we also should walk in newness of life.

But in one all important respect Paul's Jesus Mystery was different. In the mysteries of Isis and Osiris, Aphrodite and Adonis, Cybele and Attis, the goddess restores the male to life. He is a seasonal creature, he is bound by time, he is born and dies, and he is only reborn when he is united with the female who possesses zoe, eternal life. (Even in the Eleusinian Mysteries where Persephone is abducted by Hades to the Underworld, she is rescued by a woman, her mother Demeter.)

The Jesus of Paul lives and dies but returns to life because he himself is a god, in fact an aspect of God himself, the Son of the Father; no woman comes into it, not in Paul's version of the story. Like Osiris, Adonis and Attis, Jesus is mutilated and dies. On the third day he emerges from the tomb. If this were the mystery of Osiris, then his resurrection would be accomplished by Isis, protector and regenerator of the dead and guardian of tombs.

This may be why Paul makes no mention of Mary Magdalene at the tomb. In the mysteries she would be there; in the mysteries she would have zoe, the power and gift of eternal life. To avoid confusion or any doubt that anyone but Jesus can possess zoe, Paul writes every woman out of his Jesus mystery; Mary Magdalene is not mentioned even once by Paul, nor is Mary the mother of Jesus nor any other woman in Jesus' life. In Paul's version of the mysteries, women can have no place; true to Paul's Jewish monotheistic roots the mystery of rebirth and salvation belongs to Jesus Christ alone.

The Resurrection and the New Testament Canon

The New Testament as we know it only began to be crystalised at the time of Marcion, a wealthy and brilliant theologian from Sinope on the Black Sea who came to Rome around 140. Marcion was a great enthusiast for Paul's letters, finding in them a God whose love offered salvation in return for faith. But also he went further than Paul, sharing the widespread feeling in Greek culture that Christianity should cut itself free from its origins in Judaism and reject the Old Testament and its wrathful God.

What enabled and encouraged Marcion to do this was the final Jewish disaster, the Bar Kokhba revolt in AD 132-136, which the Romans put down more furiously than the revolt in AD 70, rebuilding Jerusalem as a pagan city with Roman temples while refusing Jews permission to go there. This second revolt in Judaea won the Jews no friends among the gentiles and marked the definitive separation of Christianity and Judaism. Importantly this separation freed gentile Christians from the need to accommodate Jewish beliefs and allowed them to uncompromisingly announce the resurrection of Jesus who now unequivocally became the sacrificial saviour god of Paul's preachings.

From the masses of Christian texts that had been circulating since the days of Paul's letters, Marcion set himself the task of selecting those that spoke with authority of the loving God of Jesus. He wanted to create a canon.

What he produced was a selection of letters by Paul which he called the Apostolikon accompanied by a gospel which he called the Evangelikon. The Apostolikan consisted of ten letters of Paul that Marcion decided were authentic (today seven are thought to be authentic), while the Evangelikon was a version of the gospel of Luke.

The triumphant resurrection of Jesus Christ and his raising of the dead is dramatically illustrated in this Byzantine fresco of about 1320 at the Chora Church in Istanbul.

Because Marcion believed that Jesus was not human, his version of Luke is missing the first two chapters, that is the nativity and also the stories about Jesus' childhood, so that it begins with his baptism in the Jordan by John and the start of his ministry at Capernaum.

Scholars dispute whether Marcion edited a pre-existing version of Luke or put together what he could find from various sources to write his own gospel which later developed into the Luke accepted into the canon. But the view of Church Fathers such as Tertullian, Justin Martyr and Irenaeus was that Marcion had tampered with Luke's original text – though it is unclear if any of the Church Fathers had the original text or even if they shared the same text. In 144 Marcion was summoned to Rome and excommunicated. All his writings were destroyed, or they perished, and what we know about Marcion comes from the tracts written against him by Tertullian and the others.

Nevertheless Marcion's version of Christianity proved very popular and his beliefs, together with his Evengelikon and his Apostolikan, enjoyed an audience for centuries. To counter the popularity of Marcionism the proto-orthodox body of the Church now began to decide upon a canon of its own, what we now have as the New Testament – the four gospels, the letters of Paul, other letters, and Revelation.

Apart from anything else this process of canonisation determined the literary form of the New Testament's contents, that it should consist of letters and of gospels; the one exception was the apocalyptic Book of Revelation. Gospel writing was an innovation; it was unknown until this time. Teachings, sayings, sermons, all manner of events, were put into a narrative which took a realistic and historical form. Or they were put into letters, which again allowed for clarity of teaching, of argument, and favoured realism and history.

There is significance in the way each of the gospels describes who sees Jesus at the resurrection. Except in the original version of Mark where Mary Magdalene discovers the empty tomb but Jesus makes no appearance to anyone, he always appears to the disciples, sometimes in the most painstakingly physical way, as when Thomas explores the wounds in Jesus' hands with his finger and thrusts his hand into Jesus' side. The effect of this bodily resurrection, most definitely no vision, is to validate the role of the disciples as apostles of Jesus who are to take his message to the world, who are to serve as the foundation pillars of his church.

This process continued through the second century and was settled by its end; its proponents are well known as their works have survived – Tertullian, Irenaeus, Justin Martyr chief among them. But these were figures in Rome or areas dependent on Rome. They inhabited that geographical trajectory established by the voyages of Paul, the area encompassed by the Acts of the Apostles. Not one of them came from Egypt, though soon some of the greatest figures in Christianity would indeed come from the vibrant background of Alexandria. But not now. The Church in Europe and Asia Minor determined the canon according to its way of thinking about God and it established clear markings of who was in and who was out, while at the same time establishing an order and a hierarchy of authority and power based on apostolic succession.

Of Egypt on the other hand, populous and wealthy, and Alexandria in particular with one of the largest Greek and Jewish populations in the world, little has been known of how Christianity developed during those first two centuries. What does emerge however is that Christian beliefs were varied and widely inclusive; there was nothing heretical about any of them because the very idea of a single correct point of view was unknown.

Here in Egypt Mary Magdalene thrived.

CHAPTER NINE

The Gnostic Mary
Magdalene

E ACH OF PAUL'S MISSIONARY journeys pushed westwards,
through Asia Minor and into Greece, until eventually with
what seems a sense of inevitability he reached Rome – and there
according to legend he died a martyr, though the New Testament
says nothing about this. There are other legends that Paul went farther westwards; Paul himself wrote of a desire to travel into Spain
(Romans 15:24). Paul also wrote that immediately after his conversion he went into Arabia (Galatians 1:17) where he seems to have
remained for three years. Arabia in this context is thought to mean
among the Nabataean people centred on Petra in present-day Jordan though some prefer imagining Paul retreating into contemplation and solitude in the deserts of the Negev or Sinai. But nothing
is known of that beyond Paul's brief mention of it in Galatians, and
at any rate this Arabian period seems merely a prelude to his great
missionary journeys to the West.

The movement towards Europe makes itself felt throughout the New Testament, not only in Paul's letters but in all the other epistles. The narrative of Acts leads inexorably towards Rome. Even the apocalyptic Book of Revelation is set within the historical and geographical bounds of Acts, its seven letters addressed to seven Greek churches, that is Christian communities, in Asia Minor. Also from sources outside the New Testament we have long known a great deal about the spread of Christianity through Asia Minor and into Greece and the rest of Europe.

Egyptian Mystery

But strangely nothing is known about how Christianity reached Egypt apart from the tradition, first recorded by Eusebius in his *History of the Church* in the early fourth century, that it was brought to Alexandria in the mid-first century by the Evangelist Mark. But the New Testament itself makes no mention of plans to evangelise Egypt even though it was populous and had important centres of Greek and Jewish settlement. Nor would we know from the New Testament that Christianity existed in Egypt at all were it not for a single reference in Acts which mentions a fellow missionary of Paul's, 'a certain Jew named Apollos, born at Alexandria, an eloquent man, and mighty in the scriptures, [who] came to Ephesus. This man was instructed in the way of the Lord; and being fervent in the spirit, he spake and taught diligently the things of the Lord' (Acts 18:24-25).

There is however a controversial verse in the New Testament that suggests that Christianity was brought to Egypt by the apostle Peter and the evangelist Mark – and also by a woman so well known that it was unnecessary to mention her name.

The question of Egypt turns on the meaning of Babylon in the verse. In 1 Peter 5:13 Peter addresses his fellow Christians in Asia Minor, saying, 'The church that is at Babylon, elected together with you, saluteth you; and so doth Marcus my son'. Ever since 597 BC when the Babylonian empire conquered Jerusalem and took away many of its leading citizens, Babylon had been used

According to Christian legend, St Mark the Evangelist brought Christianity to Egypt in the mid-first century AD. This mosaic in St Mark's Basilica in Venice shows Mark (on the left) arriving by sea at Alexandria with its Pharos, and then (on the right) teaching the gospel in the city. But the New Testament makes no mention of this except for one controversial verse which can be interpreted as meaning that both Mark and Peter came to Egypt together along with a woman so well known that it was not necessary to mention her name – Mary Magdalene?

by Jews as a metaphor for captivity and exile. Christians have followed suit, and so Babylon in this verse is commonly taken to mean Rome, the capital of the great empire whose influence pervaded everyone's lives, and where according to legend Peter would die a martyr's death – though none of this explains why Peter would conceal the identity of Rome behind a metaphor. The interpretation that Babylon means Rome is regarded with scepticism among some scholars and also among the Copts, that is the Christians of Egypt, who point out that Babylon was a name used in Hellenistic and Roman times and right through the Middle Ages to refer to a place that now lies within the southern quarters of Cairo, the city founded by the Arabs in 969, and is called Misr al Qadima, Old Cairo. The argument that Babylon means Rome is disingenuous, they say, and serves to appropriate Peter to Rome in order there to crown him pope and martyr, legitimising the Vatican's claim to apostolic supremacy.

In pharaonic times travellers between the great cities of Heliopolis, the religious centre of Egypt, and Memphis, its political capital, took the ferry at Babylon to cross the Nile. A settlement, perhaps even a town, sprang up on this spot on the east bank of the river opposite the southern tip of Roda island which the Greeks would later call Babylon in Egypt, probably a corruption of Roda's ancient name of Per-Hapi-en-Yun, House of the Nile of Heliopolis.

According to Jewish tradition, when the prophet Jeremiah escaped to Egypt in the sixth century BC after the destruction of Jerusalem by the Babylonians he preached and settled at Babylon; the Copts add that the presence of Jews here drew the Holy Family to Babylon during their flight into Egypt to escape Herod. For the same reason, say the Copts, Peter and Mark came here, arguing that Babylon is no metaphor for Rome but means Babylon in Egypt with its ancient Jewish and Christian associations. Retracing the flight of the Holy Family, pilgrims from all over Christendom came to this place they called Babylon right through the Middle Ages and travellers today can still see the remains of the Roman fortress of Babylon, built by Augustus in the first century BC, its towers framing the entrance to the Coptic Museum.

But the verse contains a further puzzle: 'The church that is at Babylon, elected together with you, saluteth you; and so doth Marcus my son'. That is the King James Version and many other translations also have the word church, but in the original Greek the word church is not there. More literally the verse should read 'She who is at Babylon, who is likewise chosen, salutes you, and so does Mark my son'. There is no doubt that the feminine is intended; the Greek word for likewise chosen, or the chosen-together one, is feminine. So some translations have inserted church, which is feminine in Greek; just as Peter opens chapter 5 by exhorting Christian elders in Asia Minor, so it can be argued that he ends chapter 5 by sending them greetings from similar people, members of the church, at Babylon. On the other hand numbers of scholars take the Greek as they find it and say it means she, but then they have the problem of who she can be. Some say she is the wife of Peter; they were known to travel about together, and that the person called Mark would be their son, though more usually 'Marcus my son' is thought to be Mark the Evangelist, the author of Mark's gospel, 'my son' meaning 'dear to me'. Others say that the mysterious she is some other woman who is so well-known that it was not necessary to mention her name. Could she have been Mary Magdalene?

Leaving that argument aside, we otherwise do not know how or when the Christian message was brought to Egypt, but Babylon might well have been a staging post for anyone coming overland; otherwise Alexandria would have been the natural port of entry and Christianity would have developed there, ultimately spreading throughout the country. Alexandria was the second largest city of the Roman Empire after Rome itself and with its great Library and its Museum, its scientists, mathematicians, poets and philosophers, it was the propagator of Hellenism and the intellectual and cultural capital of the Graeco-Roman world. The city's Hellenised population, predominantly Greek but also Egyptian and with the largest Jewish community outside Palestine, was famous for adapting, synthesising and propagating religious and philosophical ideas. But while the writings of various Church Fathers in Asia Minor and Europe were known from the earliest dates, such as those by Clement of Rome at the end of the first century, by Polycarp in Smyrna in the early second century, and by Irenaeus in Lyons towards the end of the second century, no Christian voices seem to have been heard from Egypt apart from Clement of Alexandria at the very end of the second century.

Yet the Roman emperor Hadrian encountered a significant Christian community when he visited Egypt in AD 130-131; in Alexandria he disputed with scholars at the Museum, while at the temple of Serapis, the Hellenised version of Osiris and the husband-brother of Isis, he confused Christians with worshippers of the pagan god.

Those who worship Serapis are Christians, and those who call themselves bishops of Christ are devoted to Serapis. As a race of men they are seditious, vain and spiteful; as a body, wealthy and prosperous, of whom nobody lives in idleness. Some blow glass, some make paper, and others linen. Their one God is nothing peculiar; Christians, Jews and all nations worship him. I wish this body of men was better behaved.

Though a great social and cultural gap lay between Alexandria with its Greek-speaking population and the rural hinterland inhabited by indigenous Egyptians whose Coptic language had been spoken since pharaonic times, by the early third century AD Christianity filled the countryside too. (Copt comes from qibt which is a corruption by the invading Arabs of Aigyptos, the Greek for Egypt.) Also from the beginning of the third century Alexandria's churchmen and its Catechetical School would take centre stage in the great theological battles of Christendom, debating, developing and refining the faith, and deciding the New Testament canon.

But early Church writers had nothing to say about the first two centuries of the Christian era in Egypt, nor about that version of Christianity called gnosticism which we now know flourished in Egypt as late as the fourth century – a silence so deafening that scholars believe that the evidence of early Christianity in Egypt was deliberately destroyed or censored by the Church itself.

Rediscovering the Lost World of Egyptian Christianity

Written works in the ancient world were laboriously produced by hand, scribes writing on papyrus, parchment or paper in the form of scrolls or on sheets that were then bound together as books. These latter, known as a codices in the plural, codex in the singular, were a Roman invention of the first century AD and within three hundred years had overtaken the use of the scroll, their rise associated with the growth of Christianity which favoured the codex for ease of reading of its sacred texts.

Under normal conditions scrolls and codices were highly perishable and the works they contained would not survive unless of
sufficient interest to warrant repeated reproduction. Though gnosticism was widespread in Egypt where it flourished as part of the
broad stream of Christian belief, its writings suffered increasingly
from an active campaign against them by the Latin church in the

A bronze head of the Roman emperor Hadrian found in the Thames in
London and now in the British Museum. Hadrian, who during his reign
travelled from one end of his empire to the other, from Britain to Syria,
visited Egypt in 130–131 as part of a lengthy tour of Rome's eastern
provinces which included visits to Athens, Palmyra and Jerusalem.
He was attempting to assimilate all the peoples of the empire into
one common Hellenistic religion, but in fierce reaction to this the Bar
Kokhba revolt broke out in Judaea in 132. After suppressing the revolt
Hadrian rebuilt Jerusalem as Aelia Capitolina, an entirely Roman city
filled with pagan temples. The revolt marked the final breach between
Jewish and gentile Christians.

West where they were condemned as heretical. And so in addition to the usual dangers of perishing through neglect they were actively destroyed.

In the course of centuries the destruction was so thoroughgoing that nothing seemed to have survived of gnostic writings; what was known about gnosticism came only from its enemies, people like the late second-century theologian Tertullian from Carthage in North Africa, the first churchman to write extensively in Latin and who has been called the father of Latin Christianity, and Irenaeus, bishop of Lyons, who wrote *Against Heresies* in about AD 180.

But in 1773 a codex known as *Pistis Sophia* was discovered in Egypt, though it was not translated from the Coptic until 1851 when it was published in German. Another codex which included the *Gospel of Mary Magdalene* was acquired in 1896 by a German Egyptologist from an antiquarian dealer in Cairo who said it had been found in Akhmim near Sohag in Upper Egypt. Unfortunately numerous vicissitudes, including two world wars, prevented its translation and publication until 1955.

The Nag Hammadi Library

By that time a momentous find had been made also in Upper Egypt. In 1945 two fellahin, the Egyptian word for peasants, were looking for fertiliser in an ancient burial site near Nag Hammadi where the desert cliffs which press close to the delicate green fields that run like a ribbon along the Nile are riddled with tombs. In a land where wood is a rarity, animal dung has traditionally been used for fuel and so other fertilisers have been sought. One of these has been the debris of the past that covers ancient towns and villages or fills burial sites. Over the centuries the debris disintegrates into a kind of earth called sebakh containing as much as 12 per cent potassium nitrate, sodium carbonate and ammonium chloride.

What the fellahin found instead was a large sealed earthenware jar containing twelve Coptic leatherbound codices, each containing several treatises, along with some loose manuscript pages, that had been preserved in their airless and bone-dry environment.

The gnostics were all but silenced for 1600 years until Muhammad al-Samman and his brother discovered their hidden trove of gospels in 1945, completely revolutionising our understanding of early Christianity. This photograph taken in 1977 shows him standing with the cliffs of the Jabal al-Tarif at Nag Hammadi in the distance behind him.

With the intention of selling off their find bit by bit, the men, who were brothers, hid them at home where their mother, fearing they carried evil powers, burnt several of the manuscripts. Fortunately a local Coptic priest recognised their significance; today the Nag Hammadi codices are housed at the Coptic Museum in Cairo.

The codices comprise fifty-two mostly gnostic treatises dating to the third and fourth centuries AD, though these were translations from the original Greek of a yet earlier date, among them the *Gospel of Thomas* composed in about AD 80 and therefore at least as old as any of the canonical gospels. The full collection was published in facsimile and English translation between 1972 and 1984.

The Nag Hammadi Library, as the find is known, probably belonged to the nearby Pachomian monastery of Pbow (present-day Faw Qibli) whose monks, rather than burn their books after bishop Athanasius of Alexandria condemned the use of non-canonical works in 367, put them aside until the climate changed. But it never changed.

Among the works in the library were the *Dialogue of the Saviour*, the *Gospel of Philip* and the *Gospel of Thomas*, all extensively featuring Mary Magdalene, as do the gnostic works acquired earlier, *Pistis Sophia* and the *Gospel of Mary Magdalene*, comprehensively reversing the silence about her which overtook the New Testament beginning with Acts.

Gnostic Gospels

The usual understanding of the word gospel is that it is a narrative account of the life and death and resurrection of Jesus which is what Matthew, Mark, Luke and John, the gospels of the New Testament, are. The New Testament is otherwise made up of letters, mostly written by Paul, which again root themselves in biography and history. As for other ways of interpreting human experience, the New Testament limits itself to a single apocalyptic work, Revelation.

This seems to have been the settled format by the end of the second century, at least everywhere that looked to Rome and fell within the geographical area of the Acts of the Apostles and the voyages of Paul.

But Egypt was different. The apocalyptic tradition largely rejected in the West flourished in Egypt along with other writings such as teachings, sayings, sermons, manuals of initiation and magical incantations that were not necessarily pressed into biographical and historical narratives or any sort of realism. Sometimes the sensation is of passing through the twelve hours of night, those hours of the Amduat, that part of the ancient *Egyptian Book of the Dead* which serves as a guide for navigating through the dark night of the underworld, filled with deities, demons and monsters, before being reborn in the morning with the rising sun. Egyptians had long known about that spiritual journey, that voyage through darkness into light – and the temples of the old gods, of Isis and Osiris and all the rest, were still filled with their ancient priesthoods. The gnostic *Gospel of the Egyptians* ends with this trinity comprised of the initiators of redemption, 'the great, invisible, eternal Spirit; his only-begotten Son, the eternal light; and his great, incorruptible consort, the incorruptible Sophia' – in which Jesus is the light of enlightenment and his consort is Sophia whom the Egyptians identified with Isis, the goddess who helps lead the dead through the perils of the night, and whom the gnostic gospels identified with Mary Magdalene.

A codex from the Nag Hammadi find. The codex, that is binding pages in book form rather than using a continuous scroll, was introduced to Egypt by the Romans and became popular because Christians found it easy to read, readily transportable and the most convenient way to spread the word.

What are called gnostic gospels are therefore not necessarily narrative gospels in the New Testament sense but in the original sense
of the word; they are the good news, god-spell in Old English, a
direct translation from the Greek evangelion (from where we get
our word evangelist), the good message of salvation delivered by
Jesus, the secret of how to escape this world and become one with
the primal God.

Gnosticism in Outline

Gnosticism is a version of Christianity that has been suppressed or
has otherwise failed to survive. But for hundreds of years the gnostics practised their rituals and beliefs alongside other Christians,
principally in Egypt but also elsewhere in the Middle East and the
Eastern Mediterranean. The destruction and loss and only recent
discovery of their works makes it seem that they belonged to a cat-
egory apart. But at the time the gnostics were part of the inclusive
atmosphere of early Christianity in Egypt and they held beliefs that
anyone was free to follow. Indeed some scholars argue that gnosticism was the original form of Christianity.

Gnosticism can be one of two things or both. Gnosticism is the
belief that people have a divine capacity within themselves and that
they can come to understand that the kingdom of God is already
upon the earth if they can come to perceive the world that way.
Jesus himself saw the kingdom of God as at hand.

Gnosticism can also be seen as a belief that differentiates the
God of this world, the God of the Old Testament, from a higher
more abstract and primal God, a belief that regards this world as
the result of an accident and under the rule of a defective or evil
demiurge, or a series of such powers or archons, whose aim is to
keep the human soul trapped in his material body, forever separated from the upper world of the spirit.

Gnosis is Greek for knowledge, in this case the intuitive process of knowing oneself, and thereby knowing human nature and
human destiny, and at the deepest level knowing God. Instead of
seeing God and humanity as separate, the gnostics saw the self and

the divine as one. Instead of discussing evil in terms of sin and repentance, the gnostics said the world was an illusion from which the escape was enlightenment. Jesus did not offer salvation by dying on the cross; he was a spiritual guide. 'If you bring forth what is within you', said Jesus according to the *Gospel of Thomas*, 'what you bring forth will save you. If you do not bring forth what is within you, what you do not bring forth will destroy you.'

Knowledge, Mystery and Evil

During the Hellenistic period the word gnosis took on a specific association with the mysteries and became synonymous with the Greek term mysterion. This gnosis was a secret knowledge that explained the way to salvation from this material world, something that a worshipper could find by attending a mystery of Isis, for example, or by hearing Paul.

Paul spoke of this quest when he told of his encounter with Jesus, his direct and personal vision of the divine, and explained that the mystery of Jesus' death and resurrection would 'deliver us from this present evil world' (Galatians 1:4). And like the gnostics he spoke of hidden wisdom. 'Howbeit we speak wisdom among them that are perfect: yet not the wisdom of this world, nor of the princes of this world, that come to nought: But we speak the wisdom of God in a mystery, even the hidden wisdom, which God ordained before the world unto our glory' (1 Corinthians 2:6-7).

Some have asked whether Paul was a gnostic or had gnostic tendencies. Valentinus, one of the greatest gnostic figures, was proud to say that his own teacher had been taught by Paul; and the gnostics held Paul in high regard, not because he was a follower of Jesus but because Jesus had revealed himself and his secrets to Paul. What this really tells us is that early Christianity was extremely fluid and that someone like Paul can be seen as the prototype of orthodoxy or the prototype of what became a heresy.

Until the discovery of the gnostic gospels little was known of the gnostics except from the writings of their proto-orthodox opponents who branded them as heretics. What can be described as

The sky goddess Nut on the vaulted ceiling of the burial chamber
of Ramses VI in the Valley of the Kings. The theme of death and
resurrection was as old as Egyptian civilisation itself. They believed
that Nut swallowed the setting sun, that it travelled through her body
illuminated by stars, and that she gave birth to the sun at the following
dawn. Likewise Ramses will travel through the darkness of death but will
emerge into the light.

the proto-orthodox position within early Christianity – that is the doctrine held by those who in the fourth century would become the victorious and therefore orthodox party – can be found in the version of the New Testament that began to take shape in the second century and was eventually agreed by the Western Church at the Council of Carthage in 397 and by the Eastern Orthodox Church several years later. In particular the letters of Paul, the four canonical gospels of Matthew, Mark, Luke and John, and the Acts of the Apostles could together be read as affirming that Jesus was divine, that his crucifixion was followed by his resurrection and that salvation lies in accepting this mystery via the apostolic Church, that is the Church that gains its authority by claiming that its highest officials are the successors of Jesus's original apostles.

The existence of evil in God's world posed a problem for early Christians, 'this present evil world' in the words of Paul. If there was only one God, and if God was the creator, and if God was good, how was it possible for there to be suffering, illness and death in his world? Christians divided into two responses. On the one hand the proto-orthodox Christians said that it was man, not God, who had introduced evil into the world, and for this they generally put the blame on Eve for eating the fruit from the tree of knowledge of good and evil. A virtue of this argument was that it spoke of the great drama which found its resolution in this world. Here man had introduced evil, yes, but by his crucifixion and resurrection Jesus had come to save him from his sins and give him eternal life.

But the crucifixion and resurrection has no place in gnostic beliefs, nor was Jesus offering salvation from the sins of mankind. For the gnostics the evil in this world came not from man; it came from God. They rejected mankind's original sin and going much further they rejected this world utterly, saying it was the creation of an evil deity, the enemy of man.

One of the most prominent gnostic teachers was Valentinus who flourished in Alexandria around AD 140. He claimed to possess the true knowledge of how the world had been created and how evil had come into being, a story that he introduced to his followers in terms of a cosmic myth. He conceived of a primal God, the centre of a divine harmony, who sends out manifestations of himself in pairs of male and female. Sophia, meaning Wisdom in Greek, the youngest of these divine emanations, tries to emulate her father, the primal God, who alone has the true power of creation, but instead she produces an abortion which after a long series of transformations evolves into the lower world of evil and decay inhabited by

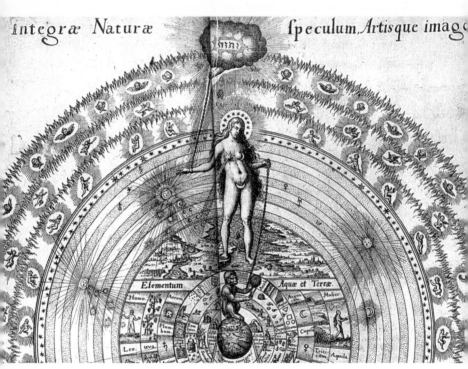

Valentinus' description of the cosmos continued to excite the minds of thinkers long after gnosticism was suppressed. Here in this frontispiece to *Utriusque Cosmi, Maioris scilicet et Minoris metaphysica atque technical Historia* (The metaphysical, physical, and technical history of the two worlds, namely the greater and the lesser), published in 1617–19 by the English physician and cosmologist Robert Fludd and illustrated by his own hand, he shows how the Anima Mundi, the World Spirit, otherwise known as Sophia, stands as intermediary between the upper world of God and the lower world of man. God's hand holds a chain which descends to her right hand, while from her left hand, in turn, the chain descends to an ape, the symbol for the arts and sciences and crafts of mankind. Pagan Egyptians identified Sophia with Isis while the gnostics identified Sophia with Mary Magdalene.

man and is ruled over by a hapless demiurge. In Valentinus' system, however, Sophia, through repentance and expiation, ultimately returns to the upper world.

The gnostics are called dualists because of their belief in these two worlds, the world of evil and decay inhabited by man, and the world of light where the primal God resides. But the gnostics also knew the secret of salvation. At the moment of her cosmic blunder, Sophia brought with her sparks of the divine light, like slivers of shattered glass, which became embedded in humankind. The gnostics saw themselves as the children of Sophia, a divinity of many names. She was the All-Mother, the Celestial Eve, the Holy Spirit. She was also She of the Left-hand as opposed to Jesus who is He of the Right-hand, she was the Man-Woman, she was Paradise, Eden, the Virgin, the Daughter of Light, the World Soul and the Soul in Man. From Sophia the gnostics had obtained the divine spark that urges them to seek the upper world, the true and perfect realm, of the primal God.

Cosmic redemption, however, and not just personal salvation, was necessary because the whole of creation had been a mistake; it had nothing to do with God who had never intended that there should be a universe and had never intended man. Creation was a defective work and so man lived in a meaningless world or in the iron control of evil powers; in any case he was caught in the trap of the material world which was sundered from the spirit of God.

Valentinus taught his followers that they could free themselves by attempting to quell their desires and by practising sexual abstinence. Bearing children would simply repeat and prolong the soul's imprisonment in this defective world, its exile from the primal God. 'Until when shall men continue to die?', Jesus is asked in the Gospel of the Egyptians, to which he replies, 'So long as women bear children'. In the polarity of the male and the female was mirrored the division, the duality, of the universe, so that the Last Judgement and the world's redemption would come – as Jesus says in the gnostic *Gospel of the Egyptians* – 'when the two become one, and the male with the female, there being neither male nor female'.

But not all schools of gnosticism promoted sexual abstinence. The Carpocratians, mentioned in Clement of Alexandria's letter about the *Secret Gospel of Mark*, had been founded in Alexandria around the time of Hadrian's visit in AD 130-131. The Carpocratians believed they could escape the shackles of this world by disregarding its rules and conventions; property was unnatural, they said, and women should be held in common; every experience, good or sinful, should be indulged, and as this could take more than a lifetime to accomplish they believed in the transmigration of souls. The licentiousness of the Carpocratians was confirmed by Clement who claimed that at their agape feast, the sacremental sharing of wine and bread and other foods practised by early Christians rather like the Eucharist, they had 'intercourse where they will and with whom they will'.

Another version of the Eucharist featured in the practices of the Phibionites according to Epiphanius, a fourth-century bishop of Salamis in Cyprus, who witnessed their practices first hand at Alexandria in his youth. In his book the *Panarion*, a treatise on heresies, Epiphanius describes how members of this gnostic sect gathered for meals where men had sex with other men's wives. Just before ejaculation the man withdrew and together with the woman collected his semen and ate it. If the woman was menstruating they mixed her blood with the semen and ate that too.

This sexual sacrament came from what the Phibionites took to be a holy scripture called the *Great Questions of Mary*, long lost and known to us only through mentions in the *Panarion*, in which Jesus takes Mary Magdalene to a mountaintop where he draws a woman out from his side, rather like Eve was first created from the rib of Adam. Jesus then has sexual intercourse with the woman, but withdraws in time to catch and swallow his own semen, saying to Mary, 'This we must do so that we may live'. The prohibition is not on sexual intercourse but on reproduction; Jesus is showing that by consuming the man's semen and the woman's blood he is stopping the cycle of reproduction which would otherwise create yet more human prisons for the soul.

Men and women break bread at the outset of an agape feast in this painting within the second to fourth-century Catacomb of Priscilla in Rome. But for at least two gnostic sects in Egypt, the Carpocratians and the Phibionites, the agape feasts were said to be more like orgies in which the men had sex with each other's wives.

That Mary Magdalene could be identified with such a range of practices, from libertinism to asceticism, shows how widely she appealed. She was a woman who could be everything to everybody – as Isis was the goddess of countless names, the all-embracing goddess. But when ultimately gnosticism became a heresy, Mary Magdalene was dethroned; from goddess Mary Magdalene became everything to everybody in a very different way; the Church turned her into a whore.

Because the gnostic mystery lay not in the crucifixion and resurrection, it undermined the rationale for the Great Commission, the command by the resurrected Jesus (found for example in Mark 9:15-16 and Matthew 28:16-20) to spread the gospel throughout the world and which became the basis for the apostolic sees and the principal of apostolic succession which is the foundation stone of the hierarichal order of the Church. Instead the gnostic approach to the divine was personal and visionary; the role of Jesus was to descend from the primal God and impart to his disciples the secret tradition of the gnosis. And according to the gnostic *Dialogue of the Saviour* found at Nag Hammadi, his best pupil, the 'woman who understood the all', was Mary Magdalene.

Mary Magdalene in the Gnostic Gospels

Mary Magdalene features prominently in *Pistis Sophia*, the *Gospel of Mary*, the *Dialogue of the Saviour*, the *Gospel of Philip* and the *Gospel of Thomas* where she is associated with Sophia, the Divine Wisdom, and is portrayed as a visionary, as the woman who 'knows all' and as the 'inheritor of light'.

The setting is usually in the period after the resurrection. The *Gospel of Thomas* is an exception in that it is a gospel composed entirely of the sayings of Jesus and therefore set outside time. Another exception is the *Gospel of Philip* in which Mary Magdalene has an explicit role in the lifetime of the historical Jesus where she is the only disciple who already understands his real character and message. She is celebrated as the chief disciple of Jesus and in the *Gospel of Philip* she is described as his koinonos, a Greek word used in the Bible to mean companion or consort or wife.

But also the relationship between Jesus and Mary Magdalene in the gnostic gospels generally suggests a profounder dimension; she is the divine syzygos of Jesus, his feminine aspect that creates a spiritual whole. In *Pistis Sophia* the disciples ask Jesus how he came down from the immortal realms to this world where everything dies, to which he replies, 'The Son of Man consented with Sophia, his consort, and revealed a great androgynous light. His male name is "Saviour, Begetter of All Things". His female name is "All-Begettress Sophia"'.

The Gospel of Thomas

The *Gospel of Thomas*, found at Nag Hammadi in 1945, dates to the very beginnings of the Christian era. Written in Coptic, it was translated from an earlier Greek version, fragments of which are known from excavations in 1897 and 1903 at Oxyrhynchus farther north along the Nile. There is growing scholarly agreement that the *Gospel of Thomas* was composed at about the same time and possibly before the four canonical gospels, and some would place it as early as AD 50. The gospel opens with these lines.

> These are the hidden words that the living Jesus spoke, and that Didymos Judas Thomas wrote down. And He said: 'Whoever finds the meaning of these words will not taste death'.

The mention of hidden words suggests gnosticism, but the *Gospel of Thomas* need not be set apart as gnostic for much of it can be found in the canonical gospels, indeed many of its lines may first have been written in Thomas rather than in Matthew, Mark, Luke or John.

The *Gospel of Thomas* is not a gospel in the New Testament sense; there is no narrative of Jesus' life, no account of his healings or miracles or teachings, nothing about his birth or death. Instead the gospel amounts to 114 sayings of Jesus as recorded by someone who calls himself Didymos Judas Thomas. The gospel of John mentions a Didymos Thomas as one of the apostles, but we really do not know who wrote the *Gospel of Thomas*, any more than we know who wrote the canonical gospels, all of them anonymous; the names Matthew, Mark, Luke and John were added in the second century.

But whoever wrote the *Gospel of Thomas* had at hand the same basic materials as appear in the canonical gospels. Most of its 114 sayings will be familiar. There are the parables of the mustard seed, of the mote in your brother's eye, of the blind leading the blind. Prophets are not recognised on their home ground, Jesus says, and he warns not to throw pearls before swine. Being shown a gold coin bearing the head of the Roman emperor, Jesus in the *Gospel of Thomas* says, 'Give the emperor what belongs to the emperor, give God what belongs to God, and give me what is mine', recalling the scene of Jesus being questioned by the priests at the Temple in the gospels of Mark, Matthew and Luke – but in the synoptic gospels the material has been worked into a narrative and a drama; in the *Gospel of Thomas* it remains a saying without context.

Instead of relying on a storyline the *Gospel of Thomas* offers bursts of revelation: 'The Father's kingdom is within you and it is outside you. When you know yourselves, then you will be known, and you will understand that you are children of the living Father. But if you do not know yourselves, then you live in poverty, and you are the poverty'.

Mary Magdalene is mentioned twice in the *Gospel of Thomas*. The first time, in saying 21, she says to Jesus, 'What are your disciples like?' and he replies, 'They are like little children living in a field that is not theirs'. The meaning of the parable is not clear, indeed it may have been poorly translated from the Greek, but what appears to happen is that the owner returns, demands his field, and the children remove their clothes and go. This can be taken to mean that the disciples, that is the children, are dwellers in this world, this creation of the demiurge, which is not their true world; in leaving, the children strip themselves of their bodies which are likewise part of the false creation of the demiurge.

Jesus continues, 'Be on guard against the world. Prepare yourselves with great strength, so the robbers cannot find a way to get to you, for the trouble you expect will come. Let there be among you a person who understands. When the crop ripened, he came quickly carrying a sickle and harvested it. Anyone here with two good ears had better listen!' Here it seems that the one who understands will know when the moment has come to harvest the gnostic wisdom. Significantly it is Mary Magdalene who has asked the question, and as though his words are meant specially for her, Jesus says, 'Let there be among you a person who understands'.

When the rubbish dumps of Oxyrhynchus, a vanished ancient city in Upper Egypt, were excavated at the end of the nineteenth and the beginning of the twentieth centuries they yielded not only the documents of everyday ancient lives such as private letters, marriage certificates, wills, accounts and land leases, but also long lost works by Sophocles, Plato and Thucydides, and they revealed also the gnostic gospels of Thomas and of Mary Magdalene.

Mary Magdalene is mentioned again in saying 114. This is the very last saying in the gospel and there is some scholarly thought that it might have been added at a later date. Abruptly, Peter says to Jesus, 'Make Mary leave us, for females do not deserve life'. Jesus replies, 'Look, I will guide her to make her male, so that she too may become a living spirit resembling you males. For every female who makes herself male will enter the kingdom of Heaven'.

THE QUEST FOR MARY MAGDALENE

The life to which Peter refers is eternal life; he is objecting to a spiritual role for Mary Magdalene and women generally. This is a complaint that Peter makes even more strongly in the *Gospel of Mary Magdalene* and *Pistis Sophia*, and the clash between Peter and Mary Magdalene is there also in the Gospel of Luke. But Jesus deals with Peter firmly, saying that he will personally ensure that she enters the kingdom of heaven. But though the language of this saying might be disturbing to modern ears – 'I will guide her to make her male' – to take it simply as evidence of misogyny is to not hear the fuller story.

A common philosophical metaphor in Hellenistic times was to describe the essence of form as male and its material element as female. 'To become male' was a commonplace phrase for becoming spiritual and pure. It was based on the notion of a continuum of being through plants and animals to men and the gods. Human males were closest to the gods along that continuum. If the aim of men was to become like gods, so for a female also to become like a god she first had to pass through being a male. Peter's prejudice against Mary Magdalene is immediately converted by Jesus into a philosophical matter; all that is earthly and perishable will be transformed into the heavenly and imperishable. Jesus is ensuring the liberation and salvation of Mary Magdalene in the same way that all must be lifted out of this material world to be liberated and saved.

There was also a Judaic aspect to this. In the original state of existence before the Fall, Adam was complete: 'So God created man in his own image, in the image of God created he him; male and female created he them' (Genesis 1:27). Woman was created when Eve was removed from Adam's side. Therefore, goes the reasoning, to restore the primal unity, to escape the pain and decay and death of the material world, woman needs to be reabsorbed into man.

There is something else going on here too, more important than any sexual politics, and that is the argument between vision on the one hand, that is the direct and personal apprehension of the divine, a quality represented by Mary Magdalene, the woman who knows, and a religion which demands the mediation of the Church, a hierarchy of officials who base their authority on apostolic succession, for whom Peter is the 'rock' – though there is no evidence whatsoever, only Church-invented legend, that Peter ever went to Rome.

The Gospel of Mary Magdalene

The codex purchased in Cairo in 1896 contains the most complete copy of the *Gospel of Mary*, as it is called in the manuscript, clearly meaning Mary Magdalene. Even so, over half the work is missing, six pages at the front and four in the middle. Copied and bound in the late fourth or early fifth century, the gospel is a translation into Coptic from the original Greek, of which two very small fragments were found at Oxyrhynchus during excavations from 1897 to 1906. The original Greek work has been dated no later than about 120 to 180, though some place it earlier, in the late first century, and one scholar, Professor Karen King of Harvard University, thinks it could date to the lifetime of Jesus – but then she is also the promoter of a tiny fragment of text to which she has given the name *The Gospel of Jesus' Wife*, though it is widely thought among scholars that she has been taken in by a fraud. As for the origins of the *Gospel of Mary Magdalene*, all that is known is that the purchase in Cairo was made from a dealer in Akhmim near Sohag, an important Coptic community in both ancient and modern times. It was held at Berlin but owing to two world wars and other difficulties it was not published until 1955, after the discovery of the Nag Hammadi Library, when a German edition appeared.

In this only gospel named after a woman, Mary Magdalene plays a central role. The gospel records an appearance of Jesus to his disciples after his resurrection in which he answers their questions about the nature of this world and of sin; then after telling them to preach the gospel of the kingdom he disappears. This is a variation on the Great Commission of the canonical gospels in which Mary Magdalene did not feature, but here she appears and takes charge. At the departure of Jesus the disciples weep in distress and ask themselves fearfully, 'How shall we go to the gentiles and preach the gospel of the Kingdom of the Son of Man? If they did not spare Him, how will they spare us?'

Now Mary Magdalene rises and speaks. 'Do not weep and do not grieve nor be irresolute for his grace will be entirely with you and will protect you. But rather let us praise his greatness for he has prepared us and made us into men. When Mary said this she turned their hearts to the Good and they began to discuss the words of the Saviour.'

But now Peter says to Mary, 'Sister we know that the Saviour loved you more than the rest of woman. Tell us the words of the Saviour which you remember which you know, but we do not, nor have we heard them. Mary answered and said, What is hidden from you I will proclaim to you'.

Mary Magdalene continues and makes clear that authority lies in vision not in apostolic succession. 'I saw the Lord in a vision and I said to him, Lord I saw you today in a vision. He answered and said to me, Blessed are you that you did not waver at the sight of me. For where the mind is there is the treasure.' Jesus is praising Mary Magdalene for her steadfastness; her advanced spiritual development means she does not waver in his awesome presence. But how does one see a vision, she asks, through the soul or through the spirit? 'The Saviour answered and said, a person does not see through the soul nor through the spirit, but the mind that is between the two that is what sees the vision.' Four pages of the codex are missing here so we lack further information about soul and spirit and mind, but it would seem that gaining a vision is not a passive matter, not something simply received, but that an active mind rules the spirit and the soul and seeks the vision, seeks the kingdom. This active visionary quality of Mary's allows her to be a leader among the disciples, to direct them away from fear and out into the world to preach the good news of the gospel.

After the four missing pages, when the account resumes Mary is telling the disciples how the human soul ascends through the heavenly spheres controlled by forces opposed to it and makes its way to its heavenly home. Then 'she fell silent, since it was to this point that the Saviour had spoken with her'. But now the brothers Andrew and Peter question whether Mary's vision can be trusted. First Andrew speaks and says to the disciples, 'Say what you wish to say about what she has said. I at least do not believe that the Saviour said this. For certainly these teachings are strange ideas'. Then Peter addresses the disciples. 'Did he really speak privately with a

In the *Gospel of Mary Magdalene*, the only gospel named for a woman, she is the disciple Jesus most loves. She displays a visionary power that allows her to take the lead, to direct the disciples away from fear and out into the world to preach the word.

woman and not openly to us? Are we to turn about and all listen to her? Did he prefer her to us?'

Mary weeps and says to Peter, 'My brother Peter, what do you think? Do you think that I have thought this up myself in my heart, or that I am lying about the Saviour?'

Levi, otherwise known as the apostle Matthew, answers and says to Peter, 'Peter you have always been hot tempered. Now I see you contending against the woman like the adversaries. But if the Saviour made her worthy, who are you indeed to reject her? Surely the Saviour knows her very well. That is why he loved her more than us. Rather let us be ashamed and put on the perfect man, and separate as he commanded us and preach the gospel, not laying down any other rule or other law beyond what the Saviour said. And when they heard this they began to go forth to proclaim and to preach.'

Though some people make much of the seeming conflict between Mary Magdalene as a woman and Peter as a man, the earlier versions of the *Gospel of Mary*, that is the ones written in Greek, show no concern with gender; the argument is over Mary Magdalene's teachings and how she came by them through her vision of Jesus. And even if later in the Coptic translation gender comes into play, nevertheless the greater matter is the value of vision and of Mary's special quality of direct apprehension of the divine. She is the most beloved disciple, but there is no evidence of a sexual relationship; her special status is due entirely to her vision of the Saviour. She shows a far greater understanding of Jesus' teaching than the other disciples, including Peter, and when the Saviour departs she comforts and encourages them, and in the Greek version she kisses each of them, an act that conveys spiritual nourishment and power. For the gnostics this is their challenge against the authority of Peter and with it the authority of priests and bishops who claim apostolic succession from Peter; the challenge is of vision over bureaucracy. As Mary Magdalene says, let us separate as he commanded us and preach the gospel, 'not laying down any other rule or other law beyond what the Saviour said'.

The Dialogue of the Saviour

The *Dialogue of the Saviour*, which was found at Nag Hammadi in 1945, is a badly damaged Coptic codex that dates from the second century, possibly as early as 120 and no later than 200. The gospel includes a description of the origin of the world, a natural history, and a vision of Hell seen by Matthew, Didymus Judas Thomas and Mary Magdalene who are told by an angel that the material world is an unintended and evil creation which will continue to perpetuate itself as long as women bear children.

Most of it, however, has Jesus answering questions put to him by these same three followers, a dialogue in which Jesus reveals the secrets of salvation while Mary Magdalene plays the leading role, not only asking more questions than the others but also saying things found in the New Testament where they are spoken by Jesus, so that again she is described as 'a woman who knows the all'.

Pistis Sophia

After Jesus himself, Mary Magdalene is the dominating figure in *Pistis Sophia* which means the Faith of Sophia, Sophia being for the gnostics the syzygy of Jesus, the female aspect of his spirit. The codex was written in a late fourth-century Coptic dialect of Upper Egypt but had been translated from an older Greek text dating from the third century, though it could be older than that; tradition attributes it to Valentinus who was writing in the early second century. But in fact the origin of *Pistis Sophia* is a mystery; it was acquired by the British physician and book collector Anthony Askew in 1773, but where it was found and how it reached his hands is unknown. Though the British Museum bought it from Askew's heirs in 1795 it remained in obscurity until its translation into German in 1851; from then until the Nag Hammadi discoveries in 1945 this was one of the very few codices of gnostic writings known to have survived obliteration by the Church.

Pistis Sophia narrates the fall of Sophia, her lamentations and her redemption through the intervention of the Saviour, that is Jesus, who recounts his journey through the splendours of the upper world after his ascension. After his return to earth and in the course of dialogues with his disciples lasting twelve years, Jesus reveals to them the secrets of the universe. He discusses with them the existence of evil, injustice, violence, riches and poverty; the varieties of animals and plants; why there is light and darkness. Everything is commented upon and explained; it is a complete spiritual exploration and a natural history of the universe, making *Pistis Sophia* one of the fundamental texts of gnosticism.

Mary Magdalene's leading role among the disciples is unmistakeable. In the dialogues with the Saviour she asks more questions and offers more interpretations of Jesus' words than all the others put together. Jesus himself affirms that her 'heart is more directed to the kingdom of heaven' than all the other disciples and says that along with John she is superior to them.

But Peter protests. 'My Lord, we are not able to bear with this woman speaking instead of us; she has not let any of us speak but often speaks herself'. When Jesus replies that he will make Mary Magdalene a man so that she can gain entry to the kingdom of heaven he is talking of returning to the original order of things, to the time when Adam was created male and female: 'So God created man in his own image, in the image of God created he him; male and female created he them' (Genesis 1:27). When the primal unity is restored death will be no more, for as the gnostic *Gospel of Philip* says, 'When Eve was in Adam there was no death; but when she was separated from him death came into being'.

The Gospel of Philip

The *Gospel of Philip*, found at Nag Hammadi in 1945, is most famous for the lines that can be interpreted to mean that Mary Magdalene was the wife or lover of Jesus. Here she does not engage with a vision or a resurrected Jesus as in other gnostic gospels; instead she is the favourite disciple of the living historical Jesus, the companion who walks beside him during his earthly existence and who alone understands his real nature and his teachings. But this is not a narrative work like the canonical gospels; rather it is an anthology of sermons and philosophical epistles as well as aphorisms and brief dialogues set down in Coptic sometime in the third century but based on an earlier Greek original, possibly an early second-century work of Valentinus.

Twice the *Gospel of Philip* portrays the intimacy between Jesus and Mary Magdalene. 'There were three who always walked with the Lord: Mary, his mother, and her sister, and Magdalene, the one who was called his companion. His sister and his mother and his companion were each a Mary'. The sister is first described as the sister of Mary but then described as a sister of Jesus; the first is probably a translation error; in both cases 'his sister' is most likely meant, and as we know from Mark 6:3 Jesus did have at least two sisters. Mary Magdalene is described as his companion, and here the Coptic text uses a variant on the Greek word koinonos which is used in the Septuagint, the Greek version of the Old Testament, to mean partner, companion, sharer, joint participant or wife. Interestingly the prominent American New Testament scholar Bart Ehrman translated koinonos as 'lover' in his version of the *Gospel of Philip* published in 2003: 'There were those who always walked with the Lord: Mary, his mother and her sister and Magdalene, whom they call his lover. A Mary is his sister and his mother and his lover'. But 2003 was also the year that Dan Brown published *The Da Vinci Code* which drew on the *Gospel of Philip* to make the assertion that Jesus and Mary Magdalene were married. That seems to have made Bart Ehrman feel that he had fallen into the camp of Dan Brown groupies, for in a 2006 book Ehrman was saying the opposite of what he had said before about the meaning of koinonos: 'This is not the Greek word for "spouse". It normally means "associate" or "companion"'. So much for what Ehrman had to say before; and so much for the Septuagint; Ehrman now tells us that what once meant lover or wife or spouse does not mean lover or wife or spouse anymore.

In the second instance the *Gospel of Philip* says, 'As for the Wisdom who is called "the barren", she is the mother of the angels. And the companion of the [Saviour was] Mary Magdalene. [Christ loved] her more than all the disciples, and used to kiss her [often] on her [mouth]. The rest of the disciples [were offended and expressed disapproval]. They said to him "Why do you love her more than all of us?" The Saviour answered and said to them,"Why do I not love you like her? When a blind man and one who sees are both together in darkness, they are no different from one another. When the light comes, then he who sees will see the light, and he who is blind will remain in darkness.'"

Wisdom being barren is apparently a reference to Sophia's abortive attempt at creation, but also Mary Magdalene is here as elsewhere in gnostic writings equated with Sophia in another guise, the bringer of light, she who brought the promise of the divine spark to mankind, and so she becomes the gnostic mother, the mother of angels. Where part of the original text is missing some translations fill in the gaps, for example by suggesting that it was 'Christ' who 'loved' Mary Magdalene more than all the disciples and used to kiss her 'often on the mouth' as in the above example – but other alternatives have been suggested such as Jesus kissing her on her hand or on her forehead or on her cheek or on her feet. Whatever the exact wording, it is clear that according to the *Gospel of Philip* Jesus and Mary Magdalene enjoyed a close and special relationship, though probably the gnostic understanding was that it was strictly spiritual. After all, as Paul said in Romans 16:16, 'Salute one another with an holy kiss'.

Looking for Mary Magdalene

So who is Mary Magdalene in these gnostic gospels and how does she compare with the Mary Magdalene of the canonical gospels? Scholars are divided, some saying it is possible to trace genuine traditions in the gnostic gospels about the Mary Magdalene who walked with Jesus in Galilee, others saying that there is no real evidence that they reflect a historical figure.

Here in these gnostic gospels Mary Magdalene appears as something of a device, asking and answering questions, but then the gnostic gospels are like that. They lack the narrative and characterisation of the canonical gospels which have the feel of being rooted in the everyday, whereas the gnostic gospels inhabit a spiritualised environment. The canonical gospels are like Dante in *Purgatory*, the gnostic gospels like Dante in *Paradise*.

Partly Mary Magdalene's purpose is polemical, to argue against the apostolic and hierarchical structure of the Church, an argument with some flesh and blood on it if Mary Magdalene really did come

The gnostic idea of dualism, of two worlds, is found in the Chnoubis, the gnostic demiurge with the head of a lion and the body of a serpent. It was often engraved on semi-precious stones and worn as a talisman against disease or harm. The lion's head represents the sun and the upper world, the seven rays round the head representing the seven planets or seven heavens, with a crescent moon and a star to the left; while the serpent's tail represents earth and the lower impulses. In this example the name of the demiurge, XNOVBIC, is written round the head in Greek; round the border of the stone the inscription reads IAWCABAWTHABPACASMIXAHLEW, which is a series of magical names including Iaw, Sabaoth, Abrasax and the archangel Michael, followed by 'I am'.

to Egypt and if Peter came too – his legendary presence in Rome being nothing more than a fiction to serve the apostolic argument of the Church bureaucracy.

But the gnostics would say that the struggle has a cosmic dimension; they would say that the Church is a creature of the demiurge whereas they are seeking the light.

From the point of view of what became in the fourth century the established Church, the need to construct and defend its hierarchy meant controlling Mary Magdalene. She was too close to Jesus; she knew too much. And unlike Mary the mother of Jesus, there was nothing passive about Mary Magdalene. The assault against Mary Magdalene in the coming centuries had less to do with her being a woman; in the gnostic gospels, as in the canonical gospels too, her powers are vision and inspiration, the antithesis of rules and dogma.

The gnostics were defeated; they buried their holy books in the sand and died. But Mary Magdalene did not die. She appears again among the Cathars who make Mary Magdalene the bride of Jesus and the Queen of Heaven – she is Isis again.

CHAPTER TEN

Changing Roles: the Virgin and the Whore

THE EARLIEST KNOWN COMPREHENSIVE attack against
Christianity was written by the pagan philosopher Celsus in
the AD 170s. The myths put about by the Christians, he wrote with
some exasperation in *The True Word*, were now becoming better
known than the doctrines of philosophers. 'Who has not heard that
Jesus was born of a virgin, that he was crucified, and that his resurrection is an article of faith among many?', he wrote, adding that
reason does not enter into their argument; instead Christians will
say, 'Do not question, but believe', and 'Your faith will save you'.
When Christians' views are challenged, writes Celsus, they retreat
behind the remark that 'to God everything is possible'.

Yet for these fables, wrote Celsus, Christians were willing to die.
Though the emperor Hadrian would not tolerate actions against
Christians for their faith, only if they broke the law, there had
been some sporadic persecutions and executions of Christians

under his predecessors Nero and Domitian in the first century and under Trajan in the early second century, and there would be more to come.

The Christian Threat

The imperial government and many citizens were anxious about Christianity, seeing it as a danger to social cohesion. Romans owed an allegiance to the state and to the emperor and occasionally performed rituals which involved offering a sacrifice, but Christians refused to participate, saying it was idolatry and the worship of a false god. This Christian refusal seemed all the more threatening after the Bar Kokhba revolt against Roman rule in Judaea in the 130s which was a rejection of any authority other than the Jewish God. But as Celsus remarked, Christians were a threat in another way; they were so divided into rival sects, denouncing one another, that simply the instability of their faith could prove harmful to social harmony and the Roman state.

Very little is known about Celsus who was probably a Greek and probably an Alexandrian. Nothing remains of his original writings and we know about *The True Word* only because Origen, an early Christian theologian and Clement's successor as head of Alexandria's Catechetical School, responded to its arguments with his own work, *Against Celsus*, written in 248. Origen so completely quotes Celsus in his refutation that it has been possible to reconstruct *The True Word* in almost its entirety.

The number of Christians in the latter half of the second century was still very small but Celsus' attack is testimony to how seriously the danger from Christianity was taken, while Origen's exhaustive rebuttal is testimony to how seriously Celsus' arguments against Christianity were taken by the Church.

Celsus compared Christians to members of other cults, to the noisy followers of the Phrygian sky god Sabazius; the acolytes of the bull-killing god Mithras; the begging priests of the fertility goddess Cybele; and to travelling rogues who called up apparitions of demons or of the triple-bodied Hecate, a goddess associated with sorcery.

Moreover, Celsus declared, 'Jesus went about with his disciples, and obtained his livelihood in a disgraceful and importunate manner', meaning sponging off Mary Magdalene and the other women. And, as for the Christians' story that when Jesus was dead 'he rose again and displayed the marks of his punishment and showed how his hands had been pierced by nails, who saw this? A frantic woman', again meaning Mary Magdalene, 'and perhaps one other person, both deluded by sorcery'. Celsus was as much against the gnostics as he was against other Christians; elsewhere in his text he mentions followers of Mary Magdalene, and knowing that she was the gnostics' visionary he attacks them by reducing her to a delusionary female. (The phrase 'gyne paroistros' in Greek is variously translated as a frantic or fevered or hysterical woman.)

Interestingly, Celsus mentions only Mary Magdalene and possibly one other person as witnesses to the risen Jesus, which suggests that the gospels in circulation in Egypt in the mid-second century were an early form of Mark and a version of John to which the final chapter 21 had not yet been added (the Church Father Tertullian writing in about 200 knew nothing about it), a late addendum which serves Rome and the purpose of apostolic succession by having Jesus appearing before the disciples and declaring Peter his leading apostle. That Celsus does not mention Matthew or Luke seems to confirm other literary sources and the archaeological record which show that while versions of John and Thomas and Mark were circulating widely in Egypt in the early second century the gospels of Matthew and Luke appear not to have circulated until the end of the century, meaning that versions of gospels carrying verses justifying apostolic succession were largely unknown in Egypt. Also as Matthew and Luke are the only two gospels that include stories of the nativity and describe Mary the mother of Jesus as a virgin, their written accounts were unknown too. So when Celsus attacks the Christian belief that Jesus was born of a virgin, and when Origen defends that belief, they might both be arguing from oral tradition, not from infancy narratives attached to the gospels of Matthew and Luke.

Geza Vermes, the leading Jesus scholar, is not alone in regarding the infancy narratives as pious fictions. The infancy narratives, he says in his *Jesus*, are 'late additions' to the main accounts in Matthew and Luke. He notes that Matthew and Luke contradict one another (the former taking Jesus off to Egypt, for example, while the latter has him go to Jerusalem and Nazareth) and are unsupported by history (such an egregious event as Herod slaughtering the infants is not remarked upon by any source other than Matthew; not even by Luke). Moreover, as Vermes observes, the idea of a virgin birth is in direct contradiction with Jewish-Christian tradition. It is unlikely therefore to have been set down before the Bar Kokhba revolt, its audience Hellenised gentiles rather than Jews. Clement of Alexandria does mention that both gospels were read in Alexandria in the late second century but we do not know their contents; the earliest known copies of Matthew and Luke discovered in Egypt date only to the third century and these are so damaged and incomplete that they tell us nothing about the infancy narratives. Not until the Codex Vaticanus and the Codex Sinaiticus, both dating to the fourth century, do we have the complete gospels of Matthew and Luke as we know them today.

Jesus a Bastard, His Mother Mary an Adulteress

The reality, writes Celsus, is that Jesus was a sorcerer and his mother Mary was an adulteress who had deceived her husband Joseph and conceived her child by a Roman soldier called Pantera. 'He invented his birth from a virgin. His mother was a poor woman of the country who was thrown out of her home by her husband, a carpenter by trade, because she was convicted of adultery; and after being driven away by her husband and wandering about for a time she disgracefully gave birth to Jesus, an illegitmate child, who having hired himself out as a servant in Egypt on account of his poverty, and having acquired there some magical powers on which the Egyptians pride themselves, returned to his own country where his sorcery won him a great following, by means of which he proclaimed himself a god'.

There are indeed hints in the gospels that stories were going round in the lifetimes of Jesus and of Mary his mother saying that he was a bastard and she was an adulteress. 'Is not this the carpenter, the son of Mary, the brother of James, and Joses, and of Juda, and Simon? and are not his sisters here with us?', says Mark 6:3. In Judaism a son would be identified by naming his father even if Joseph had been dead for a long while, but Mark, who mentions every other member of the family, leaves Jesus' father unknown. Nor does Mark mention Joseph in any other part of his gospel. And in John 8:41 during a confrontation at the Temple the Pharisees say to Jesus, 'We be not born of fornication', insinuating that he was.

In *The Illegitimacy of Jesus*, scholar Jane Schaberg argues that Matthew and Luke knew a tradition that Jesus was conceived by a rape rather than by a virginal conception and did what they could to erase the truth in their gospels, Matthew by concentrating on Joseph's dilemma and both Matthew and Luke by attributing the conception to the Holy Spirit. Schaberg, however, has simply made up the rape; as a Catholic and a feminist it seems that she prefers Mary to have been a man's victim rather than a willing adulteress. At any rate Celsus knew the story of Jesus' illegitimacy which was in general circulation among Jews, Greeks and others.

Origen in his *Against Celsus* replies to this charge of illegitimacy by writing, 'Is it at all agreeable to reason, that he who dared to do so much for the human race ... should not have had a miraculous birth, but one the vilest and most disgraceful of all?'. From 'an act of adultery between Pantera and the Virgin', from 'such unhallowed intercourse there must rather have been brought forth some fool to do injury to mankind, a teacher of licentiousness and wickedness and other evils; and not of temperance and righteousness and the other virtues'. Celsus would not have been impressed by Origen's circular reasoning, that because Jesus is the saviour of mankind then of course he would not have been the child of an adulterous relationship. But for Origen there were two kinds of faith, that of simple people (*simpliciores*) who take scripture literally, and a more

Is this the lover of Mary and the father of Jesus? Celsus was repeating a well-known story about Mary becoming pregnant by Pantera, a Roman soldier. In the nineteenth century this tombstone was unearthed in Germany. Its inscription reads: *Tiberius Iulius Abdes Pantera from Sidon, aged 62 years served 40 years, former standard bearer of the first cohort of archers lies here.* Mark, Matthew and Luke all mention Jesus going to Sidon on the coast of Lebanon from Galilee; Abdes is a semitic name, possibly Jewish; his unit the Cohors I Sagittariorum was stationed in Judaea at the right time for him to have had an affair with Mary; later it was transferred to Bingen in Germany. But Pantera, which means panther, was not an uncommon name among soldiers, and most scholars think the chances of this being the Pantera of the story are extremely remote; and anyway they prefer to accept that Mary was a virgin.

profound understanding which requires allegorical interpretation of the spiritual mysteries. The virgin birth was one such mystery.

Mary the Mother of God

Origen understood that a vital defence against the charge that Jesus was a sorcerer and a bastard was to insist that Mary his mother was a virgin. Origen further shored up the reputation of Mary the mother of Jesus by being the first to call her Theotokos, literally God-bearer in Greek, but mistranslated in the West as the Mother of God. As no original copy has survived of Origen's *Commentary on Paul's Epistle to the Romans* written in 246 in which Socrates of Constantinople, a fourth-century Byzantine historian, said Origen had used the term, some have questioned the authenticity of the claim. But the term was certainly in use just a few years later, in about 250, when it was used by Dionysius, the patriarch of Alexandria, in an epistle to Paul of Samosata. In about the same year Theotokos appeared in a Christian hymn in Egypt, preserved in a papyrus written in Greek and known in the West by its Latin title *Sub Tuum Praesidium*, literally *Under Your Protection*. One of the oldest Christian hymns and certainly the oldest to Mary the mother of Jesus, it is used in the Coptic and Eastern Orthodox liturgies to this day as well as by Catholics, Anglicans and Lutherans, and it has been rendered in Byzantine and Gregorian chants and in Mozart's K198 Offertorio.

> We fly to thy protection, O holy Mother of God; despise not our petitions in our necessities, but deliver us always from all dangers, O glorious and blessed Virgin.

The hymn states the theological doctrine that Mary the mother of Jesus is a virgin and the mother (or bearer) of the divine as chosen (blessed) by God.

Over the next century or so the use of Theotokos, or Mother of God, became widespread throughout the Church, East and West, and in 431 at the Council of Ephesus the matter was enforced:

Mary the mother of Jesus was declared the Mother of God and those who disagreed were anathematised.

Mary's elevation to Mother of God was a remarkable transition for a woman who is close to being a nonentity in the gospels. The gospel of Mark mentions her only twice, once by name (6:3), the second time as the mother of Jesus without naming her (3:31). The gospel of Matthew mentions her name five times, on four occasions in the infancy narrative (1:16,18,20; 2:11) but otherwise only once and by name (13:55). The gospel of Luke mentions Mary twelve times by name but only within the infancy narrative (1:27,30,34,38,39,41,46,56; 2:5,16,19,34); otherwise Luke has nothing to say about Mary the mother of Jesus. The gospel of John twice mentions Mary as the mother of Jesus, first at the marriage at Cana (2:1-12), which is the only time anywhere in the gospels that Jesus has a conversation with his mother, and a rather testy one at that; and on the second occasion at the foot of the cross (19:25) in the company of Mary Magdalene, Mary the wife of Cleophas, and the beloved disciple; but on neither occasion does he mention her name. Finally in Acts Mary is mentioned once and by name.

Strip away the infancy narratives and Mary the mother of Jesus is mentioned in the New Testament only six times and only three times by name. Had the infancy narratives been there from the beginning, as part of the original composition, one would expect more mentions of Mary in the later parts of the gospels. As Geza Vermes says in *Jesus*, 'The ultimate proof that the birth story is not a natural introductory section of a biography is the absence of continuity between it and the rest of the Gospel'.

In short we are left with the real possibility that the setting down of the infancy narratives with their claims of the virgin birth were a reaction to widespread criticisms and doubts as expressed by Celsus and others and also a response to the eclecticism of Christianity in Egypt. In particular it was a reaction to gnosticism which spoke of the secret message that Jesus had to bring and which valued Mary Magdalene for her vision but was not interested in the crucifixion nor in apostolic succession nor in the virgin birth which gnostics

Mary as the Theotokos, the Mother of God, with Jesus on her lap and
flanked by saints Theodore and George while angels glance heavenwards.
The icon is at the Monastery of St Catherine in Sinai and dates from the
end of the sixth century.

regarded at best as naive misunderstandings, the delusions of this world of the demiurge from which gnostics wanted to escape.

But not only was Mary a virgin, she was a perpetual virgin, which Origen also argued early on. Not that this is stated anywhere in the New Testament; indeed it is contradicted by the gospels themselves which mention four brothers by name, James, Joses, Judas and Simon, and at least two sisters (Matthew 13:55-56; Mark 6:3). Moreover Matthew 1:25 says of Mary that Joseph 'knew her not till she had brought forth her firstborn son', with its implication that after 'till', that is after the birth of Jesus, Joseph and Mary had conjugal relations and that she bore six more children. But Origen explained these verses away by claiming that the children were Joseph's from a previous marriage. That Joseph should not have to lead a chaste life with his virginal wife the fiction was invented that he was an old man who died early on, though again the gospels say absolutely nothing about his age; all we know is that Joseph does not appear after about Jesus' twelfth year by when he could have fathered all Jesus' sisters and brothers.

In these arguments put forward by Origen in Egypt more than reason and even more than faith were at work; the arguments were driven by necessity, the need to establish conformity and authority within the Church in order to counter the heterodox nature of Egyptian Christianity. By the fourth century Mary's virginity, before, during and after the birth of Jesus, was almost universally accepted as was her status as the God-bearer, the Mother of God.

The Battle for Authority

The Catechetical School of which Origen was the head was inspired by Alexandria's Museum and Library as a place to educate Christians in the faith. His predecessors were Pantaenus who is thought to have been from Sicily, part of Magna Graecia, meaning Greater Greece, which included much of southern Italy where the Greeks had established colonies as early as the eighth century BC; and Clement of Alexandria who was originally from Athens. Both men were from that part of the Christian world that looked to

Isis suckles her infant son Horus in the third-century BC temple of Isis
at Philae in Upper Egypt. Here, as elsewhere in the temple, her face has
been hacked out by early Christians but the figure of Horus is usually left
untouched, possibly because early Christians identified Horus with Jesus
but saw the Isis cult as a rival.

Rome, a world they began to impose on Alexandria through their instruction of priests and theologians at the Catechetical School. Pantaenus, who had been a Stoic philosopher before converting to Christianity, was an early and strong opponent of gnosticism while Clement, also a Stoic philosopher and influenced by gnosticism in his youth, decided in his later years that faith, not the secret knowledge of the gnostics, was required for salvation.

Origen, on the other hand, was a native Egyptian (his name derives from Horus, the son of Isis and Osiris). He was born to Christian parents and so intense was his commitment to the faith that when his father was martyred in 202 the seventeen-year-old Origen was only prevented from rushing out to join him by his mother hiding his clothes. The story comes from Eusebius writing a century later, who adds, with whatever degree of reliability, that Origen so sought the ascetic and spiritual life that he sold all his possessions and castrated himself in obedience to his interpretation of Jesus' words in Matthew 19:12: 'For there are some eunuchs, which were so born from their mother's womb: and there are some eunuchs, which were made eunuchs of men: and there be eunuchs, which have made themselves eunuchs for the kingdom of heaven's sake. He that is able to receive it, let him receive it'.

The same persecution that led to the death of Origen's father also caused Clement to flee Alexandria. The following year, though still only eighteen, Origen revived the Catechetical School and became its new head. Origen was well versed in philosophy, having studied under Ammonius Saccas in Alexandria who also taught the great Neo-Platonist philosopher Plotinus. Building on the work of Pantaenus and Clement, he countered heterodoxy and in particular gnosticism by teaching the Christian faith to new converts and to those at a more advanced level using the scriptures acceptable to Rome, especially the gospels of Matthew, Luke and John, the Acts of the Apostles and the epistles of Paul.

The man who appointed Origen as head of the Catechetical School was Demetrius, who from 189 to his death in 232 was bishop of Alexandria and patriarch of the See of St Mark. The

This fourth-century gravestone of a mother and her child from the Fayum in Egypt is an early example of the Christian appropriation of the imagery of the Isis story. Popular familiarity with the story probably contributed to Mary the mother of Jesus eventually being depicted in this form as the Theotokos.

Top: Ankhs incised in the wall of Ramses III's twelfth-century BC funerary temple at Medinet Habu across the Nile from Luxor; for ancient Egyptians the ankh was the breath of eternal life and in this case they are taking on human form. Below: this Egyptian Christian relief of the third to fourth centuries has crosses based on the ankh, again in human form.

Catechetical School provided the teachings and the canonical texts but Demetrius applied the muscle. A native Egyptian who became patriarch in 189, Demetrius was the first ecclesiastical leader in Egypt to enforce episcopal authority, that authority granted to him by apostolic succession. Determined to destroy gnosticism, he became frustrated with the patient intellectual debate of the Catechetical School and found himself increasingly at odds with Origen, who eventually decamped to Caesarea in Palestine – which is where he wrote *Against Celsus*.

Pantaenus and Clement had introduced a measure of Roman orthodoxy to Christianity in Alexandria; thereafter the task of eliminating eclecticism in Egypt was taken on entirely by native Egyptians like Origen and Demetrius and their successors. In place of Origen, Demetrius appointed Heraclas as head of the Catechetical School, and when Demetrius died Heraclas in turn became patriarch. The pattern continued with Dionysus, called the Great, a pagan who converted to Christianity. He studied under both Origen and Heraclas at the Catechetical School, eventually became its head and then succeeded Heraclas as patriarch. The interplay between the Catechetical School and the patriarch helped spread orthodoxy in Egypt, emphasising apostolic authority and circulating the canonical four gospels, especially Matthew and Luke with their infancy and resurrection narratives.

As the Church proselytised for converts among pagan Egyptians who still worshipped the old gods and as the battle against gnosticism spread deeper into the country, traditional and ancient beliefs and imagery came into play. The crucifixion and the cross were a direct challenge to the gnostics who did not accept that Jesus died for the salvation of man, but every Egyptian recognised the symbolism of the ankh, the cross-shaped pharaonic sign of life. Soon it was appearing on Christian gravestones as a symbol of resurrection; or it was made to resemble people at prayer, their arms upraised, their heads encircled by the loop of the ankh in the form of a halo – again a strike against the gnostics who offered no prayers to the demiurge but instead possessed the secret to release themselves from his evil world. Mary the mother of Jesus appeared on the throne of Isis holding Jesus as Isis held Horus, but this was Isis (whose title in ancient Egyptian was mwt ntr, meaning divine mother) transformed into the the exalted Theotokos, powerfully evocative, promoting popular devotion yet promoting also the passive role of women in imitation of the passivity of the Madonna. This was now Isis controlled and used by the Church, no longer the independent woman, the leader and the seer, the figure with whom the gnostics had identified Mary Magdalene.

These were the weapons used to impose conformity on Egyptian Christianity and to wipe out gnosticism; they also transformed Egypt into a dominating force within the wider Church, with Alexandria contesting supremacy with Rome. From Egypt many of these same images and symbols and ideas spread throughout the Christian world.

Meanwhile the monks at Pbow continued reading their holy scriptures, their gospels reminding them of the greatness of Mary Magdalene, until there came the day when they thought it best to put their gospels in a jar and bury them at Nag Hammadi.

Mary Magdalene the Whore

Gnosticism arose in precisely those places that were home to the great mysteries of the goddess and the death and rebirth of her lover – in Syria, Lebanon, Asia Minor, and even in Greece, but above all in Egypt. In Egypt the worship of Isis, already thousands of years old, would survive until AD 543 when the emperor Justinian closed her temple in the Nile at Philae, imprisoned the priests and had the cult statues carried off to Constantinople. Ten years later the temple was turned into a church, commemorated by a contemporary inscription in Greek: 'This good work was done by the well-beloved of God, the Abbot-Bishop Theodore. The Cross has conquered and will ever conquer'. It was no coincidence that less than forty years later, and with Isis appropriated by the Theotokos – who was now described as the 'sister and spouse of God, the sister of Christ', 'the lofty Pharos of light', 'our haven and anchorage on the sea of our troubles' – that Pope Gregory I, 'the Great', could safely pronounce Mary Magdalene a whore.

> She whom Luke calls the sinful woman, whom John calls Mary, we believe to be the Mary from whom seven devils were ejected according to Mark. And what did these seven devils signify, if not all the vices?... It is clear, brothers, that the woman previously used the unguent to perfume her flesh in forbidden acts. What she therefore displayed more scandalously, she was now offering to God in a more praiseworthy manner. She had coveted with earthly eyes, but now through penitence these are consumed with tears. She displayed her hair to set off her face, but now her hair dries her tears. She had spoken proud things with her mouth, but in kissing the Lord's feet, she now planted her mouth on the Redeemer's feet. For every delight, therefore, she had had in herself, she now immolated herself. She turned the mass of her crimes to virtues, in order to serve God entirely in penance, for as much as she had held God in contempt.

In these few words of his Thirty-third Homily, delivered on an autumn day in 591 at the basilica of St Clement in Rome, Gregory fixed the identity of Mary Magdalene in the ecclesiastical and popular mind for the next one thousand four hundred years. Combining several gospel verses he created Mary Magdalene the penitent prostitute. He starts with 'the sinful woman' of Luke 7:37-50 who came into Simon the Pharisee's house at Capernaum and washed Jesus' feet with her tears and anointed them with ointment. To her he adds the woman 'whom John calls Mary', that is Mary of Bethany who is described in John as anointing the feet of Jesus (John 12:3). But Mary of Bethany, says Gregory, is the same person as 'the Mary from whom seven devils were ejected according to Mark' (16:9), that is Mary Magdalene.

Gregory then goes on to say that the seven devils that were driven out of Mary Magdalene were seven vices, the seven deadly

After Gregory's homily identifying Mary Magdalene as a prostitute she was commonly portrayed in an attitude of abject submission and repentance, as in this twelfth-century relief on the west front of the abbey church of St Gilles-en-Gard in Languedoc-Roussillon.

sins which he had named the previous year as lust, gluttony, greed, sloth, anger, envy and pride. But of these, as Gregory makes clear when he says that she had 'previously used the unguent to perfume her flesh in forbidden acts', her greatest sin was lust.

But there is nothing at all sexual about Mary Magdalene's afflic-tion as mentioned in the late addition to Mark and which was taken from Luke 8:2. The word used in the original Greek of Mark and Luke is *daimonia*, which is usually translated as devils or demons. Throughout the gospels a devil or a demon refers to some serious illness or affliction like blindness or deafness, as in this example from Matthew 12.22: 'Then was brought unto him one possessed with a devil, blind, and dumb: and he healed him, insomuch that the blind and dumb both spake and saw'. Or it can refer to a psychological illness, as in Luke 7.33 where Jesus describes how John the Baptist's abstinence leads people to think he is crazy: 'For John the Baptist came neither eating bread nor drinking wine; and ye say, He hath a devil'. Nowhere in the New Testament do devils signify a person possessed by lust or other sinfulness.

But Gregory continues. To redeem herself Mary Magdalene does penance for her sins; her unguents, once used for lust, 'she was now offering to God'; once she had 'spoken proud things with her mouth', but 'she now planted her mouth on the Redeemer's feet'. Gregory's Mary Magdalene completely abases herself.

There had been some earlier confusion and questioning about the relationship between the various women in the gospels. Already in the late second century Tertullian, in his work *Against Marcion*, described the scene in John's gospel of the encounter in the garden where Mary Magdalene, 'the woman who was a sinner', reaches out to touch Jesus. Ambrose in his fourth-century commentary on Luke 10 thought it possible that Mary Magdalene and Mary of Bethany were the same woman, but he also wondered, 'Were there Mary, the sister of Lazarus, and Mary Magdalene, or more people?'. Also in the fourth century Ephrem the Syrian was writing commentaries and hymns in which he regularly had Mary the mother of Jesus appropriate the role of Mary Magdalene, as in the garden scene after the resurrection. And Augustine in *The Harmony of the Gospels* toyed with the idea that Mary of Bethany might be the sinner woman though he never entertained the possibility that the sinner woman was Mary Magdalene.

At one time or another a commentator might identify one Mary of the gospels with another and sometimes with the sinner woman but there was never anything like a settled view, and for the most part Mary Magdalene, Mary of Bethany and the sinner woman were regarded as distinct persons. Certainly that was true in the East where it remains true in the Orthodox Church to this day. But in sixth-century Rome Gregory the Great assembled these three women into one composite figure and through his authority he imposed his creation on the Western imagination.

Waiting for the Barbarians

Throughout much of the sixth century and the century before, Italy had endured barbarian invasions, and plague and famine and war. The population had declined by a third. The Roman Empire, which was divided in half in 395, had collapsed in the West; it survived in the East with an emperor enthroned at Constantinople but in the chaotic conditions of Italy the task of bringing order to society was taken up by the papacy which now established the beginnings of an anxious and ascetic temporal power.

The Church's response to gnosticism did much to shape Catholic theology and the role it gave to Mary Magdalene. The gnostics identified Mary Magdalene with Wisdom, called Sophia. But while the gnostics saw Sophia as a link between themselves and the primal god, it was also true that in her passion to create independently of her divine father Sophia gave birth to an abortion, the defective world of evil and sorrow in which we live. In the story of her cosmic calamity Sophia stood in contrast with Mary the mother of Jesus, the humble woman chosen by God to bear his son and bring salvation into the world.

For Gregory his reign as pope and the salvation of Rome from plague began with the Virgin Mary, the antithesis of Mary Magdalene. Early in 590 the river Tiber overflowed its banks and washed away many houses in the city; according to the ancient accounts it also cast up serpents and a huge dragon which were left rotting and gave rise to a great plague. Pope Pelagius, Gregory's predecessor, was the first to be stricken and died within hours; thousands more perished as the plague swept through the city, leaving many houses standing empty and silent. Gregory was a monk known for his holiness who preferred a life in the cloisters, but the people insisted he lead them and elected him pope by acclamation. He immediately launched a procession round Rome offering prayers and begging God for mercy, yet even as they marched ninety men died. Still Gregory urged them on; the plague was a chastisement from God and the people must repent of the sins and pray for their salvation; and walking at the head of the procession he held aloft an image of

In 590 Pope Gregory the Great, bearing a painting of the Virgin, led a procession round Rome imploring her to stem the plague. A year after his success, Gregory turned against Mary Magdalene whom he identified with Mary of Bethany and the sinner woman in Luke, who in the eyes of the Church all became one woman who was a whore. The painting was commissioned for an altarpiece in Spain about 1500; the artist is unknown.

the Blessed Mary Ever Virgin, supposedly painted by St Luke. Now as the procession advanced the voices of angels were heard round the image, singing 'Queen of Heaven, rejoice, allelluia, because he whom thou didst bear, alleluia, has risen as he said, alleluia', and the poisonous air fled before the image of the Virgin and a wonderful serenity and purity filled the city. 'Pray for us, we beg God', cried Gregory to the Virgin, 'alleluia!', and when the pope saw an angel sheathing his sword above the city he knew that the plague was over.

That was the immediate circumstance preceeding Gregory's Thirty-third Homily delivered the following year in which he denounced Mary Magdalene as a whore. The other Mary, the one who according to Celsus had conceived Jesus in an adulterous affair, was now the ever virgin whose powers cleansed Rome's very atmosphere of death and evil. For the gnostics the soul possesses the divine spark and can learn the secret of returning to its divine origin. But the developing Western theology said that we have fallen through original sin and must rely on virgin-born Jesus and his apostolic Church for salvation.

Order and salvation lay with the perpetual virginity of the Blessed Mary and the perpetual penitence of Mary Magdalene the whore.

CHAPTER ELEVEN

The Bride of Christ:
Magdalene of the Cathars

THE LEGENDA AUREA – the *Golden Legend* – was the most widely circulated manuscript in the late Middle Ages. Written in 1275 by Jacobus de Voragine, a Dominican and the bishop of Genoa, it gathers together the traditions about all the saints venerated at the time, their lives, their miracles and martyrdoms and the worship of their relics. Alongside the well known stories in the gospels, from the nativity and the massacre of the innocents to the crucifixion and the ascension, the *Golden Legend* also tells about Anastasia being burnt at the stake, John the Evangelist in the pot of boiling oil, Hippolytus drawn between two horses, Margaret emerging from the dragon's back, Ursula and the eleven thousand decapitated virgins, and so on. Easy to read in simple Latin and accompanied by brightly coloured illuminations depicting one horror after another, the *Golden Legend* was enormously popular; and it serves today to give us a fair impression of the beliefs inhabiting the medieval mind.

Mary Magdalene in the Golden Legend

Voragine's entry for Mary Magdalene is extensive, longer than that of Peter and nearly as long as that of Paul, though none are as long as the account of Mary 'the mother of God' whose death and ascension, unknown in the New Testament, is here a grand affair with all the apostles in attendance, including Peter, the 'most noble and sovereign of theologians', and also 'James, brother of God'. For her part Mary Magdalene conforms to the identity set out for her by Pope Gregory the Great; she is the sinner at the home of Simon the Pharisee as described in Luke and her life is one of guilt and repentance.

Yet Voragine draws on another tradition, one still alive in the Europe of the Middle Ages and suggested in the New Testament canonical gospels and celebrated by the gnostics, when he indulges in the medieval fashion of using analogy and association to interpret the meaning of her name. Playing with the sounds of words rather than their tracing their origin, he decides that Mary or Maria can be interpreted as amarum mare, Latin for bitter sea, the bitterness being the penances Mary Magdalene has endured. But also playing with the sound of amarum mare he interprets this as meaning illuminator or illuminated. And so her penances have led her to inward contemplation: 'She is called enlightener because in contemplation she drew draughts of light so deep that in turn she poured out light in abundance; in contemplation she received the light with which she afterwards enlightened others'. And she is illuminated because 'she is now enlightend by the light of perfect knowledge in her mind and will be illumined by the light of glory in her body'. And so via Isis and the Pharos at Alexandria we have travelled back to those forgotten lighthouses that once shone their beacons to fishermen at night on the Sea of Galilee.

Mary Magdalene, says Voragine, was of noble stock and her parents were descended from kings. With her brother Lazarus and her sister Martha she had inherited a considerable part of Jerusalem as well as land in Bethany and Galilee which they had divided among themselves. Lazarus held the property in Jerusalem, Martha kept the property in Bethany and Mary Magdalene owned the walled town of Magdala, but as Lazarus was devoted to the military and Mary Magdalene had given herself 'totally to the pleasures of the flesh', the estates were managed by the prudent Martha. Abundant in riches and famous for her beauty, Mary Magdalene so completely 'submitted her body to delight' that her name was forgotten and she was simply called 'the sinner'.

Voragine mentions the tradition that John the Evangelist had taken Mary Magdalene as his wife when Jesus called him away from their marriage feast and that for consolation she had thrown herself 'to all delight'. The story goes on to explain that because they lost the carnal pleasures of their marriage bed Jesus compensated them, honouring John with special affection and filling Mary Magdalene, after her plea for forgiveness, with intense spiritual delight. But Voragine dismisses these tales as 'false and frivolous'.

What Voragine does say is that after Mary Magdalene threw herself at Jesus' feet at the house of Simon the Pharisee, and after Jesus forgave her sins and drove the seven devils from her, he set her afire with love for him. She travelled by his side and looked after his needs at all times. She stood by him at the foot of the cross and at his resurrection he appeared to her and made her the 'apostle to the apostles'.

Mary Magdalene in France

Fourteen years after the crucifixion, continues Voragine's account, and long after Stephen had been stoned and the disciples had been driven from Judaea by the Jewish authorities and had begun to spread the word of Jesus throughout the nations, the unbelievers put Mary Magdalene and many other Christians, among them Lazarus and Martha, and Maximin, who we are told was one of Jesus' early followers in Galilee, in a boat without rudder or sail or provisions and sent them out to sea so that they should drown or perish from exposure and starvation – but by the will of God they landed safely at Marseilles.

There is another version of the legend not mentioned by Voragine but still alive today at the fishing village of Saintes-Maries-de-la-Mer

Carved in 1536, this wooden altar decoration at the church of Saint-Maximin in Provence shows Mary Magdalene and her companions being driven from Palestine by their persecutors. They are forced into a boat without sail, rudder, oars or provisions and left to perish. But miraculously they are borne safely across the Mediterranean to Marseilles in the South of France.

in the Camargue, about seventy miles west of Marseilles. Here, they say, Mary Magdalene landed with Mary the mother of James the Less and Joses, and Salome who was the wife of Zebedee and the mother of his sons the disciples James and John. These are the three Marys, all of them witnesses to the crucifixion, after whom the village is named. With them was Mary Magdalene's brother and sister, Martha and Lazarus, their companion Maximin, as well as Sarah who was a servant to the women, and several others. The event is celebrated by a gypsy pilgrimage every year on 24–25 May, as the gypsies identify with Sarah, who is said to have been an Ethiopian and dark-skinned like themselves.

The Greek Orthodox Church tells a completely different story, that Mary Magdalene retired to Ephesus with Mary the mother of Jesus and died there. Her relics were transferred to Constantinople in 886 and are preserved there.

But the French Catholic tradition is that recorded in the Golden Legend by Jacobus de Voragine that Mary Magdalene sailed to the South of France and came to Marseilles (the people of Saintes-Maries-de-la-Mer would say via their village) where she personally converted the governor of the province and his wife, convinced them to destroy their pagan temples and build churches in their place, and then with Lazarus, who became the first bishop of Marseilles, and Maximin, who was made the first bishop of Aix, she converted the whole of Provence.

When these things had been accomplished, and wishing to devote herself to spiritual contemplation, Mary Magdalene retreated to the remote wilderness where there were no streams, no grass, no trees, where she lived unknown for thirty years – but where everyday at the seven canonical hours angels carried her aloft to hear the celestial chants so that she nourished herself on paradise. And then when she felt her time had come she was taken by the angels to Maximin at Aix-en-Provence where, hovering in spiritual lightness two or three cubits above the floor, she asked for holy communion and the last rites. 'And Mary Magdalene received the body and blood of our Lord from the hands of the bishop with great abundance of tears, and after, she stretched her body before the altar, and her right blessed soul departed from the body and went to our Lord.' Maximin anointed her body with precious ointments and buried it, commanding that after his death his own body should be buried by hers.

The Movable Relics of Mary Magdalene

The *Golden Legend* says that Mary Magdalene was buried at Maximin's seat in Provence, but it goes on to say that in Charlemagne's time, in 769, Gerard the duke of Burgundy built a great abbey church at Vézelay and sent a monk to Aix – which had been ruined by the Arabs – with instructions to return with the body of Mary Magdalene.

And so Vézelay is where the bones of Mary Magdalene were said to lay when Jacobus de Voragine wrote the *Golden Legend* in 1275. But only four years later, in 1279, the body of Mary Magdalene was found buried back in Provence; it seems there had been some mistake, that the monk from Vézelay had never taken the body away, or had taken the wrong one, but it was now agreed by the Church that Mary Magdalene lay not at Vézelay but in the crypt of a church dedicated to St Maximin, twenty-five miles east of Aix-en-Provence. Not that the church had been dedicated to Maximin the companion of Mary Magdalene but to the fourth-century bishop Maximin of Trier in present-day Germany, a problem which the medieval flair for free association easily surmounted, making one Maximin as good as another.

The mystery of what happened between 1275 when the bones of Mary Magdalene lay at Vézelay in Burgundy and 1279 when they appeared instead at the church of St Maximin in the village of Saint-Maximin-la-Sainte-Baume (Sainte Baume being a range of mountains nearby), three hundred and fifty miles to the south in Provence, is explained by the way the Church and religious orders and kings used saints' relics for financial gain and to advance their political objectives.

This story begins with the Arabs, who in the name of Islam had invaded and occupied the entire Middle East and North Africa, all of which had been Christian, during the seventh century and crossed the Mediterranean into Spain and southern France and Italy in the eighth century. Owing to Muslim hostility and periods of instability and disorder in the East, pilgrimages to the Holy Land like that undertaken by Helena, the mother of the emperor Constantine in the fourth century, became increasingly difficult, often dangerous and sometimes impossible, factors that encouraged the development of pilgrimage sites within Europe itself.

Various well-known New Testament figures were suddenly and conveniently discovered to have travelled to the West and died there,

A 1927 photograph of a gypsy encampment by the church of Saintes-Maries-de-la-Mer in the Camargue where according to one variant of the Mary Magdalene tradition she stepped ashore after her voyage from Palestine. Among her companions was Sarah, an Ethiopian with whom the gypsies identify themselves, making a pilgrimage to this fishing village every May.

their bones unearthed by enterprising churches. Glastonbury had already laid claim to Joseph of Arimathea in this way; in Paris they announced the discovery of the bones of St Denis, a convert and student of St Paul; while St James, the son of Zebedee, had turned up in the far north of Spain at Compostela; and the remains of St Mark had been smuggled out of Alexandria in a barrel of pork and brought to safety at Venice. As well as providing new pilgrimage destinations in Europe, away from the hostile Middle East, the enthusiasm for relics also reinforced apostolic Christianity; the most favoured bones were those of the apostles themselves or people intimate with Jesus and his inner circle of followers.

But originally the great ninth-century Romanesque church at Vézelay had been dedicated to the Virgin Mary and she had risen bodily to heaven at her assumption so unfortunately there could be no question of possessing her relics. But Vézelay lay along the lucrative pilgrimage route from Germany to Compostela, and the profits to be gleaned from the passing trade, not to mention the prestige and the protection to be had, made the happy discovery of some suitable remains all but unavoidable. And who better than Mary Magdalene, the very essence of the redemptive power of the Church, both as witness to the crucifixion and the resurrection, and as a fallen woman saved by her submission to Jesus.

With her relics in their possession, the Benedictine's abbey at Vézelay, now renamed for Mary Magdalene, became immensely popular, but how, the faithful wondered, had her bones come to Burgundy? The monks response − 'All is possible to God who does what he pleases' − had theological strenghts, but as pilgrim traffic grew, and their curiosity became insistent, they offered various explanations. An early tale was that Mary Magdalene's bones were brought back from the Holy Land by Vézelay's ninth-century abbot St Badilo. Later, the monks settled on the fiction that her relics had been buried in Provence but were threatened by Arab raiders, and so were removed and brought to Vézelay for safekeeping. This new version of their story pushed the date of Vézelay's acquisition of the relics back to the eighth century, to the time of Charlemagne, and was repeated in a written account by Sigebert of Gembloux in the 1050s which was happily endorsed by a timely papal document dated 27 April 1058. But even now the monks rarely displayed Mary Magdalene's remains (not that Vézelay had a lot to show − just a few rib fragments in reliquaries looking more like a dried insect collection), telling pilgrims that their faith alone should suffice.

Still the pilgrims were not satisfied. Even if the relics at Véze-lay were real and they had been brought from Aix, they wanted to know how her bones had come to Provence in the first place. Another legend was invented to conveniently explain that Mary Magdalene and her companions had escaped from the Holy Land

An engraving from 1493 shows Mary Magdalene being taken by angels to heaven. Below is the massif where she dwelt in a cave for thirty years and where the Dominicans later built themselves a friary, declaring that Mary Magdalene was their mother, their sister and their daughter. The Dominicans were the inquisitors who helped destroy the Cathars and this was their deliberate response to the Cathars who had claimed Mary Magdalene as their own as the bride of Christ.

by sea and landed at Marseilles, or in an alternative version at Saintes-Maries-de-la-Mer, from where she made her way inland to live a solitary life of repentance and spiritual contemplation. At her death she was buried by Maximin at Aix and it was from there that a monk from Vézelay had dug up her bones and taken them for safekeeping to Burgundy.

The industry of the monks at Vézelay also ensured that Mary Magdalene's bones began performing miracles; she was associated with the liberation of prisoners, assistance with fertility and child-birth, spectacular cures and even the raising of the dead.

Such wonderful tales demanded yet wider circulation which they received from Jacobus de Voragine in his *Golden Legend*. To his account of Mary Magdalene in his compendium of saints' lives he added the plethora of new miracles put about by Vézelay and produced what very quickly became a medieval bestseller. And here the date of Voragine's work −1275 − is important. For its immediate and immense popularity attracted the attention of King Charles of Anjou who was in need of associating himself with a powerful legend. Within four years of Voragine giving his account of Mary Magdalene, Charles appropriated both the relics and the legend to his own purposes.

In the 1270s Charles of Anjou was establishing a Mediterranean empire based on Naples, Sicily and his newly-acquired territory of Provence. Learning from the *Golden Legend* that Mary Magdalene's bones had originally been associated with St Maximin, he went to have a look for himself. And what did he find? The bones of Mary Magdalene. On exactly 12 December 1279, as Charles was quick to let all the world know, at the church of someone called St Maximin. Clearly the monks at Vézelay had been mistaken. Charles and thr Vatican agreed to install the Dominican Order as caretakers of Mary's shrine, and they in turn boldly broadcast the importance of their mission by fabricating the *Book of Miracles of Saint Mary Magdalene*, documenting and backdating all the miraculous intercessions and cures the saint had wrought at her Provençal sanctuary, a publication whose success was measured by the fact that Vézelay as a centre for the miraculous soon went into decline.

A wedding party emerges from the Basilica of Saint-Maximin-la-Sainte Baume which contains the skull of Mary Magdalene. According to Father Henri Lacordaire, who reestablished the Dominican Order in France after the French Revolution, 'The tomb of Mary Magdalene at Saint-Maximin is the third most important tomb in the world. It ranks immediately after that of our Saviour in Jerusalem and of Saint Peter in Rome'.

The new shrine, however, endured. Indeed, pilgrims still come to Saintes-Maries-de-la-Mer to see where Mary Magdalene came ashore and visit St-Maximin-la-Ste-Baume to kneel before her bones.

The Bride of Christ

But the manipulation of Mary Magdalene's relics and the invention of her cult served a vastly more important purpose than making money for Vézelay or conferring legitimacy and prestige on the House of Anjou. Above all else Mary Magdalene was brought into play by the Church and by its enforcers, the Dominican order, to combat the oldest and most dangerous opponent of apostolic Christianity, the gnostics, who flourished especially in Languedoc in the South of France during the twelfth and thirteenth centuries in the form of the Cathars.

The Cathars were influenced by ideas emanating from the East which first took root in Europe among the Bogomils of Thrace and Bulgaria. The Bogomils were dualists who some trace back to the gnostics of Egypt with their belief that a portion of oneself came from God, while the material world and all its acts were evil, including the Church and its preachings about the cross, which the Bogomils rejected because they saw the cross only as the instrument of Jesus's torment.

Bogomil means Loved Ones or Friends of God; they found refuge and freedom in the mountains, but only for a while. Their rejection of the Church invited a vicious reaction from the Bulgarian and Byzantine authorities, who despatched thousands of soldiers and priests into the mountain regions where they plundered, burnt and killed everything in their path. But even as the Bogomils were being exterminated, their heresy spread westwards.

Though the Cathars were influenced by the Bogomils, they were also a native movement, disaffected from the Church which lacked anything like real sanctity, asceticism and humility, and perhaps also they were remnants of those ancient heretics mentioned by the late second-century Church Father Irenaeus of Lyons in his book *Against Heresies* where he charged that gnostics were active in his own district of the Rhone Valley. If that is so then Mary Magdalene, portrayed as the leader of the apostles in the *Pistis Sophia*, the *Gospel of Mary Magdalene* and other gnostic works, might have made herself felt in France long before the legends of Vézelay.

The Cathars insisted on spiritual purity in a world they regarded as totally evil and like the Bogomils they felt themselves especially close to God. But whatever their origin, the Cathars displayed the familiar spiritual outlook of the gnostics of a thousand years earlier in Egypt. They could not accept that if there were only one

This thirteenth-century illumination shows two Cathar perfecti administrating the consolamentum to a dying credente. The ritual will purify his soul, ensuring that he will escape reincarnation into this world and will ascend to Christ in heaven.

God, and if God was the creator, and if God was good, that there should be suffering, illness and death in his world. As in Egypt, the Cathars' solution to this problem of evil in the world was to say there were really two creators and two worlds. The Cathars were dualists in that they believed in a good and an evil principle, the former the supreme creator of the invisible and spiritual universe, the latter the demiurge who created our defective material world of suffering and pain, that is Jehovah, the God of the apostolic Church, the punishing God of the Old Testament. They called themselves Bons Hommes, meaning Good Men; they were the good Christians who worshipped the good God.

But what Catharism certainly did not get from the Bogomils was the Cathar belief that just as there are two gods, good and evil, so there are two Christs, one celestial, the other terrestrial, the one good and the other evil. The Christ born in earthly Bethlehem and crucified in Jerusalem was an evil Christ and Mary Magdalene of the gospels was his concubine. The good Christ was born in celestial Jerusalem and Mary Magdalene was his wife. These ideas seem not to have come from the Bogomils; they came either from the gnostics in Egypt or were an original Cathar tradition initiated and developed by themselves.

But though all matter was evil, the ideal of renouncing the world was impractical for everyone, and so while most Cathars lived outwardly normal lives, pledging to renounce the evil world only on their deathbeds, a few lived the strict life of the perfecti. Cathar perfecti travelled about Languedoc, ministering to ordinary believers, the credentes, by healing and caring for the sick and distributing money to the poor. One of their main tasks was to administer the consolamentum to the dying, the consolation which purified the soul, ensuring its release from the cycle of rebirth and reincarnation and allowing it to ascend to Christ in heaven. Their activities won them the support of all classes of people in Languedoc, from peasants and villagers to merchants and aristocrats. As Jesus did in the gospels, so they walked from place to place, holding services and staying in the houses of the believers. The perfecti were believed to have transcended the material as much as any human could and were looked upon almost as divine.

Women Among the Cathars

The belief that Jesus and Mary Magdalene were united in marriage was an assertion of the Cathar view that the divine world, the heaven of the ultimate creator god, brought the polarities of male and female together as one. And as in heaven so on earth, not only men but many women were perfecti. This was in contrast to the Catholic Church where women could hold no office and served only as nuns and was probably one reason for the popularity of Catharism in which a woman could achieve the prestigious and spiritualised status of the perfecti.

But how far the Cathars in their everyday lives went towards gender equality is uncertain; declared heretics by the Church which initiated a series of inquisitions against them, so much of what the Cathars believed was destroyed along with their bodies on the pyres that it is difficult to know their lives with certainty. Nevertheless, and despite the role played in their cosmology by Mary Magdalene, it is probably wishful thinking to see the Cathars as an early form of feminist society.

The best evidence comes from the inquisitor Jacques Fournier, then the local bishop of the area round the village of Montaillou in the Pyrenees; later he became Pope Benedict XII. His meticulous records were kept at the Vatican where they proved a valuable resource for the present-day historian Emmanuel Le Roy Ladurie whose *Montaillou* builds up a picture of every aspect of the villagers' daily lives over the course of thirty years, from 1294 to 1324. In fact because of the records made by Jacques Fournier more is known about this small village in the Pyrenees than about thirteenth-century Paris or London.

Ladurie makes the point that Catharism was limited by the weight of tradition in the influence it could bring to bear on peoples' lives. 'The position of a young bride in Montaillou and the other villages of the region was not a particularly attractive one', writes Ladurie of Cathar and Catholic women alike. 'Every married woman could expect a fair amount of beating some time or another.' Nor were conditions better for women of the aristocracy or the middle class and those living in the towns; their husbands too 'were heavy-handed'. Certain enlightened Cathars advocated more humane treatment of women, yet one perfectus, Guillaume Bélibaste, familiar to the people of Montaillou, who kept a mistress despite his vow of chastity, declared that a woman could never be permitted into paradise; she would first have to be reincarnated as a man. 'A man is worth nothing unless he is his wife's master', Bélibaste said, while his friend Pierre Maury, a Cathar of the village, remarked, 'Women are devils'.

There were few circumstances in which the women of the region could achieve some sort of independence; one was if the family was no longer headed by a man, usually because the man had died or had left the household; another was in a handful of occupations permitted to women, like running a shop selling wine or cheese for example, or acting as hostess at a roadside inn. It sounds like the restricted lives of Jewish women of traditional families in first-century Palestine; not at all like the freedom enjoyed by fully Hellenised women as Mary Magdalene probably was.

As for those women who were perfecti, unlike men they rarely travelled and almost never left their homes; their status was not permanent, instead normally it was laid aside and resumed as childbearing required. Girls might become perfecti a few years before puberty, were married as soon as they reached it, then became perfecti again once they were matrons or widows and their years of fertility were over. 'In other words', writes the historian R.I. Moore in *The War On Heresy*, 'whatever religious beliefs lay behind or underpinned it, this was an institution whose function was to protect the chastity of nubile females.'

The Skull of Mary Magdalene

Unlike Vézelay where the most they could ever muster were a few fragments of Mary Magdalene's ribs, the Mary Magdalene in the crypt at Saint-Maximin-la-Sainte-Baume is a beaming skull set within a robe and headdress of gold, her breast and shoulders too of gold, and her long hair of gold.

The skull said to be that of Mary Magdalene in the crypt of the Basilica of Saint-Maximin-la-Sainte-Baume in Provence. The idea behind relics was to get as close as possible to Jesus himself; given her supporting presence during his ministry and her witness at the crucifixion and the resurrection, to get this close to Mary Magdalene is as close to Jesus as you can possibly get.

Though nothing is known of who came upon the skull of Mary Magdalene, the fact that the Vatican and King Charles of Anjou immediately placed the relics under the supervision of the Dominicans suggests that they were part of the discovery from the start. The Dominicans may even have initiated the find, for Mary Magdalene was just the sort of woman they needed to destroy the Cathars.

The founder of the Dominican Order was Dominic de Guzmán, a Spanish priest who early in his career in about 1205 visited the South of France where he participated in a mission to convert the Cathars, several times engaging them in public debates, but with little effect. In his view the Cathars were alienated from the Church by its show of wealth and its lack of humility and spirituality. Deciding there was a need to combine the spiritual qualities of monastic life, including a deep training in religious studies, with an

A digital facial reconstruction based on the skull and jaw of Mary Magdalene at the Basilica Saint-Maximin by Brazilian experts in 2015. The skull belonged to a woman who died at the age of fifty-one but the face has been reconstructed to show how she looked at twenty-one – in other words, by their reckoning, at the time of Jesus' crucifixion. Apart from being used to recreate the faces of Tutankhamun and Ivan the Terrible digital forensic facial reconstruction has also been used by police forces and the FBI seeking help from the public to identify murder victims. But the accuracy is not good enough to be accepted as evidence in courts of law. Which begs the question of whose skull this is. The reconstruction might be accurate but who is she? It would not have been out of character for the Dominicans to have dug up a dead Cathar for their purposes.

active life of preaching, he obtained permission from the papacy in 1216 to found the Order of Preachers, known popularly as the Dominican Order. 'Zeal must be met by zeal, humility by humility, false sanctity by real sanctity, preaching falsehood by preaching truth', Dominic told his friars, but even so they won few converts.

Meanwhile already in 1184 the episcopal inquisition against the Cathars had begun. Ordered by the papacy but conducted by local bishops, it was intermittent and haphazard. But these persuasions were so far only sideshows compared to the brutal warfare that was undertaken in the name of the Church against the Cathars.

By 1200 Catharism had become so widespread that the papacy was alarmed. Pope Innocent III said that the Cathars were 'worse than the Saracens'. In 1209 a crusade was launched against them – the Albigensian Crusade, as so many Cathars lived around Albi – initiated by the Church and enthusiastically backed by the king of France and the nobility of the north. At that time Languedoc was not part of the French kingdom; and so the king of France and the northern nobles saw rich territorial gains to be had from a crusade against the aristocracy, the common people and the growing middle class of the south. Not all of these were Cathars but among many in the south sympathy for the Cathars ran deep. As one knight of Languedoc replied when asked by a papal legate why they did not display more zeal in pursuit of the heretics, 'We cannot. We have been reared in their midst. We have relatives among them and we see them living lives of perfection'.

The crusade began by moving against Béziers in July 1209. The population was given the chance to hand over the Cathars among them but they refused, and the Catholics of Béziers also refused the offer to freely depart. Instead the people trusted in their walls and were determined to wear down the crusader army in the course of a long siege. But as some of the townspeople were making a sally at the encircling enemy the gates were breached. When the papal legate was asked by the crusaders how to tell the Catholics from the heretics, he replied, 'Kill them all. God will know his own'.

Within hours the entire population, about 20,000 men, women and children, Cathars and Catholics, was slaughtered and the city was razed. The day was 22 July, the feast day of Mary Magdalene.

In that same first year of the crusade the core of Cathar resistance withdrew to the castle of Montségur atop a great domed hill in the eastern Pyrenees, where they withstood assaults and sieges until capitulating in 1244. Some two hundred still refused to surrender

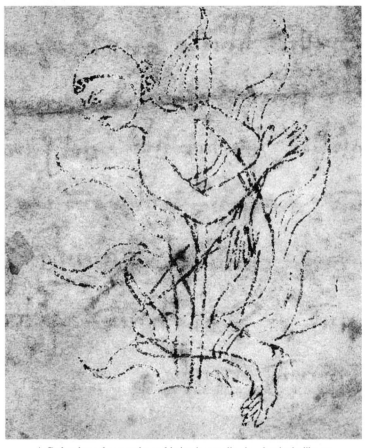

A Cathar bound to a stake and being burnt alive in what looks like an eye-witness sketch. It was found on the back of a document addressed by Alphonse, count of Toulouse, to Pope Innocent IV recommending that the pope issue what became known as the Papal Bull Ad Extirpanda of 1252 in which Innocent authorised the Dominicans' use of torture against the Cathars.

their beliefs; they were bound together within a stockade below the castle and in what Lawrence Durrell has called 'the Thermopylae of the gnostic soul' were set ablaze on a huge pyre.

Between the destruction of Béziers in 1209 and the fall of Mont-ségur in 1244 the crusade swept back and forth across southern France like a recurrent plague, killing Cathars in their thousands, destroying homes and towns. Barely more than a week after the destruction of Béziers the crusaders marched on the great walled town of Carcassonne which surrendered in the middle of August. In this case the inhabitants were permitted to go free, Catholic, Cathar and Jew, but only one by one through a postern gate, where they were stripped naked and cast out broken and barefoot into the parched landscape, their property, their livelihoods, their personal possessions left behind in the empty city. More towns fell through-out that autumn and the following year; in July 1210 the town of Minerve resisted but surrendered when its water supply was dam-aged; 140 Cathars were burnt at the stake. Likewise when Montréal surrendered in 1211 several hundred Cathars were burnt alive. And so it continued for years. In 1219 when the town of Marmande sur-rendered the crusaders nevertheless demanded a blood-price from the entire population for the Cathars they had harboured. A con-temporary account written by the unknown author of the second part of the *Chanson de la Croisade Albigeoise* describes what happened next.

> Clamour and shouting arose, crusaders ran into the town with sharpened steel; terror and massacre began. Lords, ladies and their little children, women and men stripped naked, all these were slashed and cut to pieces with keen edged swords. Flesh, blood and brains, torsos, limbs and faces hacked in two; lungs, livers and guts torn out and tossed aside lay on the open ground as if they had rained down from the sky. Marshland and firm ground, all was red with blood. Not a man or a woman was left alive, neither old nor young, no living creature, unless any had managed to hide. Marmande was razed and set alight.

The inquisitions were a supplement to this violence; they reached deep into people's lives, tormenting their minds and bodies and terrifying their hearts and souls, destroying all deviations from the authority of the apostolic hierarchy. In 1234, under Pope Gregory IX, the papacy took over the inquisition from the bishops and put the Dominicans in charge. Dominic himself had died in 1222 but not the zeal he had instilled in the Dominicans. Torture was usual though as yet unofficial, but in 1252 its use was explicitly sanctioned by Pope Innocent IV, and inquisitors and their assistants were permitted to absolve one another for the tortures they committed. There was no possible way of proving one's innocence, but there was every motivation for deciding upon guilt, for the victims' properties were confiscated and after deducting expenses – including the cost of interrogation, torture, trial, imprisonment and execution – half went to the inquisitors, half to the papacy. So lucrative was the inquisition that the Dominicans took to digging up the dead, trying and condemning them in absentia so to speak, and then dispossessing their families of their inheritances.

The most effective inquisitor, however, was Jacques Fournier, from 1317 the bishop of Pamier, who examined the people of Montaillou and elsewhere in the region, relying on close questioning rather than torture and in only five cases condemning persons judged heretics to the flames, among them the perfectus Guillaume Bélibaste who was burnt alive in 1321. By 1326 Fournier believed he had completely rooted out the Cathar heresy. In 1334 he was elected Pope Benedict XII.

Between them the crusade and the inquisition had inflicted savage and grotesque deaths on countless people and did terrible damage to the society and culture of southern France. Heresy was the excuse but independence of thought was the crime. The terror unleashed by the Church was against a whole people; the Cathars had been part of a varied and tolerant civilisation which included all manner of Christians as well as Jews; Languedoc had been the home of the troubadours, of their poetry and songs of chivalry, romance and courtly love. All this was destroyed.

Historique. - Le Château de Montségur, formidable forteresse au milieu des précipices du Pic Saint-Barthélémy (2343ᵐ); a été le dernier asile des Chefs de l'Eglise Albigeoise. Après une résistance de plusieurs années, ils furent pris par le Comte de Toulouse, Raymond VII, et brûlés vifs, sans jugement, sur la place du village (12 Mars 1244).

16. - ARIÈGE. - Village (altit. 853ᵐ) et Ruines du Château de Montségur (altit. 1.207ᵐ)

Collection V. M.

Montségur where the Cathars held out against the papal crusade for thirty-five years. When they finally surrendered in 1244 two hundred or so were brought down from the fortress atop the mountain to where the village is now and were burnt alive.

Enforcers though they were for the Church, the Dominicans' self-image was one of submission, obedience, poverty and humility and rather than identifying with the power and wealth of the Church, at whose head stood St Peter, they were drawn to Mary Magdalene. They were drawn to the very woman to whom the Cathars were also drawn, but whereas the Cathars saw Mary Magdalene as the visionary companion of Jesus in opposition to the institutionalised Church, its whole apparatus a delusion and evil, the Dominicans saw Mary Magdalene as the Church's kinder and feminised face while yet being the apostle to the apostles and therefore the upholder of apostolic authority. And they also saw her as a lure; a way of drawing Cathars back into the Catholic fold and holding them there.

Mary Magdalene, in the words of the late thirteenth-century Dominican Giovanni da San Gimignano who identified her with

Luke's sinner woman at the house of Simon the Pharisee, 'exhibited obedience to Christ because she kissed his feet. Thus her kisses were kisses of devotion and holiness. Likewise the kiss to the foot is a sign of veneration. Thus a person kisses the foot of the pope. And so did the Magdalene, out of reverence and humility, not kissing his mouth like a wife or his hand like a daughter but his feet like a servant'.

And so today the skull of Mary Magdalene shines out from her gilded reliquary in the crypt of Saint-Maximin-la-Sainte-Baume. Yet a mystery remains. Why Mary Magdalene?

For the Cathars, as it had been for the gnostics in Egypt, Mary Magdalene was the embodiment of their spiritual vision and their rejection of the structure of the Church. And for the Church, and especially for the Dominicans, Mary Magdalene was their way of grappling with and neutralising dissent.

But the fact that Mary Magdalene is there at all – that she is there regardless of being overlooked by Paul, that she found her way from Palestine to Egypt and to France – suggests that she had taken on a life of her own, that her story lives and she cannot be ignored. By her presence at the cross and the empty tomb she is forever bound up with the oldest and most fundamental mystery of mankind, the mystery of death and new life and the erotic link between the two.

CHAPTER TWELVE

The Escape from the Cave: Renaissance Magdalene

I N 1337, SIXTEEN YEARS after Guillaume Bélibaste, the last Cathar
perfectus, was condemned as a heretic by the inquisitor Jacques
Fournier and burnt at the stake, and three years after Fournier was
elected pope as Benedict XII, the Italian poet Francesco Petrarch
climbed the steep and rocky path up to Sainte Baume, the remote
cave 3,300 feet up the face of a limestone massif overlooking
Provence. Baume means cave in Provençal; in the High French used
by ecclesiastics it means balm. This was the holy cave, the holy
balm, where a repentant Mary Magdalene was said to have lived out
the last thirty years of her life in contemplation of the divine.

Petrarch's Pilgrimage of Love

No sooner had the papacy and King Charles of Anjou put the
Dominican Order in charge of Mary Magdalene's relics at St
Maximin than the friars also commandeered the cave attributed

to Mary Magdalene in the face of the mountain ridge nearby. The Dominicans, who did so much to destroy the Cathars who had venerated Mary Magdalene as the bride of Christ, usurped her for themselves, promoting and elaborating her tradition in Provence. The Dominicans after all were the Order of Preachers and Mary Magdalene was the Apostle to the Apostles who had preached the resurrection to the doubting apostles and also had preached the Christian faith to the pagans of Provence.

The Dominicans lost no time ensuring that St Maximin and Sainte Baume were celebrated throughout Europe and became famous centres of pilgrimage. Mary Magdalene's tomb at St Maximin became the third holiest site in Christendom – after the tomb of Jesus in the Church of the Holy Sepulchre at Jerusalem and the burial place of Peter at St Peter's Basilica in Rome – and the cave

The interior of the cave at Sainte Baume where according to the Provençal legend Mary Magdalene lived for the last thirty years of her life. Pilgrims have been climbing to the cave since the Middle Ages. Shrines and altars have been set up within and there is space enough to hold services for 750 people.

of Mary Magdalene at Sainte Baume was recognised as one of the oldest Christian shrines in the world. A friary and a church stood on the cliff face ledge outside the cave to service the pilgrimage traffic and several altars stood within. And the pilgrims did come. Among them was Petrarch, who is often described as the first humanist, an originator of the Renaissance, and the founder of the tradition of Renaissance love poetry; he was also a religious man and he came as a devout pilgrim to Sainte Baume.

Petrarch's family were from Florence but political disturbances forced them into exile in 1302, the same year in which Dante was driven from the city, so that Petrarch was born in Arezzo in Tuscany in 1304. When he was eight his family moved to Avignon in Provence, which was then the seat of the papacy; there Petrarch studied Latin literature and took holy orders, in 1330 becoming private chaplain to Cardinal Giovanni Colonna, whose friendship and patronage allowed Petrarch to travel widely and pursue his interests as a classical scholar. Passionate about recovering the knowledge of the classical world, Petrarch sought out ancient Latin and Greek manuscripts during his travels and discovered a previously unknown collection of Cicero's letters.

Petrarch's ecclesiatical career, however, did not prevent him fathering a son in 1337, just before his ascent to Sainte Baume, nor a daughter a few years later, both children born out of wedlock to an unknown woman. But his greatest love lay elsewhere; eleven years before his climb to the cave he met a young woman at Avignon, thought to have been Laura de Noves, who awoke in him a lifelong passion. But Laura was married to Count Hugues de Sade, an ancestor of the Marquis de Sade, and would not respond to his attentions; instead she forever lived for Petrarch as the idealised woman of his poetry.

The year before his pilgrimage to the cave of Mary Magdalene, Petrarch had climbed the 6,300-foot Mont Ventoux, the highest mountain in Provence, where he stood dazed at the spectacle of clouds passing beneath his feet, the Rhone flowing almost under his eyes, the far-off snow-capped Alps rising seemingly at the stretch of his arm, and the blue expanse of the Mediterranean filling the horizon beyond Aigues-Mortes and Marseilles several days' journey away.

But then changing his gaze from space to time, and looking within his own life, he reflected on the ten years since he had first seen Laura. The words of St Augustine came to mind, 'I desire to recall my foul past and the carnal corruption of my soul, not because I love them, but that I may the more love you, O my God'. Petrarch lived in a state of perpetual flux between the world of the flesh and the world of the spirit. 'These two adversaries', he said, 'have joined in close combat for supremacy, and for a long time a war has been waged in the field of my mind, its outcome still unknown'. That evening, after descending from the mountain, he wrote to a friend,

> Much that is doubtful and evil still clings to me, but what I once loved, that I love no longer. And yet what am I saying? I still love it, but with shame, but with heaviness of heart. Now, at last, I have confessed the truth. So it is. I love, but I love what I long not to love, what I would like to hate. Though loath to do so, though constrained, though sad and sorrowing, still I do love.

The conflict within Petrarch between the spirit and the flesh was the driving force of his work and gives movement to his *Canzoniere*, his love songs to the unobtainable Laura. Laura is forever perfect and immutable while Petrarch the lover wavers, his moods alter from passion to repentance as he travels through a range of emotions. All the while she is his constant inspiration, his muse, while for love of Laura he opens and questions and reveals himself, and presents an ever changing interior portrait of himself.

Petrarch was to enjoy great fame in his lifetime and his poems were widely circulated throughout Europe in manuscript form before their first printing in 1470. The *Canzoniere* influenced Petrarch's friend Boccaccio in Italy and parts of it were adapted by Chaucer in his *Troilus and Criseyde* around 1385. In hindsight Petrarch's account of his ascent of Mont Ventoux is said to mark the moment when the Middle Ages drew to a close and a new world

T rouommi amor del tutto difarmato
& aperta lauia per ghiocchi al core
che di lagrime fon facti ufcio & uarco
pero al mio parer non li fu honore
ferir me de faetta inquello ftato
a uoi armata non monftrar pur larco

Petarch and Laura serve to illustrate this manuscript page of the third sonnet of his *Canzoniere*. She is holding the laurel; Petrarch was recognised as the supreme poet of love. Tears, usually Laura's tears, are a frequent motif in Petrarch's poems, but in this *Canzone* the tears are his own.

> Love found me all disarmed and found the way
> was clear to reach my heart down through the eyes
> which have become the halls and doors of tears.
>
> It seems to me it did him little honour
> to wound me with his arrow in my state
> and to you, armed, not show his bow at all.

Source: *Selections from the Canzoniere and Other Works*, translated by Mark Musa, Oxford University Press, Oxford 1985.

opened. He himself was the first to use the phrase Dark Ages to describe those centuries after the fall of the Roman Empire, a dark age of closed beliefs. From the summit of Mont Ventoux Petrarch looked out upon a vast landscape, the splendour of the natural world, but his greater discovery was the world within himself. In his quest he became a moving spirit of the Renaissance.

But though Petrarch dated his letter 26 April 1336 and gave the impression that he had written it the same evening as he descended from Mont Ventoux, he did not write it until at least seven years later. Possibly he did not even climb Mont Ventoux. In fact far from being dashed off that night, the letter is a polished Latin essay and the circumstances it describes might well be a fiction. But the tension in Petrarch's mind between the carnal and the divine was real, a tension he exprienced in a heightened form the following year when he climbed to Sainte Baume, to the cave of Mary Magdalene – and which might be the real moment when the Dark Ages gave way to light.

The Tears of Mary Magdalene

Petrarch stayed three days and three nights at Sainte Baume and was deeply moved by his imaginings of the remote and solitary existence of Mary Magdalene there. After her sin, he wrote:

> She did not choose to be conspicuous to men far and wide, nor to live in palaces, but fleeing her homeland she came into these regions as if into another world; she persevered in hiding here to the end and had for her home that bare and hollow rock. ... It is a sacred place, dreadful and venerable, and not unworthy of a visit, even from a long distance. ... There the sweet and blessed hostess of Christ, living and dying, enjoyed not the services of finely dressed girls but the ministry of obedient angels.

While staying at the cavern shrine, Petrarch composed a short poem in Latin for his close friend Philippe de Cabassoles, bishop and later chancellor of the Anjou kingdom in Naples. Called *Dulcis Amica Dei*, that is *Sweet Friend of God*, Petrarch begins by calling on Mary Magdalene to look kindly on his tears which mirror the tears in which she bathed Jesus's feet. Jesus' memory of those tears, and of her clinging to the foot of the cross, and of her 'tears soaking his wounds', are the reason why Jesus made his appearance to her after his resurrection. The final lines of Petrarch's poem turn to Mary Magdalene's life as a contemplative hermit in her cave, where her 'hunger, cold and hard bed of stone were sweetened by her love and hope', and from where she is 'seven hours of the day borne upwards to hear the hymns of heavenly choirs'.

In a manner suggesting at once the spiritual and the carnal, Petrarch is calling on Mary Magdalene, who soaked the wounds of Jesus with her tears, to soak his own wounds with her tears also.

Not that Petrarch is known for this poem nor for his Latin poetry; rather he is famous for his *Canzoniere*, his 366 love lyrics which have his passion for Laura as their theme. They are personal and private and intense, and all are written in the vernacular, in Italian, considered a vulgar tongue and supposedly not suitable for the higher feelings expressed in Latin. But the tears he shared with Mary Magdalene at Sainte Baume seeped from Petrarch's Latin poem and saturated his *Canzoniere* where Laura is all the more desirable for her tears – 'When my lady weeps, desire fills me to the brim' (*Canzone* 155).

Petrarch's Laura of the *Canzoniere* was a new ideal of woman, at once alluringly beautiful and the embodiment of wisdom, who excited the passions and illuminated the poet's life and art. She became the means to his introspection and self-discovery, and he combined in her the attributes of Venus and Persephone and Athena and Mary Magdalene, the last because in his powerful emotional relationship with Mary Magdalene Petrarch found the closest and most intimate possible contact with God.

The influence of Laura and the *Canzoniere* also extended well beyond literature; it had a significant impact on the visual arts of the Renaissance, on tapestries, on sculpture and above all on painting.

Painting Laura

Painting in the Middle Ages was religious. Even into the early Renaissance only rarely did artists paint portraits of secular subjects and then it might be a benefactor to a religious institution who would be included within a religious scene, as for example the kneeling woman, probably a donor, in Fra Angelico's fresco of the *Communion of the Apostles* of about 1440 done at San Marco in Florence, reproduced on p.97.

Instead the Church followed Saint Augustine who in the fifth century had argued against images in his *Soliloquies*. Augustine was a neo-platonist, that is he believed in an ideal, an ultimate perfection, which could not be reproduced. Art could offer only false images, he said. No matter how excellent a likeness it was nevertheless a degraded likeness of the ideal and therefore it was false. In fact the idea of art and artists hardly existed in the Middle Ages; painters and sculptors were largely anonymous craftsmen who devoted their talents to images meant to excite devotion; their job did not include putting forth anything of themselves nor trying to bring their subjects to life.

Petrarch, who was deeply immersed in the works of Augustine, agreed with this view. He condemned images. Sometimes he even used Augustine's words verbatim to attack the falseness and the empty pleasure of visual representations.

And yet Petrarch commissioned his friend Simone Martini, a pupil of Giotto and the most famous Sienese artist of his day, to paint a portrait of Laura. The painting is lost but we know about it because Petrarch refers to it in canzoni 77 and 78 of his *Canzoniere* and because Giorgio Vasari, a painter himself and the author of the *Lives of the Artists*, mentions it in his life of Simone.

Petrarch found his way round the problem of images. The attempt to represent Laura, felt Petrarch, did not result in falseness, rather it demonstrated a yearning to capture the truth of love and beauty though it was a yearning that could never be fulfilled. Even so, according to Vasari, Petrarch found Simone's painting of Laura 'as beautiful as he had desired', and Petrarch himself wrote in his

Canzoniere that Simone 'must have been in Paradise, from where this lady came, and portrayed her in paint'.

But unlike Dante's untouchable Beatrice in the *Divine Comedy*, an ethereal creature who consorts with the Virgin Mary in Paradise, Petrarch writing a generation later enumerates Laura's palpable attractions, her lovely body, her skin like ivory and roses, her fingers soft and long, her tears like crystals, her sighs like flames, her golden hair flowing free in the breeze.

Palpable she may be but Laura's earthly beauty is derived by nature from a heavenly ideal.

> From what part of the Heavens, from what Idea
> did Nature take the model to derive
> that lovely face of charm by which she chose
> to show down here her power up above?
>
> *Canzone 159* (translated by Mark Musa)

For Petrarch beauty is the link between man and the divine, and in writing of the tears in her eyes, her golden hair flowing free in the breeze, he was thinking as much of Mary Magdalene as of Laura.

Emerging from the Cave

The legend of Sainte Baume returned Mary Magdalene to the empty tomb, but not that tomb in Jerusalem where she experienced the mystery of the divine, instead a cave in a remote cliff face where she was entombed for her supposed sins. The legend replaces wonder with grief and repentance – sensations easier for the Church to manipulate and control.

Mary Magdalene's emergence from that prison began with Petrarch's visit to Sainte Baume and his love poems to Laura. Where the beauty of women was condemned in the Middle Ages for its association with sin, Petrarch celebrated their beauty for its association with the divine. Throughout Europe Mary Magdalene was still vastly popular as a penitent hermit, dressed in rags or covered with hair like a creature of the wild and hardly human; but over the next two centuries she would be transformed from

Mary Magdalene, carved from poplar wood by Donatello in about 1454, is shown as remarkably tall at 6 foot 2 inches (188 centimetres), but ravaged by a lifetime of self-lacerating penance. Her naked body is entirely covered by her long hair, streaked with gold; her skin is brown and leathery from enduring the elements for thirty years.

a grieving, penitent, self-punishing sinner to an alluring, beautiful and knowing woman – even a goddess.

The most dramatic and extreme example of a penitent Mary Magdalene was the wooden statue carved in about 1454 by Donatello that stood within the Baptistry at Florence. A creation of the early Renaissance, its genius and power lies in its emotional realism. She is shown as an old, emaciated and toothless woman, her hands seemingly shaking with palsey as she holds them together in prayer, her nakedness entirely covered by her long hair. This is a woman worn down by years of hard solitude in her cave, her soul wracked by penitence, her unfocused eyes searching for salvation. The statue itself has been worn by time and flood but recent restoration shows that it was originally painted and that Mary Magdalene's hair was red and streaked with gold. Before her suffering she had been a beautiful woman.

But Donatello's image of Mary Magdalene as a fiercely devout and determined woman (or as a self-abusing religious psychotic as others would have it) was one of the last to depict her as a suffering penitent.

Renowned as the supreme poet of love, Petrarch had found a way of combining his Christian faith with his passion for pre-Christian classical culture and had developed a new sensibility through his poetry that slowly began to spread throughout Europe. That sensibility found a response and was further developed in Florence where beauty as the link between man and the divine was the central idea of Marsilio Ficino who in 1459, a few years after Donatello's ravaged and haunted Mary Magdalene, was chosen by the Florentine ruler Cosimo de Medici to establish the Platonic Academy in emulation of Plato's original fifth-century BC Academy in Athens. But the immediate inspiration for the Florence Academy came from the Byzantine neoplatonist philosopher Gemistus Plethon.

In the summer of 1439 the leaders of the Greek Orthodox and the Catholic churches met with each other at the Council of Florence in a desperate effort to unite Christianity, East and

West, against renewed aggression by the armies of Islam. The Byzantine emperor John VIII Palaeologus came to Florence in person at the head of a delegation of more than seven hundred Greeks, both lay and ecclesiastical, from throughout Asia Minor and the Balkans. The emperor's need was to win Western help to save what remained of his empire from the Ottoman Turks who threatened his capital Constantinople on all sides. Their immediate task was to negotiate with their Cathholic counterparts, headed by the pope, and overcome the various theological differences and conundrums that had grown up between the Eastern and Western churches, and, in the course of hundreds of years, helped to drive them apart.

Ultimately the council proved a failure but its historical legacy was nonetheless profound thanks to the presence among the Greek delegation of Gemistus Plethon to whom an incalculable debt is owed for the progress achieved by humanism in Italy, that is the movement to recover and assimilate the language, literature, knowledge and values of the ancient Graeco-Roman world. In their passion for inquiry and learning, in their assertion of the dignity and genius of man, fellow humanists from Byzantium and Italy brought the Renaissance to full flower.

The contribution made by Plethon was born out of his despair as he witnessed the dying days of the Byzantine Empire, that is the Roman Empire in the East, the half that had survived the barbarian invasions and had once extended from North Africa and the Middle East through Asia Minor and the Balkans and into northern Italy (the oldest standing structure in Florence in Renaissance times was a Byzantine tower; it still stands there now). For centuries its capital, Constantinople, was the largest, wealthiest, most cultivated and learned city in the world. But with its passing, Plethon feared that the Greeks would lose their civilisation, their very world.

Yet in its last years and right up to its conquest by the Ottomans in 1453 Constantinople experienced a brilliant renaissance. This revival in learning had started long before the birth of Petrarch

Humanism played a powerful role in shaping perceptions of Mary Magdalene. The six Italian humanists in this 1544 painting by Giorgio Vasari (1511-1574) were not all alive at the same time but all were prime movers of the Renaissance. The two central figures in the foreground are Petrarch (1304-74) who is trying to attract the attention of Dante (1265-1321), who is holding up a copy of his *Divine Comedy* for his friend and fellow poet Guido Calvacanti (c1255-1300). Behind Petrarch and Dante is Boccaccio (1313-75), the author of the *Decameron*, biographer of Dante and friend of Petrarch. Behind Petrarch are two men belonging to a later generation, Marsilio Ficino (1433-1499) on the right who was the founding head of the Platonic Academy in Florence, and on the left his successor Cristoforo Landino (1424-1498). Petrarch and Ficino in particular associated female beauty with the divine and elevated love over sin.

in the West and amounted to a greater intensification than ever before in the study of ancient Greek literature, philosophy and science, while in art it expressed a new realism in mosaics and painting.

Byzantium might die but Greek civilisation must not. Plethon had long since come to the conclusion that Christianity offered no solutions, not with its emphasis on sin and repentance; in lectures he gave during his time in Florence he proposed instead the salvation of society through a return to the ideals of ancient Greece, supported by a revived Hellenic religion and an ethical system based on neoplatonic philosophy.

In 1453 Constantinople fell to the Turks and an entire civilisation which could trace it roots back to the Hellenistic world of Greece and Rome was lost except for what could be preserved of its teachings in the West. Six years later, in 1459, Cosimo de Medici, who had been inspired by Plethon's lectures, founded the Platonic Academy of Florence and appointed Masilio Ficino as its head. With remarkable energy and urgency Ficino translated the entire body of Plato's work into Latin and at the same time attempted a synthesis of Hellenistic thought with Christian belief, a task that brought him very close to condemnation for heresy and burning at the stake.

Though Augustine had said that the ideal could never be reproduced, Ficino said that the ideal was love. The relationship between man and God was based on love and man could realise this love through his contemplation of the divine. But also as man found spiritual completion by loving God, so by loving one another people were expressing divine love.

Ficino called this Platonic love, a term which nowadays is drained of any sensual content, but Ficino did not rule out a carnal, erotic or sexual dimension. Beauty was the expression of spiritual harmony. To celebrate beauty and to love was divine. The monasteries of Florence were filled with devotional images of Mary Magdalene, sinful and grieving and repentent. But humanism emphasised contemplation of God and the beauty of womankind.

Naked Mary Magdalene

With the recovery of Graeco-Roman cultural values painters and sculptors turned to the female nude. Most famously Botticelli painted his *Primavera* in 1482 and the *Birth of Venus* two years later. Yet within a decade Botticelli had become an earnest follower of the Dominican religious fanatic Girolamo Savonarola who established Florence as a theocracy with himself as ruler.

Savonarola railed against the Florentines for their sinful ways, their passion for gambling, their perfumes and extravagant clothes, their dissolute carnivals and their sensual pleasures. All of which were destroying their souls and making it impossible for them to enter the Kingdom of God. Prostitutes must be beaten to make them virtuous, he thundered; homosexuals must be burnt alive; the books of Plato and Aristotle must be kicked into the gutter; and all those paintings of voluptuous women must be destroyed. The Florentines must war against sin and live the austere and simple life of the Early Church. And the Florentines must repent.

To purify the city and impose his ascetic regime, Savonarola organised armies of children to march about the streets, even going into homes, inspecting and confiscating belongings. Scent bottles, mirrors, fans, necklaces, packs of cards, profane books such as the stories of Boccaccio, musical instruments, portraits of beautiful women, furniture too lavish, sculptures too bare – all such things were seized and burned. The most famous immolation took place in February 1497, when tens of thousands of objects were piled high in the Piazza della Signoria and set alight in what became infamous as the Bonfire of the Vanities.

The poor and middle class were among the preacher's warmest supporters, but also many artists, writers and scholars had been deeply impressed by Savonarola's sermons, his sincerity, his vision of a City of God. Among the objects blackening in the flames were paintings considered sensual by the artists themselves, including, it was said, works by Botticelli, who had become a true believer.

If Mary Magdalene must be a penitent in a cave then she is a voluptuous penitent in this 1522 painting by Antonio Correggio, and a self-improving one, her nipples delicately touching the open pages of a book. The Provençal legend about Sainte Baume allows this figure to be identified as Mary Magdalene; otherwise she is a classical nymph, a child of nature, one of Jupiter's many delights. These sorts of paintings would adorn bedchambers and studies where they could appeal to the pious and secular alike.

Eventually the city turned against Savonarola; he was accused of heresy and in 1498 he was dangled by the neck above a great pile of wood in the Piazza della Signoria and burnt to death.

But the outburst of Savonarola's fundamentalism was a warning and where a man might have commissioned a painting of Venus he might now have a painting of Mary Magdalene. Paintings of undressed Mary Magdalenes proved popular in the sixteenth century as they allowed artists and their secular patrons to combine eroticism and religion without exposing themselves to threat or scandal. Produced for private display in studies and bedchambers, Mary Magdalene was depicted as living in her cave at Sainte Baume, still a supposedly penitent Magdalene; she weeps, she raises her eyes to heaven, she shows her earnestness by opening a book and proves her awareness of the passing of temporal things by leaning against a skull. But her hair is allowed to fall in such ways as to reveal and emphasise the beauty of her body, to draw attention to her femininity. Or her hair covers nothing at all. Nor does she really seem penitent; instead she luxuriates in her warmly seductive appeal.

Leonardo Da Vinci's Mary Magdalene

Until recently Leonardo Da Vinci was not thought to have done a painting of Mary Magdalene (leaving aside those who think that the rather feminine figure leaning against Jesus in Leonardo's *Last Supper* is Mary Magdalene – see p.100). And in Leonardo's forty or so known paintings only very few are nudes, one being *Leda and the Swan*. But those understandings changed in 2005 when Carlo Pedretti, the world's leading authority on Leonardo Da Vinci, identified a painting of a bare-breasted Mary Magdalene, previously thought to have been done by Giampietrino, as an authentic original by Leonardo. Giampietrino, a student of Leonardo's and a prolific painter of Magdalenes, has been accused of doing no more than turning out nudes with 'a veneer of sanctity', their hair carefully draped to expose their breasts as they raise their eyes to heaven. Not that he was a slacker; his works are held by major museums around the world including the Hermitage in St Petersburg, the Louvre in Paris, the Metropolitan Museum of Art in New York and London's National Gallery.

This newly identified Leonardo painting, done in 1515, four years before his death, and which depicts Mary Magdalene bare-breasted, wearing a red robe and holding a transparent veil over her belly, has long been in private hands and has been on public view only twice in the last hundred years or so, in 1949 in New York and

This bare-breasted Mary Magdalene has recently been identified as a painting by Leonardo Da Vinci, done in about 1515. The exposed breasts associate her with the goddess Venus and also suggest that she is preparing to consummate her marriage. She is entirely frank about her sensuality; her smile is a promise, and soon her fingers will let her robe fall away entirely. There is not an ounce of sin or repentance in this Mary Magdalene.

in 2005 in Ancona. Its recent appearance at an exhibition in Italy was therefore the first chance that Pedretti had to see the painting in person. 'It is not I who says the painting is by Leonardo; the painting itself forces me to say it', he said, adding, 'one extraordinary thing is that it is painted on an intact wood panel, just like the Mona Lisa'.

Though there are similarities between Mona Lisa and this Mary Magdalene, they are fundamentally different. The Mona Lisa is aloof and self-possessed, but with a sense of mystery and sensuality in her slight smile. Mary Magdalene's hair falls loose on her shoulders, she throws open her robe to expose her breasts, her right hand tugs at the diaphanous veil across her lower abdomen. She also smiles but not with mystery; she is promising herself to the unseen figure off to her left. At any moment the fingers of her left hand will open and let her robe fall entirely away.

There was no secret about the meaning of Leonardo's Mary Magdalene. Portraits of women revealing their breasts were not uncommon in Florence at the time. They were inspired by ancient statues of the Greek Aphrodite, the Roman Venus, as Botticelli was famously inspired; they spoke of chastity, beauty and love. Exposing the breasts was also associated with a wedding, with a virginal bride who is about to consummate her marriage.

Leonardo's Mary Magdalene is a woman who repents of nothing, who feels no shame or guilt. She feels no contradiction between the spiritual and the erotic as she prepares to consummate her relationship. She is the creation of the greatest humanist and artist of the Renaissance and she has escaped from a world of sin.

CHAPTER THIRTEEN

Modern Mary Magdalene

IN 1517, ABOUT TWO YEARS after Leonardo Da Vinci painted his bare-breasted Mary Magdalene, Jacques Lefèvre d'Etaples, a French theologian and philosopher, and a Dominican scholar who had trained in humanist criticism in Florence, published his argument that there was no historical basis for saying that Mary Magdalene was the sinner woman in Luke nor was she Mary of Bethany. In making his case against the composite Mary Magdalene he called on the works of Origen, Jerome and other Church Fathers, and in flatly rejecting the homily of Gregory the Great he declared that the authority of the gospels is greater than that of the pope. Lefèvre d'Etaples was censured by the Sorbonne and accused of heresy, and for a while he had to go into exile, but he never gave up his Catholic faith. Had the Church been receptive to what he had to say history might have turned out very differently, not because it would have averted the Reformation but it might have had some effect on the evolution of Catholic thought, particularly towards women.

Instead, and also in 1517, Martin Luther nailed his Ninety-Five Theses to the door of All Saints' Church in Wittenberg, the act that began the Protestant Reformation. Influenced by humanist critical thinking which had spilled over from Renaissance Italy into Germany, Luther argued – as Lefèvre d'Etaples had done – that the gospels had greater authority than any opinion of the pope's. He began by criticising the selling of indulgences, saying the pope had no authority over purgatory, and he was scathing about the cult of saints, saying that their efficacy had no foundation in the New Testament. As for the means to salvation, Luther dismissed confirmation, holy orders, extreme unction, matrimony and penance, five of the seven sacraments of the Catholic Church; the Eucharist, he said, was merely symbolic, a commemoration of the Last Supper. Salvation lay only in baptism. Neither confession nor penance was necessary; baptism removed the stain of original sin.

Martin Luther holds up his Ninety-Five Theses to ward off a monstrous beast representing the pope.

The Persistence of the Penitent

Yet despite the assault on penance and the cult of saints, Mary Magdalene remained a revered saint for Lutherans and Anglicans and many other Protestants, just as she had been in the Catholic and Orthodox churches. Moreover, Luther himself retained his belief in the composite Mary Magdalene – that she was also Mary of Bethany as well as the sinner woman of Luke – and much Protestant literature continued to emphasise the penitent whose sins had been forgiven because of her love for Jesus.

In response to the Protestant Reformation, the Catholic Church launched its Counter-Reformation with the Council of Trent, held from 1545 to 1563, which reaffirmed the efficacy of saints but pared down the many attributes that had adhered to them over the ages, preferring to emphasise just one and basing that as much as possible on history rather than legend. In Mary Magdalene's case her role as apostle to the apostles was dropped as it was regarded as legendary and the entire focus was put on her penance – specifically at Sainte-Baume, despite that fact that the story of Mary Magdalene at the cave lacked any historical pedigree.

For both Protestants and Catholics, Mary Magdalene as a penitent was too important and useful to drop. Paintings of Mary Magdalene proliferated, her innocence the excuse for her nakedness, her sensuality too alluring to discard. Both the Reformation and the Counter-Reformation confirmed the naked and ecstatic and penitent Mary Magdalene luxuriating in her cave at Sainte-Baume as a popular and acceptable religious pin-up, an image that remains in the Western mind to this day.

The Great Social Evil

With the growth of cities from the late Middle Ages and into the seventeenth and eighteenth and nineteenth centuries, prostitution became more prevalent and visible. Cities meant opportunity but they were also places to which people were driven when the old social and economic order was breaking down – and in the case of women they could be a place of anonymity and refuge when their

Mary Magdalene by French figure painter Jules Joseph Lefebvre in 1876.
The naked, ecstatic and penitent Mary Magdalene luxuriating in her
cave became a popular and acceptable religious pin-up.

lives had been ruined by careless love or the persuasions or insist-
ence of a farm hand or the master of the house.

Prostitution in the Middle Ages was a matter for the secular
authorities but the Church also involved itself. The Church saw
prostitution as a grave sin but also as a necessary evil for direct-
ing the desires particularly of young men who could not yet afford
to marry. As St Augustine had said in *De Ordine*, 'If you eliminate
prostitutes from society, you will disrupt everything through lust'.
Instead the Church looked to the harvest: a fallen woman was a
soul to save. Mary Magdalene was pressed into service as the saint
who herself had once been a sinner and the saint's name was given
to half-way houses for prostitutes.

In London the first such institution was founded in Whitechapel
in 1758 by a committee of merchants. The women had to be under

thirty years of age and sincere in their desire to give up prostitution; preference for admission was given to the youngest and least experienced. The committee proposed that the place be called the Magdalene House for the Reception of Penitent Prostitutes.

One of their number, James Hanway, objected to the name. 'It does not appear to me', he said, addressing the committee, 'that Mary Magdalene was deficient in point of chastity, as is vulgarly understood. I rather imagine she was not. It is certain she was a lady of distinction, and of a great and noble mind. Her gratitude for the miraculous cure performed upon her was so remarkable that her story is related with the greatest honour, and she will ever stand fair in the records of fame.' In the event, Hanway accepted that their patron should be Mary Magdalene, reasoning that St Luke's Hospital had been founded to house madmen, 'but that would not occasion our posterity to consider this Evangelist as a madman'. Anyway, he observed, 'the dedication of your institution to her memory is entirely consistent with the honour due to her character'.

Hanway's sympathy for prostitutes is expressed in the rulebook he wrote for Magdalene House:

> There cannot be greater Objects of Compassion than poor, young thoughtless Females, plunged into ruin by those Temptations to which their very youth and personal advantages expose them ... What virtue can be proof against such formidable Seducers, who offer too commonly, and too profusely promise, to transport the thoughtless Girls from Want, Confinement, and Restraint of Passions, to Luxury, Liberty, Gaiety, Joy? and once seduced, how soon their golden dreams vanish! Abandoned by the Seducer, deserted by Friends, contemned by the World, they are left to struggle with Want, Despair, and Scorn, and even in their own defence to plunge deeper and deeper into sin, till Disease and Death conclude a human Being.

Yet come the nineteenth century that compassionate approach would change; the idea that young women were the victims of circumstances or of their own innocence or of predatory seducers was dismissed and instead they were were accused of being predators themselves, deliberately attempting to destroy society. A passage in *The French Lieutenant's Woman* by John Fowles tells how extensive prostitution had become in London and of the hypocrisy with which it was met:

> What are we faced with in the nineteenth century? An age where woman was sacred; and where you could buy a thirteen-year-old girl for a few pounds – a few shillings, if you wanted her for only an hour or two. Where more churches were built than in the whole previous history of the country; and where one in sixty houses in London was a brothel (the modern ratio would be nearer one in six thousand). Where the sanctity of marriage (and chastity before marriage) was proclaimed from every pulpit, in every newspaper editorial and public utterance; and where never – or hardly ever – have so many great public figures, from the future king down, led scandalous private lives.

Fowles drew his information from William Acton's contemporary book *Prostitution, Considered in Its Moral, Social, and Sanitary Aspects, in London and Other Large Cities and Garrison Towns, with Proposals for the Mitigation and Prevention of Its Attendant Evils*, published in London in 1857. But Acton expresses no such compassion as that of Hanway a hundred years earlier. Instead he warns of the dangers posed by prostitutes:

> Such women, ministers of evil passions, not only gratify desire, but also arouse it. Compelled by necessity to seek for customers, they throng our streets and public places, and suggest evil thoughts and desires which might otherwise remain undeveloped. Confirmed profligates will seek out the means of gratifying their desires; the young from a

craving to discover unknown mysteries may approach the
haunts of sin, but thousands would remain uncontami-
nated if temptation did not seek them out. Prostitutes have
the power of soliciting and tempting. Gunpowder remains
harmless till the spark falls upon it; the match, until struck,
retains the hidden fire, so lust remains dormant till called
into being by an exciting cause.

In Victorian Britain prostitution was seen as the single greatest threat to society. Contemporaries called it the Great Social
Evil. Certainly the country was undergoing a great upheaval;

Ostensibly offering flowers but selling something more, this madeline, as
street girls were called after Mary Magdalene, was one of 80,000 prostitutes in London in the 1850s. The Great Social Evil was seen as the
greatest threat to British society in the nineteenth century.

agricultural reforms and the industrial revolution saw a massive increase in the population which doubled from 1812 to 1851 and by 1900 had doubled again, an explosion that was accompanied by a great migration of the population from the countryside to factory towns and cities. The young in particular, men and women, were drawn into urban life where instead of finding opportunity they often faced unemployment and poverty and lived in overcrowded and unhealthy conditions. The effect on women could be devastating. In 1885 the investigative journalist W.T. Stead published a series of articles called *The Maiden Tribute to Modern Babylon* in which he compared London to the Minotaur's labyrinth, awash with women sacrificed to the monster of modern society.

Poverty and degredation were a problem and could not be hidden; urbanisation meant that the rich and poor lived close together. But instead of seeing a threat coming from the lower classes generally, the Great Social Evil came from women in the form of prostitution. The 1864 Contagious Diseases Act subjected prostitutes to a fortnightly internal examination. Nevertheless the notion took hold that prostitutes were about to wipe out the population. One doctor calculated that 500 women could annually infect 3,304 men which would lead to a total of 1,652,500 men and women becoming infected in the year. A campaigner declared that three quarters of all British men had a venereal disease, while talk went round that prostitutes were no better than paid murderers, committing their crimes with impunity. The collapse of an entire generation was expected and with it the fall of the British Empire.

But what seems to have been the great fear at the heart of the Great Social Evil was not disease, which was effectively controlled by the successive Contagious Diseases Acts of the 1860s, nor even immorality, rather the apparent freedom from male control enjoyed by prostitutes. Instead of filling the roles of obedient wife and mother at home, financially dependent on their husbands, it was complained that prostitutes boldly walked about in public, soliciting business and selling sex – and though it went unmentioned, managing their financial independence. Whether prostitutes lived as freely and comfortably as that was not the point; they challenged the rules and structure of society; their ability to survive without men was a threat.

Victorian women were expected to fulfill the ideals of chastity and submissivness. Yet prostitutes made an independent living by violating both, and furthermore did so in the most public and pro-vocative way. Victorian society depended on knowing one's place, but prostitutes made a highly visible point of being morally, socially and financially out of place. In defying the rules of a world regulated by men, prostitutes demonstrated the possibility of turning society on its head.

Approachable Mary Magdalene

The Victorians' preoccupation with prostitutes was expressed by artists and writers who during the second half of the nineteenth century turned to Mary Magdalene as they questioned the relationship between women and men and society. This took place against a backdrop of the Vatican's renewed assertion of its authority. Britain was a Protestant country and there was no shortage of people who looked askance at the declaration by the pope in 1854 of the dogma of the Immaculate Conception, finally settling an issue that Origen had argued against Celsus more than one thousand six hundred years before, that the Virgin Mary, far from herself having been a fallen woman, was unique among all people in having been born free of Original Sin. Conveniently the Virgin Mary herself appeared at Lourdes in 1858, telling Bernadette that 'I am the Immaculate Conception'. Seventy-five years later Bernadette was made a saint, and meanwhile Mary the mother of Jesus, passive, pliable and pure, was being used by the Catholic Church in its reassertion of dogma over humanist and Enlightenment reason. As if to underline the point, in 1870 the dogma of papal infallibility was declared, a direct if belated rejection of the charge made by Jacques Lefèvre d'Etaples and Martin Luther that authority did not lie in the pope but in the gospels.

This new prominence given to Mary the mother of Jesus contrasted with the image of Mary Magdalene, imperfect perhaps but a woman active and strong, and faithful among the faithless when

she followed Jesus to the cross, a model for womanhood which the
ever more perfect Virgin Mary could never be.

Just as Hanway had done, many Protestants, including numbers
who were trying to alleviate the problem of prostitution, were saying that Mary Magdalene was not the same woman as the sinner in
Luke. But many artists and writers adopted her especially in that role.
In the guise of penitent she served to explore the position of fallen
women, and women downtrodden, dependant or marginalised.

Numerous popular nineteenth-century novels in one way or
another used her story or her name; they are mostly forgotten now,
but there are two by the incomparable Wilkie Collins, author of
the first thriller, *The Moonstone*, and also *The Woman in White*, and
who also wrote *The New Magdalen* about a fallen woman who, conventionally, is rescued by a clergyman and then, unconventionally,
marries him, and *No Name* which deals with the issue of illegitimacy
and in which the heroine is a courageous, lively and independently-
minded young woman called Magdalen.

The most famous images of Mary Magdalene, fallen but definitely a new woman, are those by the Pre-Raphaelites, in particular
by Dante Gabriel Rossetti. In his *Mary Magdalene at the Door of Simon
the Pharisee*, drawn in 1858, we see an extraordinary coup de fou, the
sudden emotional and spiritual recognition by Mary Magdalene
of Jesus. She has been revelling in the streets but as she passes the
house of the Pharisee she catches a glimpse of Jesus and is trans-
fixed; breaking free of her lover and tearing the roses from her hair,
she presses her way within, telling her lover to let her loose, that she
is drawn, as Rossetti says in his accompanying sonnet, to her 'bridegroom's face'. She is a beautiful woman, confident and sensual and
powerfully built, and she knows what she wants.

> Oh loose me! Seest thou not my Bridegroom's face
> That draws me to Him? For His feet my kiss,
> My hair, my tears He craves to-day:—and oh!
> What words can tell what other day and place
> Shall see me clasp those blood-stain'd feet of His?
> He needs me, calls me, loves me: let me go!

Mary Magdalene at the House of Simon the Pharisee by Dante Gabriel Rossetti. She is casting off her lover, tearing the roses from her hair, and is about to throw herself at the feet of the man she has instantly recognised as her bridegroom.

The Resurrection of Mary Magdalene

Mary Magdalene moves with the times, or rather the times call upon Mary Magdalene. The Great Social Evil in the nineteenth century had less to do with prostitutes than it had to do with the position of women in society generally. To the extent that their challenge was reflected in writing and the arts, Mary Magdalene was the almost unconscious choice of expression. Her strength of character is there in the gospels and perhaps an undercurrent of sensuality is too, and though she has still not shaken off her false reputation as a sinner, it lends itself to her humanity.

In contrast Mary the mother of Jesus, a minor figure in the gospels, has been reinvented by the Church outside the pages of the Bible and stripped of the most basic human qualities. She is a perpetual virgin immaculately conceived, nothing less than the mother of God, in all ways perfect – entirely inhuman and completely unreal. Her idealised unreality allows the Church to maintain its cult of virginity and its ban on contraception; also the notion that women are subordinate to men and can never be part of the priesthood. Social developments have moved beyond the Virgin Mary; she has inspired in an abstract way but she cannot be a model for women today. In *Alone of All Her Sex*, her biographer Maria Warner believes that the Virgin Mary is beyond engaging with the modern world and will recede into legend, an empty relic of another age.

But that is not true of Mary Magdalene who is rising again to the forefront of peoples's minds when they think of the mystery and meaning of Jesus' teachings.

The Da Vinci Code

It is almost certain that Dan Brown had no idea that his book *The Da Vinci Code*, published in 2003, would provoke such a worldwide reaction. After all, the plot of his previous book, *Angels and Demons*, published three years earlier, included the murder of a pope who had had an illegitimate child, the murder of his four nominated successors, and a bomb placed on the tomb of St Peter that was set to blow up the entire Vatican and probably most of Rome as well. But that book had only modest sales until the extraordinary success of *The Da Vinci Code* – which by comparison has a rather sedate plot; there is an intriguing murder in the Louvre and a lot of driving around Paris, but mostly it is talk.

The talk, however, is extraordinary, and the more so in that it focuses largely on theology. It is about everything written since the gospels, and about the writing of the gospels themselves, and how much of it can we trust; and it is about the two figures who stand at the centre of the Christian story, Jesus and Mary Magdalene, and what became of them. The novel touches on something that turns out to be terribly important to people, that is the nature of Christianity, which stands at the heart of Western civilisation and influences everyone regardless of our individual beliefs.

Industrious academics have written thousands of monographs about these things; in fact people have been writing about these things for the last two thousand years. But when expressed within the pages of a novel it seems to become immediate, tangible, personal. *The Da Vinci Code* readers found themselves talking about the nature of Christ, the resurrection, Constantine, the gnostic gospels. It was reminiscent of Gregory of Nyssa's observation on the intensity of theological interest in the nature of Christ in fourth-century Constantinople:

> The city is full of mechanics and slaves who are all of them profound theologians, and they preach in the shops and the streets. If you desire a man to change a piece of silver, he informs you wherein the Son differs from the Father; if you ask the price of a loaf you are told by way of reply that the Son is inferior to the Father; if you inquire whether the bath is ready, the answer is that the Son was begotten out of nothing.

The Sacred Feminine

Arguably the most interesting discussions in *The Da Vinci Code* concern the 'sacred feminine'. As the novel's characters point out, seeing God in solely masculine terms misrepresents and limits the divine – which is precisely what happens in Christianity with its vocabulary of Jesus the Son of God the Father. That is the starting point of those who argue for recognition of the sacred feminine and what they see as the restoration of spiritual balance to the world. True, the Virgin Mary as Mother of God brings something of the feminine to the Christian godhead, but it is not a full partnership and entirely lacks that element of Eros in which the feminine and the masculine most intimately meet.

The argument for recovering the sacred feminine finds a tradition of sacred union in ancient cultures in which the feminine and masculine were celebrated as intimate and equal partners; examples include Isis and Osiris, Astarte and Tammuz, Cybele and Attis, and Aphrodite and Adonis. In these sacred pairings there is the theme of death and new life, with the female playing an active and restoring role, raising her dead lover or bringing forth new life by bearing his child. Yet this role of the sacred feminine is missing from Christianity, and there are those who in searching for Christianity's 'lost bride' find her in the figure of Mary Magdalene, and who say the time has come to listen to her story.

Pseudo-Histories

Dan Brown did not pull his ideas out of a hat. Just about everything he has to say about Leonardo da Vinci comes from *The Templar Revelation* by the London-based writers Lynn Picknett and Clive Prince. It is in this book, a thriller really, that we learn of 'the secret code of Leonardo da Vinci' found throughout his works, and particularly in *The Last Supper*, and which links him to the Templars, the Freemasons and the Priory of Sion. So when Dan Brown writes about *The Last Supper* and asserts that the figure of John is really that of Mary Magdalene, that this figure and Jesus are 'joined at the hip', that together they describe the shape of the letter M, that there is a disembodied hand holding a dagger – all this and more comes from *The Templar Revelation*.

In *The Holy Blood and the Holy Grail* by the British trio Michael Baigent, Richard Leigh and Henry Lincoln, Dan Brown read about the great secret, hidden supposedly in code, that Jesus was married to Mary Magdalene, who after his crucifixion escaped to the South of France where she gave birth to their child and propagated his bloodline – the Merovingian dynasty of kings. This is the explosive secret that Sophie Neveu, a leading character in *The Da Vinci Code*, claims would 'crumble up the Church'.

A work of pseudo-history and a careless one at that, *The Holy Blood and the Holy Grail* introduced the Priory of Sion, a shadowy secret society promulgating the holy bloodline, and the mystery of Rennes-le-Château, a church in Languedoc. Rennes-le-Château, the book claims, was lavishly endowed by a nineteenth-century priest on the proceeds of hush money from the Vatican to hide his evidence of the marriage of Jesus and Mary Magdalene. The mundane reality is that the priest. Bérenger Saunière, had been selling masses on an industrial scale. Canon law permits three to be said a day and donations for them accepted, but Saunière accepted money for thousands of masses which were never performed.

As for the Priory of Sion, in 1993 Pierre Plantard, a draughts-man and fabulator with a background in far-right politics, admitted inventing the evidence supporting its existence and planting it in the Bibliothéque Nationale in Paris as part of a hoax to advance his claim as the king of France. But the real success of the hoax was that it worked on Baigent, Leigh and Lincoln, and through them on Dan Brown and millions of people who read his book and believe what he wrote on the opening page of *The Da Vinci Code*, that the Priory of Sion was a 'fact'.

Jesus' Wife

If all this nuttiness reminds you of something, it might be the sto-ries cranked out by the monks at Vézelay, and the Dominicans at Sainte-Baume. But more lies behind *The Da Vinci Code* than *The Templar Revelation* and *The Holy Blood and the Holy Grail* and several other 'alternative' works that Dan Brown has cited, even if the material has reached popular writers indirectly, almost by osmosis one might say.

A fundamental source of the ideas behind the reappraisal of Mary Magdalene is located in the religious studies departments of several of the world's most prestigious universities, where a circle of scholars – among them Elaine Pagels, Jane Schaberg, Richard Bauckham, Bruce Chilton, Karen King and Ann Graham Brock – have shed new light on the feminine in the New Testament. Their writings have percolated down, probably much to their chagrin, into the New Age writings of people like Margaret Starbird and finally into popular thrillers.

A spur to the new scholarly interest in Mary Magdalene and the feminine was the discovery of the Nag Hammadi codices in 1945 which presented an alternative Christian tradition, one that was opposed to the proto-orthodoxy that eventually became dominant and formed the institutional hierarchy of the Church – a hierarchy that was and has remained overwhelmingly male. To some writers, especially those with a feminist perspective, scenes of Peter's anger or jealousy towards Mary Magdalene in these gnostic Gospels are taken as proof of an early sex war. Peter may be the rock upon whom the Church is built, but Mary Magdalene is the one whom Jesus kisses. Jesus has been betrayed by the Christian Church.

But there are other ways of looking at this. The argument presented by the gnostic gospels between Peter and Mary Magdalene was about how to attain knowledge of the authentic spirit. Peter seems to be arguing that authority is passed down through a hierarchy, as in apostolic succession, whereas Mary Magdalene has been inspired directly by Jesus. That is clear from the fact that Jesus appears to her in a vision and not to the apostles, and it is also clear from the kisses he would give her, the kisses of inspiration, of divine breath, before his crucifixion. Whether the argument was primarily over how to attain the authentic spirit or how to build the Church into a durable institution, the sex of Jesus' apostles might have been secondary.

To say that the depreciation of Mary Magdalene has been caused by a conspiracy of men against women might be missing the point. Rather Mary Magdalene has fallen foul of a profound argument over the apprehension of the divine, in which the established, ritualised and hierarchical Church requires that God be mediated through itself, whereas everything about Mary Magdalene suggests a more immediate and personal experience of the divine. The alternative is to do without the hierarchy; there was no hierarchy when Mary Magdalene was alone in the empty tomb.

But the suggestion that Jesus, together with Mary Magdalene, had other ideas about life and the spirit than those put about by Christian churches does not go away.

'Jesus said to them, "My wife ..."' Those are the words written in Coptic, the language of ancient and Christian Egypt, on a small piece of papyrus that was placed in the hands of professor Karen King of Harvard University. King herself named the papyrus fragment *The Gospel of Jesus' Wife* and when she announced its discovery in September 2012 it had a sensational impact round the world. The fragment raised the possibility that Jesus was married, which would prompt a radical reconsideration of the New Testament and of biblical scholarship.

There were some sceptical voices and so a series of tests were run in 2014 and published by Harvard University on their *Gospel of Jesus' Wife* website, seemingly authenticating the ink and the papyrus itself. However, the information posted on the website raised new questions and within days numerous authorities in Coptic and early Christianity were saying that King's papyrus was a forgery, that it had come from the same hand, using the same ink and the same writing instrument as a supposed *Gospel of John* fragment that is widely considered to have been copied from a papyrus fragment published by University College London in 1924.

Professor Karen King of Harvard holds up a fragment of sixth to ninth-century papyrus bearing in Coptic text the words 'Jesus said to them, "My wife..."'. This is not proof, as King points out, that Jesus was married, only that whoever wrote the text apparently thought that he was.

Faced with the charge that the *Gospel of Jesus' Wife* is a forgery, both King and Harvard went mute. Professor King failed to come forward with everything she knows about the *Gospel of Jesus's Wife*, including the full circumstances under which it was bought and sold several times before it came into her possession, and its shady history in Communist East Germany. Quite possibly Professor King knows nothing, for the papyrus fragment was apparently put into her hands without any proof of its provenance, and she never seemed to think that mattered.

But if the papyrus fragment and the writing upon it are genuine then it would appear that there were people in ninth-century Egypt who thought Jesus had a wife.

It would tell us nothing more, however.

The Future of Mary Magdalene

What is to become of Mary Magdalene? In 1969 the Roman Catholic Church ceased to recognise a composite Mary Magdalene; the Vatican decided that she and Mary of Bethany and the sinner woman were separate people in the gospels. But at the same time it decreed that Mary Magdalene would be venerated only as a disciple. The Church has corrected one error by no longer associating her with the sinner woman, and has possibly committed another error by dissociating her from a plausible identification with Mary of Bethany, and it has confirmed the decision at the Council of Trent that she is not the apostle to the apostles. Not that separating her from the sinner woman has removed the association zealously cultivated by the Church for over fifteen hundred years; there is considerable popular pleasure in relating to Mary Magdalene as a penitent.

Also persistent in the popular mind is the notion that Jesus and Mary Magdalene were married. Forget about *The Da Vinci Code*. It is there in professor Karen King's fragment of papyrus, in Rossetti's poem about Mary Magdalene at the door of Simon the Pharisee, and it is there among the Cathars, and there have been suggestions about it going back to the gospels themselves.

Whatever the Catholic Church or other churches decide, the future of Mary Magdalene looks secure in the public imagination, more secure than Mary the mother of Jesus. That is how it was in the gospels and that is how it is now; in the beginning was Jesus and Mary Magdalene.

And if and when the Church should pass away, when formalised Christianity itself should pass, what then of Mary Magdalene? I prefer to believe there really was a Mary Magdalene. The reality seems stronger than everything ever written by Paul. She is the authentic figure. Jesus ends in her and in those who have listened in the silence of the empty tomb.

Further Reading

BIBLES

King James Bible
http://www.kingjamesbibleonline.org
The King James Version of the
Bible is used throughout this book.
It can be accessed and searched
online at the dedicated website King
James Bible Online.

Bible Hub
http://biblehub.com/
You can read and search different
English translations of the Bible,
– King James, New International
Version, Douay-Rheims, etc – at
this website. It also has Bibles in
various languages and provides
Greek and Hebrew interlinears
of English-language Bibles so that
you can read verses of the Old and
New Testaments in their original
languages.

Scripture 4 All
http://www.scripture4all.org/
A dedicated website for Hebrew
and Greek interlinears of English,
German and Dutch Bibles.

MARY MAGDALENE

Mary Magdalene: A Biography by
Bruce Chilton, Doubleday, New
York 2005. Chilton, a professor of
religion and a priest in New York
state, sees Mary Magdalene as an
anointer and healer; he identifies her
with Mary of Bethany.

*Peter, Paul and Mary Magdalene:
The Followers of Jesus in History and
Legend* by Bart D. Ehrman, Oxford
University Press, New York 2006. A
highly readable general book by a
New Testament scholar.

*Mary Magdalene, The First Apostle: The
Struggle for Authority*, by Ann Graham
Brock, Harvard University Press,
Cambridge, Massachusetts 2003.
Apostolic succession and the
marginalisation of Mary Magdalene.

*The Making of the Magdalen: Preaching
and Popular Devotion in the Later
Middle Ages* by Katherine Ludwig
Jansen, Princeton University Press,
Princeton 2000. The development

of Mary Magdalene as sinner and a penitent leading to her cult at Sainte-Baume.

The Golden Legend by Jacobus de Voragine, translated by William Granger Ryan, Princeton University Press, Princeton 2012. The medieval bestseller on the lives of the saints, including Mary Magdalene.

Mary Magdalene: Iconograpic Studies from the Middle Ages to the Baroque edited by Michelle A. Erhardt and Amy M. Morris, Brill, Leiden and Boston 2012. The continuous reinvention of Mary Magdalene's image in art to suit the needs of the Church and of private patrons.

The Resurrection of Mary Magdalene: Legends, Apocrypha, and the Christian Testament by Jane Schaberg, Continuum, New York and London 2002. Considered a landmark work in feminist studies, Schaberg attempts to theologically resurrect Mary Magdalene, interweaving her story with that of Virginia Woolf.

Mary Magdalene Understood by Jane Schaberg with Melanie Johnson Debaufre, Continuum, New York and London 2006. A shorter and easier to read version of *The Resurrection of Mary Magdalene*.

Mary Magdalen: Myth and Metaphor by Susan Haskins, Harper Collins, London 1993. Only the first chapter, less than thirty pages, deals with Mary Magdalene of the gospels; the rest is an exhaustive account of her legendary afterlife up to modern times.

Searching for Mary Magdalene: A Journey through Art and Literature by Jane Lahr, Welcome Books, New York and San Francisco 2006. A beautifully produced coffee table book.

Mary Magdalene, or Salvation in *Fires* by Marguerite Yourcenar, translated by Dori Katz, Aidan Ellis, London 1982. Yourcenar tells the story attributed to Jerome in the fourth century of Mary Magdalene being jilted by John the Evangelist at the marriage of Cana, falling into prostitution, and finally devoting herself to Jesus.

JESUS

Jesus: Nativity, Passion, Resurrection by Geza Vermes, Penguin Books, London 2010. The gospels carefully described, tested and analysed by the leading Jesus scholar of recent times.

Jesus: An Historian's Review of the Gospels by Michael Grant, Macmillan, London 1977. Grant, an outstanding classical historian, admits the extreme difficulty of drawing historical accounts from the gospels but manages a well-judged and readable account.

Jesus by A.N. Wilson, Sinclair-Stevenson, London 1992. A somewhat iconoclastic biography of Jesus which dismisses the story of his birth in Bethlehem, his life as a carpenter, his betrayal by Judas, and takes Paul to task for inventing a Jesus cult. This book was written when Wilson, now a Catholic, was an atheist.

How Jesus Became Christian by Barrie Wilson, Weidenfeld and Nicolson, London 2008. Barrie Wilson, a professor of religious studies in Canada, shows by examining the gospels that Jesus was never anything other than an observant Jew but who was turned into a god by Paul. Which explains much about Mary Magdalene too.

MARY, MOTHER OF JESUS

Alone of All Her Sex: The Myth and the Cult of the Virgin Mary by Marina Warner, Weidenfeld and Nicolson, London 1976. Warner's outstanding book traces the historical development of Mary as Virgin, Bride, Mother, Queen of Heaven and Intercessor, and how these aspects have affected and been depicted in literature and art, as well as their influence on the lives of both men and women. She is also ample in her treatment of Mary Magdalene and the 'muddle of Marys' in the gospels.

Mary Through the Centuries: Her Place in the History of Culture, by Jaroslav Pelikan, Yale University Press, New Haven and London 1996. The other important account of Mary the Mother of Jesus. Pelikan describes the developed traditions and then traces them back to their biblical and doctrinal sources, seeking what he calls the 'eternal feminine' at the heart of all that is holy. He also ventures into Black Madonnas and Mary the Mother of Jesus in Islam.

THE GOSPELS

Jesus and the Eyewitnesses by Richard Bauckham, William B. Eerdmans, Grand Rapids, Michigan, and Cambridge, England 2006. Bauckham argues the case that the gospels are largely based on reliable eyewitness accounts.

Gospel Women: Studies of the Named Women in the Gospels by Richard Bauckham, William B. Eerdmans, Grand Rapids, Michigan, and Cambridge, England 2002. An examination of women's lives in Palestine, the credibility of their stories in the gospels, in particular a valuable look at Joanna the wife of Chuza, and also a consideration of *The Secret Gospel of Mark*.

Clement of Alexandria and a Secret Gospel of Mark by Morton Smith, Harvard University Press, Cambridge, Massachusetts, 1973. The full-blown academic study by Smith of the Secret Gospel.

The Secret Gospel: The Discovery and Interpretation of the Secret Gospel According to Mark by Morton Smith, Victor Gollancz, London 1974. Smith's popular history of the Secret Gospel.

PALESTINE AT THE TIME OF JESUS

The Archaeology of Society in the Holy Land edited by Thomas E. Levy, Leicester University Press, London 1998. Good on the Hellenisation and Romanisation of Palestine, and field towers such as that at Migdal Eder.

THE WORLD OF EARLY CHRISTIANITY

Lost Christianities: The Battles for Scripture and the Faiths We Never Knew by Bart D. Ehrman, Oxford University Press, New York 2003. A great variety of Christianities flourished when the new religion began; eventually this diversity was replaced by orthodoxy and dissent was persecuted as heretical.

Lost Scriptures: Books that Did Not Make It into the New Testament by Bart D. Ehrman, Oxford University Press, New York 2003. Provides readers with all the relevant apocryphal and gnostic gospels of the lost Christianities.

Early Egyptian Christianity: From its Origins to 451 CE by C. Wilfred Griggs, Brill, Leiden 1990. This academic work is one of the very few books about the poorly documented and elusive subject of early Christianity in Egypt.

Contested Issues in Christian Origins and the New Testament by Luke Timothy Johnson, Brill, Leiden 2013. Johnson, an historian of religion and a Catholic who takes issue with several teachings of the Church, examines in these essays the Jewish and Graeco-Roman contexts of early Christianity, gnosticism, Marcion, Paul and the quest for the historical Jesus.

Introduction to the New Testament, volumes 1 and 2, by Helmut Koester, Walter de Gruyter, New York and Berlin 1987. This is regarded as the standard reference work on the New Testament. Koester suggests that in the earliest version of the story only Mary Magdalene discovered the empty tomb; the account was later diluted by the gospel writers who added the names of other women.

Christian Beginnings: From Nazareth to Nicaea, AD 30-325 by Geza Vermes, Penguin Books, London 2013. This book relates how there were many streams of Christianity in the early centuries and they only began to be channelled into one great instrument of faith and state under the Roman emperor Constantine at the Council of Nicaea.

Christ's Resurrection in Early Christianity and the Making of the New Testament by Markus Vinzent, Ashgate, Farnham, Surrey 2011. Vinzent, a professor at King's College London, argues that the resurrection was unknown or of no interest to the earliest Christians and only became so when Marcion revived the letters of Paul in the 130s; he also says that the gospels were written at about that same time.

On the True Doctrine: A Discourse against the Christians by Celsus, translated by R. Joseph Hoffmann, Oxford University Press, Oxford and New York 1987. The famous attack on Christianity by a second century Greek philosopher.

Jews and Christians: Graeco-Roman Views by Molly Whittaker, Cambridge University Press, Cambridge 1984. Judaism and mystery religions; the environment in which Christianity took shape.

Isis in the Ancient World by R.E. Witt,
The Johns Hopkins University
Press, Baltimore and London 1997.
Witt stresses the influence of Isis
worship on Christian thinking,
practice and iconography.

GNOSTICISM, CATHARS AND DUALISM

*The Gospel of Mary of Magdala: Jesus
and the First Woman Apostle* by Karen
King, Polebridge Press, Salem,
Oregon 2003. Translated and
elucidated by professor Karen King,
Mary's gospel rejects Jesus' suffering
and death as a path to eternal life
and replaces that with the inner
spiritual knowledge possessed by
Mary Magdalene.

*Montaillou: Cathars and Catholics
in a French Village 1294-1324* by
Emmanuel Le Roy Ladurie,
Penguin Books, Harmondsworth
1980. The classic account of
the Cathars in their own words,
drawn from their testimony to the
inquisition.

The Gnostics by Jacques Lecarrière,
Peter Owen, London 1977. A
beautiful and poetic book about the
gnostics with an introduction by
Lawrence Durrell.

*The Woman Jesus Loved: Mary
Magdalene in the Nag Hammadi Library
and Related Documents* by Antti
Marjanen, Brill, Leiden 1996.
Among other things, this treats with
how the anointing episodes in the
gospels were run together by the

early Church as the acts of one
woman, with the effect that Mary
Magdalene became one and the
same as the sinner woman at the
house of Simon the Pharisee and
so was identified as a prostitute,
and later became a penitent, rather
than the apostle to the apostles –
and how this narrative has been
contradicted by the discovery of the
gnostic gospels.

*The War on Heresy: Faith and Power
in Medieval Europe* by R.I. Moore,
Profile Books, London 2012. The
Cathars were persecuted and
destroyed, says Moore, not because
of their beliefs but because of
the needs and ambitions of their
persecutors.

*The Perfect Heresy: The Life and the
Death of the Cathars* by Stephen
O'Shea, Profile Books, London
2000. A good popular history,
including the place of Mary
Magdalene in Cathar beliefs.

The Gnostic Gospels by Elaine Pagels,
Weidenfeld and Nicolson, London
1980. The first and still one of
the best popular but scholarly
presentations of the Nag Hammadi
gnostic gospels.

*The Other God: Dualist Religions from
Antiquity to the Cathar Heresy* by Yuri
Stoyanov, Yale University Press,
New Haven and London 2000. A
sweeping account of the recurring
struggle between the one god and
the periodically dying and rising
other god.

Photo credits

The author and publisher gratefully acknowledge permission to use copyright images in this book. Copyright holders are acknowledged below. Every effort has been made to trace and contact copyright holders. If there are any inadvertent omissions we apologise to those concerned, and ask that you contact the publisher so that we can correct any oversight as soon as possible.

PHOTO CREDITS

p.84 *Jesus' entry into Jerusalem* by Giotto. Wikimedia Commons.
p.87 *Jesus attacks the moneychangers. Illustrations of the Life of Christ* by Alexandre Bida, New York 1874.
p.89 *The anointing of Jesus at Bethany. The Engravings,* by Eric Gill, edited by Christopher Skelton, London 1990.
p.92 *The Raising of Lazarus* by Giotto. Photograph by Michael Haag.
p.94 *The Pool of Siloam. Picturesque Palestine, Sinai and Egypt* by Wilson, Charles William, Sir; Lane-Poole, Stanley. London 1881-84.
p.97 The *Communion of the Apostles* by Fra Angelico. Wikimedia Commons.
p.99/100 The *Last Supper* by Leonardo Da Vinci. Wikimedia Commons.
p.102 The *Last Supper* by William Blake. Wikimedia Commons.

Chapter Six
p.105 *Trial of Jesus.* Wikimedia Commons.
p.109 *Ecce Homo* by Antonio Ciseri. Wikimedia Commons.
p.111 The Via Dolorosa. *Picturesque Palestine, Sinai and Egypt* by Sir Charles William Wilson and Stanley Lane-Poole. London 1881-84.
p.114 *Jesus Stripped* by Eric Gill. *The Engravings,* by Eric Gill, edited by Christopher Skelton, London 1990.
p.117 The *Crucifixion* by Gustave Doré. Wikimedia Commons.
p.121 The *Deposition* by Sebastiano del Piombo. Photograph by Michael Haag.

Chapter Seven
p.125 The *Resurrection* by Eric Gill. *The Engravings,* by Eric Gill, edited by Christopher Skelton, London 1990.
p.127 The *Resurrection*, detail, by Meister Francke. Wikimedia Commons.
p.128 The women go to the tomb. *Illustrations of the Life of Christ* by Alexandre Bida, New York 1874.

p.131 Nuptials of God by Eric Gill. *The Engravings,* by Eric Gill, edited by Christopher Skelton, London 1990.
p.135 *Nicodemus with Jesus* by Rembrandt. Wikimedia Commons.
p.142 Mar Saba. *Picturesque Palestine, Sinai and Egypt* by Sir Charles William Wilson and Stanley Lane-Poole. London 1881-84.
p.146 *Fleeing Youth* by Correggio. Wikimedia Commons.
p.149 Church of Lazarus at Bethany. Library of Congress.
p.152 The tomb of Lazarus. Library of Congress.
p.155 *Noli Me Tangere* by Giotto. Photograph by Michael Haag.

Chapter Eight
p.160 *The stoning of Stephen* by Gustave Doré. Wikimedia Commons.
p.163 Paul's conversion in the *Nuremberg Chronicles.* Wikimedia Commons.
p.165 The Arch of Titus. Wikimedia.
p.167 Peter and Paul in a Roman catacomb. Wikimedia Commons.
p.170 Tetradrachm showing Isis Pharia. Bibliotheca Alexandrina.
p.173 Isis Capitoline. Photograph by Carole Raddato.
p.174 Piè di Marmo. Photograph by Carole Raddato.
p.177 Isis copulating with Osiris. Wikimedia Commons.
p.180 Anastasis fresco in the Chora Church, Istanbul. Photograph by Michael Haag.

Chapter Nine
p.185 Mosaic of St Mark arriving at Alexandria. Tour Egypt.
p.189 Bronze head of Hadrian. Wikimedia Commons.
p.191 Muhammad Al-Samman. Le Gnosticisme Universal.
p.193 Nag Hammadi codex. Le Gnosticisme Universal.

Index

Page references for illustrations are given in *italics*

I

H

J

N

R

S